ROUTLEDGE LIBRARY EDITIONS:
CHARLES DICKENS

DICKENS AT WORK

DICKENS AT WORK

JOHN BUTT AND KATHLEEN TILLOTSON

Volume 1

LONDON AND NEW YORK

First published in 1957

This edition first published in 2009 by
Routledge
2 Park Square, Milton Park, Abingdon, Oxon, OX14 4RN

Simultaneously published in the USA and Canada
by Routledge
270 Madison Avenue, New York, NY 10016

Routledge is an imprint of the Taylor & Francis Group, an informa business

Transferred to Digital Printing 2009

British Library Cataloguing in Publication Data
A catalogue record for this book is available from the British Library

Library of Congress Cataloging in Publication Data
A catalog record for this book has been requested

ISBN 10: 0-415-48232-1 (hbk)
ISBN 10: 0-415-56909-5 (pbk)
ISBN 10: 0-415-43595-1 (Set)

ISBN 13: 978-0-415-48232-5 (hbk)
ISBN 13: 978-0-415-56909-5 (pbk)
ISBN 13: 978-0-415-43595-6 (Set)

Publisher's Note

The publisher has gone to great lengths to ensure the quality of this reprint but points out that some imperfections in the original copies may be apparent.

Disclaimer

The publisher has made every effort to trace copyright holders and would welcome correspondence from those they have been unable to trace.

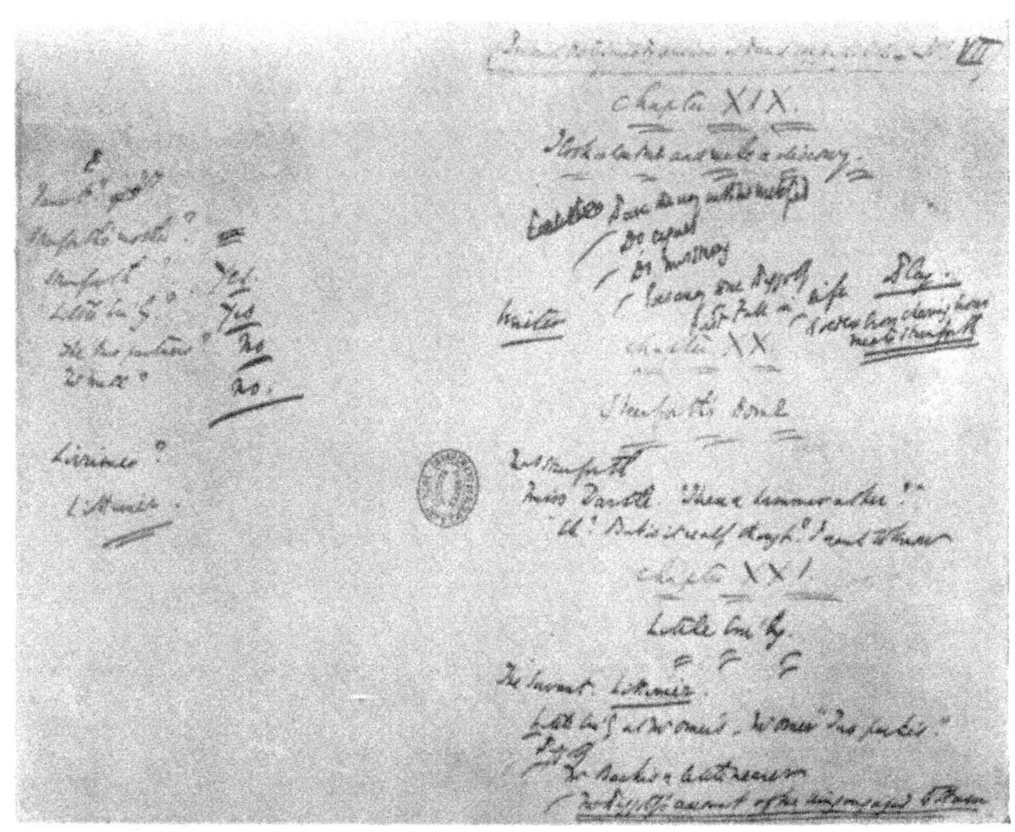

Dickens' 'Number Plan' for *David Copperfield*, No. VII
(Victoria and Albert Museum)

Dickens at Work

JOHN BUTT

AND

KATHLEEN TILLOTSON

METHUEN & CO. LTD

36 ESSEX STREET · LONDON W.C.2

First published in 1957
Printed in Great Britain by
The Broadwater Press Ltd
Welwyn Garden City, Herts
Catalogue Number 5888/U

Contents

Illustrations

Abbreviated Titles

of works frequently referred to

COUTTS LETTERS = *Letters from Charles Dickens to Angela Burdett-Coutts, 1841–1865*. Selected and edited . . . by Edgar Johnson (London, 1953).

FORSTER = John Forster, *The Life of Charles Dickens* (Library edition, 2 vols., revised, 1876; originally published in 3 vols., 1872–4). [Reference is by book and section.]

HATTON AND CLEAVER = Thomas Hatton and Arthur H. Cleaver, *A Bibliography of the Periodical Works of Charles Dickens* (1933).

JOHNSON = Edgar Johnson, *Charles Dickens, his Tragedy and Triumph* (2 vols., London, 1953).

LETTERS = *The Letters of Charles Dickens*, edited by Walter Dexter (3 vols., 1938, the Nonesuch Dickens).

Preface

In this book we have examined several of Dickens's novels in the light of the conditions under which he wrote them. The surviving evidence of these conditions is extensive and has been generally neglected hitherto, but if we are right in our estimate of the importance of this material, it suggests more than one new direction in the criticism of his work.

Many writers, taking their point of departure from Dickens's childhood reading, have seen him as continuing the tradition of Fielding and Smollett; but he also continues another eighteenth-century tradition. In the original Preface to *Nicholas Nickleby* (1839) he chose to call himself a 'periodical essayist', and took leave of his readers in the words of Henry Mackenzie in the last paper of the *Lounger*:

> Other writers submit their sentiments to their readers, with the reserve and circumspection of him who has had time to prepare for a public appearance. . . But the periodical essayist commits to his readers the feelings of the day, in the language which those feelings have prompted.

It is to the recovery of Dickens as a writer of 'periodical' novels that this book is especially devoted: how he responded to and conveyed 'the feelings of the day', what methods of work he evolved as best suited to his own genius and to the demands of monthly or weekly publication, and above all, how he eventually defeated Mackenzie's antithesis by learning to combine the 'circumspection' of preparation with the immediate and intimate relation to his readers which he valued so highly.

Our emphasis accordingly falls upon the process rather than the result, upon Dickens's craft rather than his art; but the inspiration and justification of our work is none the less a conviction of Dickens's greatness as a creative artist. This is widely shared. Yet, despite some excellent interpretative criticism and much zealous biographical enquiry, Dickens studies have hardly passed beyond the early nineteenth-century phase of Shakespeare studies; while the study of his text seems arrested in the early eighteenth century. With the lifting of this spell, which can only come with a full critical edition, much that Dickens originally wrote and had to discard, but would have retained had he been writing three-volume novels, will be restored to readers, as well as passages in the early works which for a variety of reasons he removed or revised in later editions. In some of our chapters we give a few examples of such passages; more will be found in recent issues of *The Dickensian*, and in *Dickens Romancier* (1953) by Professor Sylvère Monod, whose approach resembles ours in his use of the rich material of the Forster collection in the Victoria and Albert Library.

All of Dickens's writings have claims to be included in a study of 'Dickens at work', but our present choice fairly represents different stages of his career and different kinds of work. The variations and development of his method of work in early and late novels, in weekly and monthly instalments, are thus indicated; and also the persistence of his journalistic response to events of the day, from the 'no popery' cry of the late eighteen-thirties to the war in the Crimea—a response which is more varied and more extensive than is usually recognized or than we have had full opportunity of showing.

We arrived at our common concern in these matters by rather different routes: one of us starting from a specific interest in the effect of serial writing upon Dickens's novels, and the other from a more general interest in the conditions of publication of Victorian fiction. Some results of our earlier and largely independent investigations are to be seen in John Butt's article 'Dickens at Work' in 1948, and Kathleen Tillotson's *Novels of the Eighteen-Forties* in 1954. The beginnings of collaboration appeared in John Butt's centenary articles on *David Copperfield* in 1949-50, and in the same year we converged upon *Dombey and Son*—the earliest of the fully-documented novels—on which we published a jointly-written essay.

The other studies were written in close association. Chapters i, vi, vii, and viii are mainly the work of John Butt, chapters ii, iii, iv, and ix mainly the work of Kathleen Tillotson; but we are jointly responsible for the whole book, and for chapter v in particular. That chapter is the only one which has been published hitherto in substantially its present form: it appeared in *Essays and Studies 1951*, published for the English Association by John Murray. Parts of chapters i, vi, and vii have appeared in *The Durham University Journal*, *The Listener*, *The Dickensian*, *The Review of English Studies*, and *Nineteenth Century Fiction*. Chapter iv incorporates most of the introductory essay to *Barnaby Rudge* in the New Oxford Illustrated Dickens. To the editors of the journals mentioned, to the English Association, John Murray Ltd, and the Oxford University Press, we are indebted for permission to reprint.

For quotations from manuscripts, proof sheets, and memoranda in the Forster collection we acknowledge the permission of the Director of the Victoria and Albert Museum. Letters owned by the Henry E. Huntington Library, the Pierpont Morgan Library, the Albert A. Berg Collection of the New York Public Library, and the Rare Book Department of the Free Library of Philadelphia are quoted by permission of the owners. Permission to quote from hitherto unpublished material has been given by Mr Henry C. Dickens, O.B.E.

We are also grateful to Professor Geoffrey Tillotson for his constant advice and assistance; to Mr K. J. Fielding and Mrs Madeline House for several details which their unrivalled knowledge of unpublished letters could alone supply; to Miss Margaret Cardwell for valuable help in checking quotations and references; and generally, to members of discussion classes on Dickens at King's College, University of Durham, and Bedford College, University of London.

J. B.
K. T.

CHAPTER I

Dickens as a Serial Novelist

I

IT is a commonplace in the criticism of early drama that the conditions in which a dramatist worked must be taken into account. He wrote for a theatre of a certain shape, with certain structural features, which permitted him to use certain dramatic effects. The analogy can be applied to the novelist who, though he has greater freedom than the dramatist, must also suit what he has to say to the current conventions of presentation. Just as Shakespeare thought in terms of a theatre without drop curtain, artificial lighting, or scenery, and of a theatrical company of male actors only, so Dickens was accustomed to think in terms of publication peculiar to his time. Today novels are customarily published in single volumes. A hundred and fifty years ago this form of publication was unusual. In the eighteenth century, novels had appeared in five volumes, or even in as many as seven; but by the time of Scott and Jane Austen the usual number was three or four. The prices varied: it was not uncommon to charge as much as half a guinea a volume, which made novel-reading exceedingly expensive to those who did not belong to a circulating library. These were still the conditions ruling when Dickens began to write. His first novel, *Pickwick Papers*, shows him attempting to reach a larger number of readers by cutting the price to suit their pockets. The method chosen was to publish in 'what was then a very unusual form, at less than one-third of the price of the whole of an ordinary novel, and in shilling Monthly Parts'.[1]

1. Dickens's address announcing the 'cheap edition' of his works (1847). It is preserved in a scrap-book of cuttings in the British Museum (shelf mark K.T.C. 1.b. 5 (21)), and is reprinted in the 'National' edition, XXXIV (1908), p. 433.

After the first few numbers of *Pickwick*, each monthly 'part' or number consisted of three or four chapters, covering thirty-two pages of print, with two plates, and several pages of advertisements. It was issued in green paper covers and was published at a shilling, nominally on the first day, actually on the last day, of each month. This form of publication was chosen for *Pickwick* by Chapman and Hall, but Dickens found it so suitable that he adopted it for *Nicholas Nickleby*, *Martin Chuzzlewit*, *Dombey and Son*, *David Copperfield*, *Bleak House*, *Little Dorrit*, *Our Mutual Friend*, and *Edwin Drood*. Each of these novels, except *Edwin Drood*, was planned for completion in nineteen monthly numbers, the last being a double number priced at two shillings, and containing, besides forty-eight pages of text and four plates, the title-page, frontispiece, preface, and other preliminaries. *Edwin Drood*, of which only six numbers were written, was planned for completion in eleven, the last to be a double number. Five of the other six novels were published in serial in weekly magazines and produced distinct problems of composition and form, which are touched upon in later chapters.

Although it might be supposed that Dickens would wish to complete a novel before permitting serial publication to begin, in fact he never wrote more than four or five numbers before the first was published, and by the middle of the novel he was rarely more than one number ahead of his readers. As might be expected, his practice differed at different stages of his career. Whereas *Little Dorrit* III was finished before the first number appeared and an even larger portion of *Our Mutual Friend* was ready before publication day, he had lightly embarked upon *Pickwick Papers* with nothing in hand;[1] and it seems that no more, or very little more, than the first numbers of *Nicholas Nickleby* and *Martin Chuzzlewit* were complete when publication began.[2] Furthermore, the writing of *Pickwick Papers* overlapped with *Oliver Twist*, and *Oliver Twist* with *Nicholas Nickleby*. In circumstances such as these, it is not surprising to learn that each number of *Nickleby* had been completed 'only . . . a day or two before its publication';[3] and

1. See Forster, VIII i, IX v, and below, p. 66.

2. 'The first chapter [of *Nicholas Nickleby*] is ready . . . so you can begin to print as soon as you like. The sooner you begin, the faster I shall get on' (*Letters*, I 161; 22 Feb. 1838). The first number of *Martin Chuzzlewit* was 'nearly done' on 8 Dec. 1842, with a little more than three weeks to go before publication day (*Letters*, I 493).

3. *Letters*, I 170.

this in turn meant that when something compelled him to stop working for a prolonged period, a gap in the series supervened. Thus the death of Mary Hogarth, his sister-in-law, on 7 May 1837 moved him profoundly, and the effect upon his serial publication was immediate: there were no June numbers of *Pickwick Papers* and *Oliver Twist*. On the other hand, when he himself died on 9 June 1870 there was enough of *Edwin Drood* written to permit the publication of three more numbers, the third being only two pages short of the normal complement.

The disadvantages of this method seem obvious. As Trollope remarked, 'an artist should keep in his hand the power of fitting the beginning of his work to the end'.[1] And the difficulties seem equally great. Writing in serial involved maintaining two focuses. The design and purpose of the novel had to be kept constantly in view; but the writer had also to think in terms of the identity of the serial number, which would have to make its own impact and be judged as a unit. Incident and interest had therefore to be evenly spread, since 'the writer . . . cannot afford to have many pages skipped out of the few which are to meet the reader's eye at the same time'.[2] Chapters must be balanced within a number in respect both of length and of effect. Each number must lead, if not to a climax, at least to a point of rest; and the rest between numbers is necessarily more extended than what the mere chapter divisions provide. The writer had also to bear in mind that his readers were constantly interrupted for prolonged periods, and that he must take this into account in his characterization and, to some extent, in his plotting. So early as the original preface to *Pickwick*, Dickens showed his recognition that not every story is suited to this type of publication.[3]

Great as these difficulties were, they were felt to be worth overcoming. To the reader the system meant not merely eager expectation of the day which brought a fresh batch of green covers to the bookstall, but also the impression that the story was in the making from month to month. Thus Lady Stanley is found addressing a friend in 1841 about the weekly progress of *The Old Curiosity Shop*:

> How *can* you read Humphrey's last number and not *indulge* me with an ejaculation or two about it? Are you satisfied with the disposal of Quilp? My Lord is not, says it is too easy a death and that he

1. *Autobiography* (World's Classics revised text), p. 127.
2. Ibid., p. 132. 3. See below, p. 65.

should have more time to *feel* his punishment. Will Nelly die? I think she ought.[1]

To the author it meant a larger public, but also a public more delicately responsive, who made their views known during the progress of a novel both by writing to him and by reducing or increasing their purchases. Through serial publication an author could recover something of the intimate relationship between story-teller and audience which existed in the ages of the sagas and of Chaucer; and for an author like Dickens, who was peculiarly susceptible to the influence of his readers, this intimate relationship outweighed the inherent disadvantages of the system.[2]

II

Yet the disadvantages were none the less apparent, and they could be mastered only by more systematic planning than this impulsive man has been credited with. Publication day was the last day of each month, known in the trade as 'magazine day'.[3] By that date Dickens had to plan and write the equivalent of thirty-two printed pages and to give his illustrator instructions for two engravings. The manuscript had to be sent to the printer in London, perhaps from Broadstairs or the Isle of Wight, or even from as far off as Lausanne.[4] Proofs were to be corrected and sent to press, and copies were to be sewn and distributed to booksellers. The publishers' agreement for *Nicholas Nickleby* specified that the manuscript should be delivered on the fifteenth day of each month.[5] During the progress of this novel it seems to have been recognized that the twenty-fourth would serve as the last

1. *The Ladies of Alderley*, ed. N. Mitford (1938), p. 2.

2. On serial publication see Kathleen Tillotson, *Novels of the Eighteen-Forties* (Oxford, 1954), pp. 21–47.

3. For an account of the scene on 'magazine day' in Paternoster Row see Charles Manby Smith, *The Little World of London* (1857), pp. 45–6. The arrangements were different for weekly serials. When W. H. Wills, the assistant editor of *All the Year Round*, was arranging for contemporaneous publication of a German version of *Great Expectations*, he told the German publishers that the translated portion was not to anticipate the original: 'we publish on the Wednesdays before the date upon our numbers, which is that of each Saturday. Therefore you can bring out each weekly portion every Wednesday after Wednesday the 28th Instant; when (and not before) you may issue the first portion.' (copy, dated 15 Nov. 1860, in the *All the Year Round* letter-book, Henry E. Huntington Library.)

4. Part of *Copperfield* was written at Broadstairs, part in the Isle of Wight; part of *Dombey* was written at Lausanne, part in Paris.

5. Forster, II ii.

date for a number,[1] but Dickens's subsequent practice was to aim at the twentieth. Frequently he had to go straight from one number to the next; but often he could allow himself a few days' respite at the end of the month before beginning the next month's instalment. Occasionally he resumed work as late as the seventh day.[2] Thus he had about a fortnight for writing his three or four chapters.

He did not always complete his number before sending it to the printer. Sometimes it was delivered in batches with instructions for a proof to be forwarded to the illustrator.[3] Hablôt Browne was accustomed to work to orders. At best he had a proof to go upon; at worst his instructions were verbal.[4] Sometimes he had a letter such as this, which embodies directions for the first illustration in *Dombey* VII:

> . . . The first subject which I am now going to give is very important to the book. *I should like to see your sketch of it, if possible.*
>
> I should premise that I want to make the Major, who is the incarnation of selfishness and small revenge, a kind of comic Mephistophilean power in the book; and the N° begins with the departure of Mr. Dombey and the Major on that trip for change of air and scene which is prepared for in the last Number. They go to Leamington, where you and I were once. In the Library the Major introduces Mr Dombey to a certain lady, whom, as I wish to foreshadow dimly, said Dombey may come to marry in due season. She

1. *Letters,* I 177.

2. Occasionally even later. On 9 Mar. 1847 he told Miss Hogarth that he had 'not yet written a single slip' of *Dombey* VII (*Letters,* II 17).

3. Thus Dickens wrote to Evans from Broadstairs about *Copperfield* No. IV (10 July 1849): 'I send you, by this Post, 9 slips of copy, containing Mr. Browne's second subject. Get it up *with all speed,* and send a proof to him. . .' (*Letters,* II 160).

4. 'It is due to the gentleman, whose designs accompany the letterpress, to state that the interval has been so short between the production of each number in manuscript and its appearance in print, that the greater portion of the Illustrations have been executed by the artist from the author's mere verbal description of what he intended.' Original preface to *Pickwick Papers.* David Croal Thomson, *Life and Labours of Hablôt Knight Browne 'Phiz'* (London, 1884), pp. 63f, 73f, prints instructions for *Dombey,* plate VII, and *Nickleby,* plate XXXIII; manuscript instructions for the plates XVIII, XXXVII, and XXXVIII, frontispiece, and title-page vignette of *Martin Chuzzlewit* are preserved in the Henry E. Huntington Library. On the instructions for plate XVIII, *The thriving city of Eden as it appeared in fact,* Browne has pencilled a mild protest: 'I can't get all this perspective in—unless you will allow of a long subject—something less than a mile'. Nevertheless he produced a sketch, on which Dickens commented 'The stump of the tree should be *in* the ground in fact a tree cut off two feet up. Too wide—cannot it be compressed by putting Martin's label on the other side of the door, and bringing Mark with his tree forwarder. Qy is that a *hat* on his head?'

is about thirty, not a day more—handsome, though *haughty* looking —good figure. Well dressed—showy—and desirable. Quite a lady in appearance, with something of a proud indifference about her, suggestive of a spark of the Devil within. Was married young. Husband dead. Goes about with an old mother, who rouges, and who lives upon the reputation of a diamond necklace and her family. Wants a husband. Flies at none but high game, and couldn't marry anybody not rich. Mother affects cordiality and *heart*, and is the essence of sordid calculation. Mother usually shoved about in a Bath chair by a Page who has rather *outgrown and outshoved his strength*, and who *butts at it* behind like a ram, while his mistress *steers herself languidly* by a handle in front. *Nothing the matter with her to prevent her walking*, only was once *sketched* (*when a Beauty*) *reclining in a Barouche*, and having *outlived the beauty and the barouche* too, still *holds on to the attitude* as becoming her uncommonly. Mother is in this machine in the sketch. Daughter has a *parasol*.

The Major presents them to Mr. Dombey, gloating within himself over what may come of it, and over the discomfiture of Miss Tox. Mr. Dombey (in deep mourning) *bows* solemnly. Daughter bends. The Native in attendance, *bearing a camp-stool and the Major's greatcoat*. Native evidently afraid of the Major and his thick cane.

If you like it better, the scene may be in the street or in a green lane. But a great deal will come of it: and I want the Major to express that, as much as possible in his apoplectic Mephistophilean observation of the scene, and in his share in it.

Lettering: *Major Bagstock is delighted to have that opportunity.*[1]

The letter is typical of the attention to detail which Dickens paid in all his undertakings. At a time when it might be expected that his energies would be fully expended upon writing his monthly instalment, he must turn aside to create a scene in Browne's imagination, letting him into secrets, appropriately enough, which less privileged readers were left to guess, and speaking out straight on matters which in the novel he is content to hint at, but embodying here and there with little verbal change significant details from the manuscript before him.[2] Browne responded rapidly. The directions were dated 10 March 1847; on the evening of 15 March Dickens was writing to express his delight at the sketch which Browne had furnished, and to ask him to re-dress the Native ('who is prodigiously good as he is') in European costume ('He may wear ear-rings and look outlandish,

1. D. C. Thomson, op. cit., pp. 68–71; *Letters*, II 17–18.
2. We have italicized these passages in the second and third paragraphs.

and be dark brown') and to make the Major older, and with a larger face.[1]

The last book which Browne illustrated was *A Tale of Two Cities*. For *Our Mutual Friend*—neither the weekly serial nor the first 'volume' edition of *Great Expectations* was illustrated—Dickens chose Marcus Stone, the son of an old friend. Though Stone was only twenty-five when he began work on *Our Mutual Friend*, Dickens seems to have given him a freer hand than he allowed Browne. Stone used to get proofs and select his own subjects, though Dickens reserved the right to criticize and to demand alterations, and was always 'ready to describe down to the minutest details the personal characteristics, and . . . life-history of the creations of his fancy'.[2] But though Stone was allowed to draw the cover of *Our Mutual Friend* without more than the first two monthly numbers to go upon, Dickens's son-in-law Charles Collins, who drew the cover of *Edwin Drood*, admitted that he did not in the least know the significance of the various groups in the design, which were drawn from instructions given him personally by Dickens.[3]

III

Much is known about Dickens's habits at the desk. In the middle of his career, it was his normal custom to work in the mornings only from nine o'clock till two; but he was no clock-work performer like Trollope. He described himself beginning *Little Dorrit*, in a letter to Mrs Watson (21 May 1855),

> walking about the country by day—prowling about into the strangest places in London by night—sitting down to do an immensity—getting up after doing nothing—walking about my room on particular bits of all the flowers in the carpet—tearing my hair (which I can't afford to do)—and on the whole astonished at my own condition, though I am used to it. . .[4]

1. D. C. Thomson, op. cit., p. 65; *Letters*, II 19. Thomson (p. 234) also prints a table of work, without mentioning book or year, which shows that Browne received his instructions for the first plate on Friday, 11 Jan., posted his sketch to Dickens on Sunday, received it back on Monday evening with instructions for the second plate, forwarded his sketch for that on Tuesday, and received it on Wednesday. The first plate was finished on Tuesday, 22 Jan., and the second on Saturday, 26 Jan.

2. Notes of an interview with Stone, quoted in *The Dickensian*, Aug. 1912, pp. 216–17.

3. Luke Fildes in *The Times*, 3 Nov. 1905.

4. *The Dickensian*, June 1942, pp. 165–6.

As a young man he had been a fluent writer, able to drive himself to work all day; and the surviving sheets of manuscript of his earliest novels suggest a hand racing to keep pace with the mind's conceptions. As Heminge and Condell said of Shakespeare, 'We have scarce received from him a blot in his papers.' His letters to Forster written at this time suggest that eleven or twelve of these sheets, or 'slips' as he called them, could be written in a day, or, at a push, as many as twenty.[1] But at the height of his powers, he found more difficulty in satisfying himself, and from *Dombey and Son* onwards his manuscripts are characterized by frequent erasures and interlineations. Of these slips Georgina Hogarth is witness[2] that an average day's work was two or two-and-a-half, and 'a very, *very* hard days work was 4 of them'. The different shades of ink which he used from time to time show that his habit was to correct as he wrote, sentence by sentence, and that though he subsequently read through the whole of his chapter, he rarely needed to make any later alteration.

IV

The manuscripts he sent to press were these corrected first drafts. He never dictated to an amanuensis, nor used a secretary to make a fair copy, and only in a few instances can we be sure that he took the trouble of rewriting a much-corrected slip.[3] Indeed there was no time for what a modern printer regards as normal courtesy from his author; and as for dictation, it would only have hindered him, for he relied upon the knowledge that he had to fill about thirty slips in his normal handwriting to com-

1. Forster, II ii, iii, iv.

2. Letter to F. Harvey, 15 Dec. 1880, accompanying the MS. of *The Battle of Life* (Pierpont Morgan Library).

3. When sending Charles Edward Lester a sheet of the MS. of *Oliver Twist* on 19 July 1840, he remarked, 'I should tell you perhaps as a kind of certificate of the Oliver scrap, that it is a portion of the original and only draught.—I never copy' (letter in the New York Public Library, Berg Collection). But this does not represent his invariable practice later in life. The sheet on which Staggs's Gardens is described in *Dombey and Son*, ch. vi, is so clean and so conspicuously different from its neighbours in that respect as to suggest that he had decided to make a fair copy of a passage which had involved him in unusually heavy corrections. On the same reasoning it seems likely that he rewrote the first MS. slip of *Hunted Down* and of *A Holiday Romance* (both in the Pierpont Morgan Library), and certain passages in *Barnaby Rudge* (see p. 81 n.). In the MS. of *Little Dorrit* there are traces of rough draft on the versos of some sheets of the first and last numbers; three leaves of the last number have been pasted on to slips concealing an earlier version.

plete a monthly number. Thus Bradbury and Evans, his printers, had to make do with 'copy' obscure enough to daunt the most experienced compositor. Not only was it written in a small hand with all too little space left between lines for the numerous interlineations, but the text was sprinkled with peculiar proper names —not Cox but Tox, not Tomlinson but Towlinson—and with phonetic spellings of standard English. The difficulties presented even to a compositor accustomed to Dickens's hand may be gauged from the printer's setting up 'Mr. Dick was very partial to going abroad' for 'Mr. Dick was very partial to ginger bread'. But the compositors were picked men,[1] clean, quick, and accurate. To ensure rapid despatch they were accustomed to distribute copy amongst several hands by dividing each slip across the centre and endorsing the lower half with a starred numeral corresponding to the number of the original slip.[2] Their accuracy cannot be properly attested until the manuscripts have been carefully collated with the proofs by some future editor of a standard text of the novels; but it may be said that neither Dickens nor Forster, who also read the proofs, found much to need correction.

Surviving copies of proof sheets suggest that the printer was instructed to provide galley-proof when time permitted. Thus corrected proofs of *Copperfield*[3] consist of two sets of galley-proof of Number I, one set of page-proof of Numbers II to XVIII, and two sets of page-proof of Number XIX–XX. It seems unlikely that Numbers II to XIX–XX were first set up in galley, for time was short; and, as will be seen, the bulk of correction was necessarily done in page. We can be almost certain that Number II (chapters iv–vi, published on 31 May 1849) was not set up in galley, for Dickens sent the end of the number to Evans on 5 May 1849 with the note, 'If it should make a little too much (as I think it may) let them begin Chapter 5 on page 46, where there is now a great blank.'[4] A reasonable inference is that he had already seen page-proofs of at least chapter iv and possibly of chapter v as well.

There was not infrequently 'a little too much', for though he used the numbering of his slips as a guide to quantity—30 slips would yield about 32 pages of print—the reckoning was only

1. Mamie Dickens, *My Father as I recall him* [1897], p. 63.
2. See letter to Mrs Procter, 29 Oct. 1865 (*Letters*, III 442).
3. Victoria and Albert Museum Library, 48 B 16. 4. *Letters*, II 152.

approximate. In every number of *Copperfield* except V, X, XI, XIV, XVI, XVIII, and XIX–XX, the proofs show what was called 'over-matter' extending, in Number VI, to as much as 96 lines of print. Dickens was so well accustomed to this happening that he could write to a correspondent on 28 January 1848, when *Dombey and Son* was drawing to a close:

> I never accept an engagement for about this day in the month: being always liable, if my *proofs are late, to have to revise them at the printers*, and if there is too much matter (as is the case this month) to take it out, and put them all to rights and leave them on the press.[1]

But the amount taken out rarely corresponded at all exactly with the amount of 'over-matter'. Thus in *Copperfield* VI Dickens saved little more than 50 of the 96 lines excess; and in Number IX, where there were 58 lines excess, he saved 40 but inserted the equivalent of six more, adding as a note to the printer, 'the over-matter must be got in somehow—by lengthening the page'. This expedient was needed only in extreme cases, a 51-line page then taking the place of a page of 50 lines of type. Where the over-matter was small, less drastic methods were employed. In *Copperfield* XIII, for example, where there were a mere 11 lines too many, the printer preferred to save the space by resetting a letter, quoted at the end of chapter xi, in smaller type; and on numerous occasions a small saving was readily made where the final words of a paragraph overlapped into a new line.

When forced to lop and crop, Dickens was accustomed to make his cuts at the expense of the comedy. In *Dombey and Son*, where passages of greater significance were also removed, Mrs Chick, Miss Tox, and Major Bagstock originally had longer parts;[2] so had Skimpole in *Bleak House* II and Honeythunder in *Edwin Drood* V; and in *David Copperfield*, chapter xxi, he had to remove a capital scene in which Steerforth successfully exerted his charms upon the lugubrious Mrs Gummidge and entered into a league with her to be lone and lorn together.[3] The future editor of Dickens will have to consider restoring these passages to the text, since they were removed only because of the fortuitous demands of serial publication.

1. *Letters*, ii 70. 2. See below, pp. 97, 98.

3. First published in *Review of English Studies*, new series i (1950), p. 251. It is obvious, too, that space is most easily saved in dialogue, where short lines of print are frequent.

But too little copy was even more troublesome than too much. 'Fancy!' Dickens wrote to Forster[1] early in July 1865, while *Our Mutual Friend* was on the stocks, 'fancy my having under-written number sixteen by two and a half pages—a thing I have not done since *Pickwick*!' He had forgotten *Dombey and Son* VI and *Bleak House* XVI where in each instance he was two pages light, and numerous other numbers deficient by half a page or more, notably *Little Dorrit* X, which concludes the first book with the release of Old Dorrit from the Marshalsea Prison. On that occasion he was the best part of a page too short even after he had added in proof a long paragraph describing the friends who assembled at the prison gate to welcome Mr Dorrit on his discharge. He disliked giving his readers short measure. The text of a number must usually end well down on the thirty-second page. 'Couldn't the end of the *next* chapter, which is crowded, be brought over to the following page?' he asked on the proofs of *Copperfield* XV, 'then, the blanks at the end of the No would be avoided'.

Proofs also provided opportunity for other types of alteration. Sir Leicester Dedlock's hair is turned from white to grey in *Bleak House* I, Richard Carstone's age is increased from seventeen to nineteen, and it is only at this stage that Skimpole's first name is changed from Leonard to Harold—one of a number of changes designed to weaken the resemblance to Leigh Hunt—that Jobling's assumed name is altered from 'Owen' to 'Weevle', that Matthew Bagnet's nickname is changed from 'Number Seventy Four' to 'Lignum Vitæ' and Minnie Meagles's from 'Baby' to 'Pet'. It is more surprising to discover that until proof Miss Flite had been 'Maggie'—a name to be used in *Little Dorrit* for another crazy woman[2]—and that even then Dickens had toyed with 'Flighty'.

Forster had also been accustomed to lend a hand ever since 1837.[3] He provided another pair of eyes for detecting errors of the press, and he was trusted as a judge of what the average reader would stand. Proofs show that he softened such expletives as Dickens himself had overlooked, and removed the description of Miss Tox ejecting the bugs from the wainscoting of her house by means of a brush dipped in paraffin. Furthermore, Forster was

1. Forster, IX v.
2. Her surname also is changed in proof—from Flinx to Bangham.
3. Forster, II i.

usually in London and could deal with last-minute adjustments sent from Broadstairs or further afield. Thus in July 1841 Dickens wrote from the Highlands—a 'place which no man ever spelt but which sounds like Ballyhoolish'—inquiring 'whether the blind man, in speaking to Barnaby about riches, tells him they are to be found in *crowds*. If I have not actually used that word, will you introduce it? A perusal of the proof of the following number (70) will show you how, and why.'[1] The addition was needed in chapter xlvii in the next number. A few years later on, as the last number of *Dombey* was going to press, he recollected that in the final parade of his pantomime one character had been overlooked—the dog Diogenes; he therefore sent Forster alternative versions, leaving to his judgement which was to be inserted in proof. There is no evidence of his consulting anyone else at proof-stage, except for a mystifying reference in a letter of 15 May 1861, where he tells Lytton that 'a woman' had frequently shown, when proofs were read to her, 'an intuitive sense and discretion that I have set great store by'.[2]

V

Such were the conditions in which he worked from writing the first words of the novel till the moment of publication. But the system only began to work when planning was completed. The nature of his planning is very largely revealed in the notes bound with his manuscripts. Those of *Pickwick Papers*, *Nicholas Nickleby*, and *Oliver Twist* are imperfect;[3] but judging by the sparseness of notes in the first complete manuscript, that of *The Old Curiosity Shop*,[4] the notes for these early novels are likely to have been very slight indeed. The beginnings of a change in practice are first noticeable in the manuscript of *Martin Chuzzlewit*, and it is not

1. Forster, II ix.

2. *Letters*, III 220. Could the unknown woman have been anyone but Georgina Hogarth?

3. Fragments of *Pickwick* are in the British Museum and in the Berg Collection of the New York Public Library; about two-thirds of *Oliver Twist* is in the Victoria and Albert Museum, and a page in the Berg Collection; and the Dickens House in Doughty Street has some fragments of *Nickleby*.

4. This MS. and those of all subsequent novels, with two exceptions, were bequeathed by Forster to the Victoria and Albert Museum. The MS. of *Great Expectations* was given by Dickens to Chauncy Hare Townshend and by him to the Wisbech Museum where it still lies. The MS. of *Our Mutual Friend* was given by Dickens to E. S. Dallas, and is now in the Pierpont Morgan Library.

without significance that Dickens claimed in the original preface to this novel:

> I have endeavoured in the progress of this Tale, to resist the temptation of the current Monthly Number, and to keep a steadier eye upon the general purpose and design. With this object in view, I have put a strong constraint upon myself from time to time, in many places; and I hope the story is the better for it, now.

Some evidence of this growing restraint is to be found in the manuscript notes for contents of two numbers of *Martin Chuzzlewit*, IV (chapters ix and x) and VI (chapters xiii–xv). Thereafter each novel from *Dombey and Son* to *Edwin Drood*, except for *Great Expectations* and *A Tale of Two Cities*,[1] has its full quota of notes, one page to each number.

The precise function which these notes fulfilled is difficult to determine. Dickens himself never mentions them; and Forster, who reproduced in his *Life of Dickens* part of the notes prepared for the first monthly numbers of *Little Dorrit* and *David Copperfield* to show 'in the former the labour and pains, and in the latter the lightness and confidence of handling',[2] was either ignorant of their function or insufficiently curious about them.

From *Dombey and Son* onwards the notes are uniform in appearance. A sheet of paper has been folded across the centre, thus forming two conjugate half-sheets. The left-hand half-sheet is invariably filled with general memoranda: the right-hand sheet is invariably headed by the title of the novel and the number of the monthly part, and is then sub-divided into chapters. A glance at the photograph of the notes relating to *David Copperfield* VII will show that the chapter numbers and chapter titles have been written down before the succeeding notes, since Dickens has left himself insufficient space between chapter xix and chapter xx for all the jottings he wanted to make. The *Edwin Drood* notes confirm that this was his practice, for the notes for Numbers V and VI contain no more than the chapter numbers and chapter titles.

What Dickens did after mapping out his memoranda sheet into chapters may be inferred from the appearance of the ink. He seems to have had three sorts in general use, one a blue-black, another a vivid blue, and a third which has now faded to a

1. It is not easy to account for Dickens's abandoning his practice in his last two weekly serial novels. The MS. of *Great Expectations* contains notes of other kinds; see below, pp. 30–1.

2. Forster, VIII i.

watery yellow. The supplies appear to have been uncertain, since changes from one to another occur with baffling irregularity. But though the irregularity is puzzling in itself, the frequency of change in ink in some of the manuscripts throws some light upon the process of composition. Thus the supply of watery ink with which *David Copperfield* was begun gave out on the eleventh leaf of Number IV, three-quarters way through chapter x, and Dickens then changed over to vivid blue which lasted him until the end of Number VII; but in Number VIII (chapter xxii) he reverted to the watery ink. We should expect the ink with which the notes were written to alter with these changes, if we assume that Dickens wrote the notes at the same desk at which he was writing the novel. But this does not happen. In the notes for Number IV[1] the chapter titles of chapters xi and xii, the line 'on my own account, and don't like it' on the left-hand side, and the passage 'neglect Quinion.–arrangement/"Behold me" &c' on the right-hand side are written in vivid blue ink unlike the surrounding notes, which are written in watery ink. This suggests that the passages written in vivid blue were jotted down after the supply of watery ink had temporarily failed and therefore *after* Dickens had begun to compose the number. But it also suggests that the notes under the headings of chapters xi and xii were written *before* the chapters were composed. More surprising is to find the resumption of watery ink in Number VIII anticipated in the summary for Number VII, where the only jottings in vivid blue are the memoranda on the left-hand side, the three chapter numbers, and the first two chapter titles. The inference is that all the notes on the right-hand side and the last chapter title ('Little Em'ly') were written after finishing the monthly number itself.

There is further evidence to support this. On the left-hand side Dickens can be seen trying out two names for Steerforth's servant: 'Lirrimer? Littimer'. 'Lirrimer' was his first choice; and so the name stands, though corrected to 'Littimer' on its first two occurrences in the second paragraph of chapter xxi—'Nothing could be objected against his surname, ⟨Lirrimer⟩ Littimer, by which he was known. Peter might have been hanged, or Tom transported; but ⟨Lirrimer⟩ Littimer was perfectly respectable.' But by the time he came to write the fourth paragraph of the same chapter, he was quite decided upon the name. 'Littimer was in my room in the morning' needed no correction, and 'Lit-

1. See below, pp. 126–7.

timer' he was from that point onwards. But 'Littimer' was also the form used in the notes to chapter xxi, showing that the notes for this chapter—or at least a part of them—were written after the chapter was completed.

It will be recalled that Mr Vholes in *Bleak House* supported an aged father in the Vale of Taunton. The manuscript reveals that he was originally intended to support an aged mother: 'father' is a correction in the manuscript, but it is the word 'father' we find in the summary for that chapter. Similarly, a comparison of chapter titles in the notes and in the text of *Bleak House* and of passages from the text quoted in the notes shows that the version in the notes often, but not invariably, records the corrected and not the original version.

It is clear, therefore, that Dickens was not entirely consistent in his practice. Sometimes he wrote his chapter notes before the corresponding chapter was written, sometimes after. And this inconsistency in his practice seems to imply an inconsistency of purpose. For while those chapter notes which were written after the chapter was finished cannot have been intended to help him in the composition of the chapter, those which were written before the composition of the chapter they relate to may well have been intended as a rough plan of the direction the chapter was to take. The closing notes for chapters vii and ix in *Copperfield* III are almost certainly notes of this kind.[1] But that he should have taken the trouble to jot down chapter notes after the chapter was written suggests that though he did not always need a rough plan to work by in composing his chapter, he did feel the need of a summary of the chapter afterwards. The function of this summary may have been to refresh his memory of the details of the preceding number before embarking upon the next.

The chapter notes on the right-hand side, then, seem to fill a double purpose. Sometimes they serve to rough out the direction the chapter will take and to emphasize its salient points; but except for the last numbers, they always serve to summarize the contents and to put Dickens into the mood of the last monthly number when beginning upon another.

The function of the notes on the left-hand side seems to have been different. They are jotted down haphazardly and bear no relation to the chapter divisions on the right-hand side. Dickens is seen in the process of meditating what ingredients shall go into

1. See below, p. 123.

the number to be written. Both the form of the entries and the quality of the ink show that there were frequently two stages in this process. The questions represent the stage of indecision; and the conviction of the replies, often underlined more than once, suggests that the shape of the number was rapidly forming in his mind.

This indecision must not be read as evidence of mere opportunism, as though Dickens relied upon the inspiration of the moment for filling his number. That indeed must have been his temptation in the days of *Pickwick* and *Nickleby*, and we learn from Forster that the theme of *The Old Curiosity Shop* took gradual form as he wrote it, 'with less direct consciousness of design on his own part than I can remember in any other instance throughout his career'.[1] But from *Martin Chuzzlewit* onwards readers could feel assured that though a Sairey Gamp or a Wilkins Micawber might wrest temporary control of the story, yet the novel was proceeding in however leisurely a fashion to some predestined end. 'The whole pattern . . . is always before the eyes of the story-weaver at his loom', he said in the Postscript to *Our Mutual Friend*; and it is hoped that later studies in this volume will confirm the remark. The master plans of *Dombey and Son*[2] and of subsequent novels almost certainly existed, but they have not survived on paper and in all probability they were never written down. 'I never commit thoughts to paper', he told a correspondent, about the time of *Copperfield*, 'until I am obliged to write, being better able to keep them in regular order, on different shelves of my brain, ready ticketed and labelled to be brought out when I want them.'[3]

The number plans were not primarily concerned with these master plans. At most they drew occasional attention to some prominent thread in the pattern, as when Dickens notes in the plan for *David Copperfield* XII: 'Carry the thread of Agnes through it all', or 'Carry through, the unravelling of Uriah Heep. always by Mr Micawber' in the plan for Number XVI, or 'The man who, being utterly sensual and careless, comes to very much the same thing in the end as the Gradgrind school', a sentence in which he characterizes James Harthouse in the first number plan of *Hard Times*. In short, the number plans show us Dickens not in the moments of creation, but in the moments of translating ideas

1. Forster, II vii. 2. See below, pp. 90, 94.
3. *Harper's New Monthly Magazine*, June–Nov., 1862, p. 379.

into practice,[1] deliberating how best to achieve a certain effect ('Louisa to be acted on by Harthouse, through Tom? Yes', *Hard Times* IV), when to introduce a predetermined theme ('Dora in declining health. First intimation? Yes', *David Copperfield* XVI), how to finish off a number ('Little Em'ly and Mr Peggotty. qy. To close the N° with her discovery? Yes', ibid.), or defining the dominant theme of a number ('David's Marriage to Dora', Number XIV; 'The Emigration N°', Number XVIII). Sometimes he will review possible characters and defer their re-entry to a subsequent number; thus Miss Mowcher's claim is rejected in Number X (chapters xxviii–xxxi) with the note 'Impossible. Try next time', and Mr and Miss Murdstone are kept waiting in the wings for a call which is deferred from month to month from Number XIII till the final number. Sometimes, when at work on one number, he can be discovered turning to consider an episode in a future number. Thus in the memoranda for *Little Dorrit* XVIII there is an entry 'The Merdle Image smashed?'. But it had been smashed in the previous month, and a later entry, '(Done last N°.)', takes account of the fact. This can only mean that the original entry, and presumably the two preceding entries, on the plan for Number XVIII were written before Number XVII was finished. Such evidence, however, is exceptional; and equally exceptional is the use of these memoranda to plan a scene at some length, as the storm scene in Yarmouth Roads is planned in *Copperfield* Number XVIII.[2] Often the briefest of notes suffices: 'Miss Murdstone comes on a donkey' is enough to suggest that generously comic incident in chapter xiii. Though indeed the majority of these jottings are related to incidents in the story, almost as many record the names of characters only. Their names, it would seem, were enough to suggest the parts the characters were to play.

1. For several years Dickens kept a notebook in which he jotted down notions as they darted into his mind; for example, 'The unwieldy ship taken in tow by the snorting little steam Tug', subsequently endorsed 'Done in Casby and Panks'. This notebook, which was used by Forster for his *Life of Dickens*, is now in the Berg Collection of the New York Public Library. He is also reported to have kept 'a series of small paper bags, filled with scraps of paper containing various memoranda' upon his writing-table (F. G. Kitton, *Charles Dickens by Pen and Pencil*, 1889, pp. 173–4, on the authority of Arthur Locker, a contributor to *All the Year Round*); but no memoranda other than those mentioned in this chapter have survived.

2. See below, pp. 168–9.

VI

Such would seem to have been the purposes Dickens had in mind when making these memoranda. Other notes associated with the memoranda can be more confidently accounted for. There are several sheets on which possible titles have been drafted. Occasionally—but this is rare—he makes a calculation about the age of a character so as to assure himself that all the evidence tallies. Thus there is a note on Florence's age in *Dombey and Son* XV based on the statement in Number VI that she was then not yet fourteen. An even more detailed calculation is made of the ages of the ten principal characters 'in the last stage of Pip's Expectations'.[1]

For *Great Expectations* he had been able to manage without number plans, but he found that he could not entirely dispense with all memoranda. In addition to the note on the ages of the characters, there is a calculation on the state of the tides for use in the great scene of Magwitch's recapture (chapter liv),[1] and there is a sketch of the conclusion of the novel[1] headed 'General Mems' which reads as follows:

> Miss Havisham and Pip, and the Money for Herbert. So Herbert made a partner in Clarriker's.
> Compeyson. How brought in?
> Estella. Magwitch's daughter.
> Orlick and Pip's entrapment—and escape
> —To the flight
> Start
> Pursuit
> Struggle—Both on board
> together—Compeyson drownd [sic]—
> Magwitch rescued by Pip. And
> taken—
> Then:
> Magwitch tried, found guilty, & left for
> Death
> Dies presently in Newgate
> Property confiscated to the Crown.
> Herbert goes abroad:
> Pip perhaps to follow.
> Pip arrested when too ill to be moved—lies in the
> Chambers in Fever. Ministering Angel Joe.

1. Printed in *The Dickensian*, Mar. 1949, pp. 78–80.

recovered again, Pip goes humbly down to the
old marsh Village, to propose to Biddy.
Finds Biddy married to Joe
So goes abroad to Herbert (happily married to Clara
Barley), and becomes his clerk.
The one good thing he did in his prosperity,
the only thing that endures and bears good fruit.

Although there is no comparable sketch for the conclusion of any other novel, it is not altogether surprising that one was needed for a novel written without the help of number plans. The last double number had often proved to be troublesome. In *Dombey and Son* the final number plan is dense with notes; two or three scenes are sketched in some detail; and as each memorandum is used, a tick is placed against it in the plan. The last of these reads 'Qy Order of chapters—'. An answer was found in the customary manner on the right-hand side of the number plan. But when the same problem arose in *David Copperfield*, the solution was reached only after canvassing three different orders in the memoranda.[1] In *Little Dorrit* also the order of chapters had to be settled ahead; but there the difficulty was, in the words of the chapter summary, to 'tell the whole story, working it out as much as possible through Mrs Clennam herself, so as to present her character very strongly'. Even the author himself seems to have been hard pressed to recall the precise connexion between Arthur Clennam, his father, his uncle, and Frederick Dorrit, Mrs Clennam, Flintwinch, and Flintwinch's brother. Accordingly an additional memorandum in two columns was compiled for the double number, one column being entitled 'Mems: for working the story round.—Retrospective' and the other 'Mems: for working the story round.—Prospective'. The 'retrospective mems.' summarize what was already known to the reader, and append page references; the 'prospective mems.' succeed, after what was clearly a struggle, in finding an answer to the initial question, 'How [were the Clennams] connected with the Dorrits?'

The conclusion of *Great Expectations* was straightforward by comparison, though 'the general turn and tone of the working out and winding up, will be away from all such things as they conventionally go', and 'the planning out from week to week' was declared to be unimaginably difficult.[2] The interest of the

1. See below, p. 174. 2. *Letters*, III 216–17.

sketch printed above lies in the stage of the story at which Dickens took his bearings, and the details which he altered in the course of writing. The last stage of Pip's expectations begins in chapter xl with Magwitch's return. Of the succeeding twelve chapters—dealing with Magwitch's story, Estella's marriage to Drummle and her parentage, the arrangements for Magwitch's escape by river, and Miss Havisham's death—the summary has little or nothing to say. It is only after Pip's entrapment by Orlick in chapter liii and his rescue that the events are forecast in detail. It would therefore appear that the sketch was written either immediately before or immediately after the completion of chapter liii, and that the first three entries are notes about matters still to be kept prominently in view. It was in chapter xxxvii that Pip had begun to buy Herbert a place in Clarriker's business, and the transaction was completed by Miss Havisham in chapter xlix. But it remains a live issue; for this was, in the words of the sketch,

> the one good thing he did in his prosperity, the only thing that endures and bears good fruit.

That this was not a mere afterthought, but one of the 'morals' of the book, is shown by the anticipation of these words at the end of chapter xxxvii:

> At length, the thing being done, and he having that day entered Clarriker's House, and he having talked to me for a whole evening in a flush of pleasure and success, I did really cry in good earnest when I went to bed, to think that my expectations had done some good to somebody.

'Compeyson. How brought in?' This query seems to refer to a problem of tying up loose ends at the conclusion of the novel, for Compeyson had been 'in' from the beginning. He had been actively shadowing Pip and Magwitch since the first chapter of the final stage, and his relations with Miss Havisham had been explained at a time when Dickens was still calling him 'Compey'. It was in chapter xlii that he was first given a name, and the last three letters are first added to it in the manuscript of chapter xlv. Not until chapter xlvii, where he next enters, is the name 'Compeyson' written without hesitation, as it is written in the 'General Mems'. On any explanation of them, therefore, the memoranda cannot have been drawn up until after chapter xlii was written, in which Magwitch tells the story of his life. 'How brought in?' must refer to something other than Compeyson's connexion with

Miss Havisham, and to what else can it refer but to the scene of Magwitch's capture?

'Estella. Magwitch's daughter' was almost certainly a part of the original design: it bears at least as closely upon the 'moral' of the book as the purchase of Herbert's partnership. Though the parentage is revealed before chapter liv, it was still to be kept in mind for use in the scene of Magwitch's death and later.

The sketch seems therefore to have been designed to cover the course of the last six chapters, or what is called in the manuscript the 'Ninth Monthly Portion'. The course as planned was not strictly followed. Magwitch and Compeyson were not on board together, nor was Magwitch rescued from drowning by Pip. Herbert's departure occurs before the trial, and there is no hint given of Wemmick's wedding or of the last meeting with Uncle Pumblechook. The variations are small, the additions mentioned are scarcely significant; so narrowly does Dickens diverge from the path he had plotted.

But there was to be one other addition to the scheme, the final scene with Estella. In the novel as we read it, all but the opening paragraphs of chapter lix, describing Pip's visit to the old forge, are a revised version urged upon Dickens by Bulwer Lytton.[1] The original was preserved and published by Forster,[2] who regarded it as 'more consistent with the drift, as well as natural working out, of the tale'. From this we see that the book was to end with a casual meeting between Pip and Estella. 'I was very glad afterwards to have had the interview', Pip commented,

> for, in her face and in her voice, and in her touch, she gave me the assurance, that suffering had been stronger than Miss Havisham's teaching, and had given her a heart to understand what my heart used to be.

Perhaps this seemed obvious before Lytton made his sentimental plea—something which could be left, like Wemmick's marriage, for the improvisation of the moment. It was at least more appropriate that Pip, who had lost Magwitch's money, should also lose his daughter, than that he should marry her in the end.

These were the kind of notes which experience showed that his system of publication and his manner of work required of him. They do not determine the pattern of the novel, they do not define the path of the story, but they ensure that, the pattern

1. *Letters*, III 225. 2. Forster, IX iii.

once determined, the threads do not go awry, and, the path once set, there is no serious deviation in a course of as much as nineteen months. Furthermore, they have an abiding interest in that they shed light on the design in the pattern and serve to show the measure of control which Dickens exercised. They reveal a calculated emphasis at one point, a calculated suspense at another, a problem of arrangement solved or a conclusion settled; they will accordingly be examined more closely in subsequent chapters in relation to the novels whose composition they served. The first ten years of Dickens's career present problems of a different kind. Though the documentation is sparser, enough evidence survives to answer some of the more interesting questions raised, and to these the next three chapters are devoted.

CHAPTER II

Sketches by Boz: Collection and Revision

I

EVERY biographer has described how Dickens began by contributing tales and sketches to magazines and newspapers, later collected and enlarged in the two series of *Sketches by Boz*; and many since Forster have followed Dickens's own cue in high-lighting that dramatic moment in December 1833 when the twenty-one-year-old gallery reporter bought a copy of the *Monthly Magazine* and his eyes were 'dimmed with joy and pride' on seeing his first story 'in all the glory of print'.[1] But there are many aspects of this crucial first phase of his writing that have been under-emphasized or even neglected: not only the sheer merit of the *Sketches*, but their signal importance as an event in literary history, and the effect of their contemporary fame on Dickens's literary career; and, most neglected of all, the care which he took in revising them. That revision—its extent, direction, and probable motives—is the primary concern of this essay; it deserves a fairly full treatment, both for its obvious relevance to the theme of this book and for the light thrown on the inter-relations of journalistic and creative writing, a question of central interest to Dickens's early career, and perhaps to the whole.

The *Sketches by Boz* are too apt to be seen as a mere prelude to *Pickwick Papers*, instead of as, in Forster's words, 'a book that might have stood its ground, even if it had stood alone'.[2] They have been seen from a distance as 'early Dickens', and seldom as writings which suddenly appeared to dazzle the 1830s with their brilliance. And this has affected the whole interpretation of those

1. Preface to 1847 edition of *Pickwick Papers*. 2. Forster, I v.

first three years; too exclusive an emphasis has been laid on the 'ascent of the rocket'[1] with the fame of *Pickwick* and its immediate consequences, whereas it was the success of the *Sketches*, first in periodicals and then more decisively in book form, that really inaugurated Dickens's career as a writer. Indeed, as subsequent chapters suggest,[2] it appeared as the beginning of a different kind of success. When we try to recover Dickens's own point of view in the winter of 1835–6 and that of the contemporary readers who gave the First Series of the *Sketches* its glowing reception in February and March, we see that the *Pickwick* project cut across the planned career at an unexpected and slightly disturbing angle; and it was not of *Pickwick* that Dickens was thinking when he promised 'connected works of fiction of a higher grade' as a result of the 'unlooked-for success' of the *Sketches*.[3] The deflection of his ambition was, as we know, permanent; against all probability and expectation he discovered in that 'monthly something' his full creative powers and the beginnings of his large-scale constructive powers; he also, almost accidentally, initiated his characteristic mode of publication; and that is certainly one reason[4] why in maturity he tended himself to belittle the *Sketches*, and left too many later readers content to take them at the author's retrospective valuation. 'They were written', said Dickens, looking back from the peak of 1850, the year of *David Copperfield*, 'when I was a very young man . . . sent into the world with all their imperfections (a good many) on their heads . . . I am conscious of their often being extremely crude and ill-considered, and bearing obvious marks of haste and inexperience'.[5] This is very different from the tone of the original Preface of February 1836, which, despite its tactful modesty—the *Sketches* are a 'pilot balloon' in which the author ventures with the 'assistance and companionship' of an already famous illustrator, 'GEORGE CRUIKSHANK'—

1. The phrase, adapted from the review in the *Quarterly* (Oct. 1837), is used by Johnson as a chapter heading for III 3, in the year following the completion of *Pickwick* (1838). This criticism applies less to him than to other post-Forster biographers.

2. See pp. 63, 76 below.

3. Preface to second edition of First Series, 1 Aug. 1836; that is, just before *Pickwick* began to succeed.

4. Another reason may be that the later history of the *Sketches* involved him in his first disillusioning clash with a publisher.

5. Preface to 1850 edition (reprinted without change in all subsequent editions); this was the seventh volume in the 'Cheap edition'. It was Dickens's wish to put it late, since otherwise 'the Sketches would make a dangerous break in the continuity of the Sale, and perhaps damage what followed' (*Letters*, II 148).

asserts a high claim in the classic phrase of all literary revolutions —'his object has been to present little pictures of life and manners as they really are', which is echoed in the challenge of the subtitle: 'Illustrative of Every-Day Life, and Every-Day People'. As such they were applauded on all sides: next to the 'variety', the mingling of the exquisitely ridiculous and the grim, what was most praised was the 'startling fidelity';[1] '"Boz" is a kind of Boswell to society.'[2] The *Sketches* were acclaimed for their novelty and accuracy both in the kind of life observed, and the penetration of the observer accepting and transforming the commonplace, 'bringing out the meaning and interest of objects which would altogether escape the observation of ordinary minds',[3] 'the romance, as it were, of real life'.[4] Throughout the reviews there is gratitude for the discovery of 'every-day life' in neglected but immediately recognized pockets of urban and suburban society. This sense of revelation cannot be fully recovered by readers unaware of the deficiency of such a quality in the popular prose-literature of the time, of the sharpness of the difference between the world of Boz and the worlds of 'silver-fork' novels, of the Annuals, of romantic-historical thrillers and 'political-economy' tales, or of the less sharp but still distinctive difference from the comic worlds of Hood and Hook[5] and the lower-grade imitators of Egan's *Life in London*. Unlike *Pickwick*, which for all its incidental topicality is upheld in timeless splendour by the illusion of a self-sustaining world, the *Sketches* have more to give to a modern reader who knows something of their literary and social context. But this approach, though helpful, is by no means indispensable. The tales and sketches themselves, without annotation, give us the world which the young Dickens saw; and what is more import-

1. *Metropolitan Magazine*, Mar. 1836, p. 77.
2. *Court Journal*, 20 Feb. 1836, p. 123. 3. *Examiner*, 28 Feb. 1836, p. 133.
4. *Spectator*, 20 Feb. 1836, p. 183.
5. Some reviewers compared Boz's 'caricature of Cockney life' with Hook's; others found it noticeably superior, and the *Sunday Times* (21 Feb. 1836) predicted that Boz 'would one day make Tom Hood look to his laurels'. None mentions what seems much more akin to Dickens's work, the tales in John Poole's *Sketches and Recollections* (1835; mainly from the *New Monthly Magazine* of 1826–34). Sketches on the recreations of Londoners (such as Greenwich Fair, Astley's, Vauxhall Gardens) were very common, but the likeness here is merely of substance.

The closest contact, recognized by several reviewers, was between the tales and contemporary theatrical comedy; they do not suggest derivation, but note Boz's promise as a comic dramatist. Two tales were soon to be dramatized, 'The Bloomsbury Christening' and 'The Great Winglebury Duel', the latter by Dickens himself as *The Strange Gentleman*.

ant, they give us Dickens seeing it, with that curious, all-absorbing eye—the child's eye of David Copperfield, which he never lost.

Contemporary reviews are cited here, because the comments of critics saluting an almost unknown writer have a special value as testimony; but Forster's summary,[1] which includes and recalls their sense of discovery, has also the distinctive authority of its date and writer, and much of it deserves to be quoted for its general critical direction as well as its information:

> The *Sketches* were much more talked about than the first two or three numbers of *Pickwick*, and I remember still with what hearty praise the book was first named to me by my dear friend Albany Fonblanque, as keen and clear a judge as ever lived either of books or men. Richly did it merit all the praise it had, and more, I will add, than he was ever disposed to give to it himself. He decidedly underrated it. He gave, in subsequent writings, so much more perfect form and fullness to everything it contained, that he did not care to credit himself with the marvel of having yet so early anticipated so much. But the first sprightly runnings of his genius are undoubtedly here. . . The observation shown throughout is nothing short of wonderful. Things are painted literally as they are; and, whatever the picture, whether of every-day vulgar, shabby genteel, or downright low, with neither the condescending air which is affectation, nor the too familiar one which is slang. . . Of course there are inequalities in it, and some things that would have been better away: but it is a book that might have stood its ground, even if it had stood alone, as containing unusually truthful observation of a sort of life between the middle class and the low, which, having few attractions for bookish observers, was quite unhacknied ground. It had otherwise also the very special merit of being in no respect bookish or commonplace in its descriptions of the old city with which its writer was so familiar. It was a picture of every-day London at its best and worst, in its humours and enjoyments as well as its sufferings and sins, pervaded everywhere not only with the absolute reality of the things depicted, but also with that subtle sense and mastery of feeling which gives to the reader's sympathies invariably right direction, and awakens consideration, tenderness, and kindness precisely for those who most need such help.

II

'He decidedly underrated it'. This underrating has already been illustrated from Dickens's 1850 Preface; and his view, how-

1. Forster, I v.

ever disputable, is a valid personal judgement, a fact about Dickens in 1850. But two other statements in that Preface, both coloured by this critical view, are open to objection from their manipulation of facts.

> The whole of these sketches were written and published, one by one, when I was a very young man.

But since six[1] out of the total of over fifty had made no previous periodical appearance,[2] and since his letters of 1835–6 show that some at least were written especially for the collection, this is only an approximate statement; and his exaggeration is probably motivated, consciously or not, by a wish to extenuate their 'obvious marks of haste'. What follows is misleading, if not disingenuous:

> They were collected and republished while I was still a very young man; and sent into the world with all their imperfections (a good many) on their heads . . .
>
> But as this collection is not originated now, and was very leniently and favourably received when it was first made, I have not felt it right either to remodel or expunge, beyond a few words and phrases here and there.

This description would not lead one to suppose that when Dickens first collected his sketches he made extensive cuts, rewrote whole paragraphs, and made innumerable minute changes both of substance and style; nor that he continued to revise in successive editions including the very one for which this Preface was written. Only an edition with heavy textual apparatus could exhibit the full extent of these changes; but a general account of them is for the first time[3] attempted here. The docu-

1. Three tales ('The Black Veil', 'The Great Winglebury Duel', and 'Sentiment', first appearing in First Series); and three sketches ('A Visit to Newgate', First Series, 'Our Next-door Neighbours' and 'The Drunkard's Death', Second Series).

2. Fifty-three items were previously published; all but one are recorded by Hatton and Cleaver, pp. 91–103, and 'Brokers' and Marine Store Shops' was further noted by W. J. Carlton (*The Dickensian*, Mar. 1951, p. 67) as published in the *Morning Chronicle*, 15 Dec. 1834. The fifty-three are reduced to fifty when collected, as two tales originally appeared in two instalments each, and two sketches were later combined into one.

3. Some of the cut passages are given, and the fact of revision noted by Hatton and Cleaver; and F. J. H. Darton (*Dickens, Positively the First Appearance*, 1933) reprinted the original version of 'A Dinner at Poplar Walk' ('Mr. Minns and his Cousin'). W. J. Carlton (*The Dickensian*, June 1954, pp. 100–9; see below, p. 52, n. 2) makes some use of the original versions of 'A Parliamentary Sketch'. The intermediate revisions of 1837–9 ('monthly parts') and 1850 have, so far as we know, never been mentioned; Darton even says (p. 131) that 'the earliest volume texts

ments are straightforward; no manuscripts or proof sheets survive, but all the periodicals are accessible in national libraries,[1] and also most of the important editions:—First Series, [February] 1836;[2] Second Series, 1837 [December 1836]; Monthly Parts of combined series, November 1837 to June 1839, complete in one volume, May 1839;[3] 'Cheap edition', October 1850.

The story necessarily begins with the process of collection and selection. The plan of a collection was evidently formed, at the suggestion of the publisher John Macrone, early in the October of 1835. By 27 October[4] the scheme was well under way: Cruikshank had been secured as illustrator, and the title was being discussed. Something like 'Bubbles from a Brain' had apparently been considered;[5] but Dickens now put forward, as 'more modest', 'Sketches by Boz and Cuts by Cruikshank', a title which shows his appreciation of his good fortune[6] as well as his awareness of the strikingly visual quality of his own writing.[7] He offered to write additional sketches 'if the whole collection falls short of the two volumes', mentioning several possible topics from his 'memoranda'; his enthusiasm makes it plain that he meant to

(1836) remained virtually the same in all later editions'. Yet the 'monthly parts' were actually advertised as 'revised by the author'. The Macmillan edition of 1892, which purports to reprint the 'first' edition, gives the 1839 text.

1. The British Museum lacks the 1833–4 volumes of the *Monthly Magazine*.

2. The second edition appeared in Aug. 1836, the third in Mar. 1837 (see below, p. 50, n. 3).

3. We have not seen the actual monthly parts in wrappers, but there was no possibility of revision between these and the volume edition.

4. *Letters*, I 46–7 (letter to Macrone); this is the first known reference to the collection. Dickens was introduced to Cruikshank by Macrone in Nov. (I 49, 52), not, as Johnson (p. 104) implies, by Ainsworth.

5. 'Are you particularly attached to the retention of the word "Brain"—when we can't preserve the parody on Head's title?' (*Letters*, I 46). This must refer to *Bubbles from the Brunnens of Nassau*, By an Old Man [Sir Francis Bond Head], published by John Murray in 1834. The reason against such 'parody' was that both Dickens and Macrone now saw that the notion of 'bubbles coming direct from a steel instrument' was unacceptable; which suggests that some pun on 'springs' may have been thought of.

6. Cruikshank had been before the public as caricaturist and illustrator for some twenty-five years. He had illustrated, for example, John Wight's *Mornings in Bow-street* (1824–7), *Sunday in London* (1833), and *The Comic Almanack* (1835–47), all works showing some general likenesses of material to Dickens's tales and sketches. By this time he had probably also agreed to illustrate the fourth edition of Ainsworth's *Rookwood*, which Macrone published in 1836.

7. Apart from the quasi-pun, 'Sketches' was a natural choice, as Dickens had used it for two of the newspaper series; it was also fashionable (especially for accounts of travel) and appropriately recalled Washington Irving's *Sketch-Book* (1820), which Dickens greatly admired (*Letters*, I 315), as well as a popular success of the year, John Poole's *Sketches and Recollections* (1835).

write 'A Visit to Newgate' whether more material was needed or not. There was no thought at this stage of publishing anything less than 'the whole collection'; but the letters show that Dickens had not yet looked over the available material as a whole, and it was more extensive than he evidently remembered.

The sketches proper, as distinct from the tales, fell into two distinct and complete series; the five 'Street Sketches' which had appeared in the *Morning Chronicle* in the autumn of 1834;[1] and the twenty 'Sketches of London' in the *Evening Chronicle* from January to August 1835.[2] Soon after the conclusion of the latter, Dickens had begun a new series of twelve 'Scenes and Characters', in *Bell's Life in London*,[3] over a new signature, 'Tibbs'; these too were no doubt also regarded as possible material, though in fact only four of the twelve got into the first collected series, as against twenty-two of the earlier twenty-five. Besides the sketches, there were the seven tales which had appeared in the *Monthly Magazine*.[4] The last of these was published in February 1835, Dickens having notified the editor of the *Monthly* that he could no longer contribute without payment; he seems however to have expected to publish 'The Great Winglebury Duel' there in December[5]

1. 'Omnibuses', 26 Sept.; 'Shops and their Tenants', 10 Oct.; 'The Old Bailey', 23 Oct.; 'Shabby and Genteel People', 5 Nov.; 'Brokers' and Marine Store Shops', 15 Dec.

2. 'Hackney-coach stands', 31 Jan.; 'Gin Shops', 7 Feb.; 'Early Coaches', 19 Feb.; 'The Parish', 28 Feb.; 'The House', 7 Mar.; 'London Recreations', 17 Mar.; 'Public Dinners', 7 Apr.; 'Bellamy's', 11 Apr.; 'Greenwich Fair', 16 Apr.; 'Thoughts about People', 23 Apr.; 'Astley's', 9 May; 'Our Parish' (ctd), 19 May; 'The River', 6 June; 'Our Parish' (ctd), 18 June; 'The Pawnbroker's Shop', 30 June; 'Our Parish' (ctd), 14 July; 'The Streets by Morning', 21 July; 'Our Parish' (ctd), 28 July; 'Private Theatres', 11 Aug.; 'Our Parish' (concluded), 20 Aug.

The 'Parish' sketches, though irregularly spaced, form a kind of serial, and were probably intended as a novel variation of that popular success, Miss Mitford's *Our Village* (1824–32).

3. 'Seven Dials', 27 Sept.; 'Miss Evans and "the Eagle"', 4 Oct.; 'The Dancing Academy', 11 Oct.; 'Making a Night of It', 18 Oct.; 'Love and Oysters', 25 Oct.; 'Some Account of an Omnibus Cad', 1 Nov.; 'The Vocal Dress-Maker', 22 Nov.; 'The Prisoners' Van', 29 Nov.; 'The Parlour', 14 Dec.; 'Christmas Festivities', 27 Dec.; 'The New Year', 3 Jan. 1836; 'The Streets at Night', 17 Jan. 1836.

As biographers are uninformative about *Bell's Life*, it may be worth noting that it was a four-page sevenpenny weekly, liberal in politics but non-party, giving sporting and comic features as well as news; according to James Grant (*The Great Metropolis*, first series, 2 vols., 1836, II 134) it had a larger circulation than any daily or weekly except the *Dispatch*.

4. 'A Dinner at Poplar Walk', Dec. 1833; 'Mrs. Joseph Porter over the way', Jan. 1834; 'Horatio Sparkins', Feb. 1834; 'The Bloomsbury Christening', Apr. 1834; 'The Boarding House', May and Aug. 1834; 'The Steam Excursion', Oct. 1834; 'Passage in the Life of Mr. Watkins Tottle', Jan.–Feb. 1835.

5. *Letters*, I 47.

(perhaps changing his mind when he decided to dramatize it as 'The Strange Gentleman'); and he may have kept 'Sentiment' by him with the same purpose.[1] The other newly published tale, 'The Black Veil', is known to have been written in November,[2] expressly for the collection. The addition of these three, and of the long new sketch, 'A Visit to Newgate', suggests that where Dickens rejected earlier sketches it was not merely for lack of space; though it may of course have been thought advisable to attract readers by the inclusion of some unpublished material.

On the whole, it seems fair to regard work published by the beginning of November and omitted from the First Series of *Sketches by Boz* as deliberately rejected; though sketches published later might be left out simply for lack of space, since the new ones were by then already written. (One published as late as 27 December 1835 was in fact included, but probably as an afterthought—'Christmas Festivities', now called 'A Christmas Dinner', which concludes the first volume.) The 'rejected' material therefore consists of seven sketches: 'The Streets—Morning', 'Seven Dials', 'Some Account of an Omnibus Cad', 'The House', 'Bellamy's', 'The Old Bailey', and 'Love and Oysters'; and one tale, 'A Dinner at Poplar Walk'. Of these the first represented half a pair, and appears in the 'memoranda'[3] quoted in Dickens's letter of 27 October as 'The Streets—Noon and Night'; he did not publish its companion piece until 17 January 1836, too late for inclusion. 'Some Account of an Omnibus Cad' was eventually expanded into twice its length, as 'The Last Cab-driver and the First Omnibus Cad'; it may be that Dickens already had this expansion in mind, but had not time to effect it. 'The House' and 'Bellamy's', two *Evening Chronicle* sketches, were later combined into 'A Parliamentary Sketch', with some drastic rewriting to make them less allusive and topical; while 'A Dinner at Poplar Walk' was, when it finally appeared in the Second Series as 'Mr.

1. Its position, last in Vol. II, rather favours the supposition that it was written late; but in substance and manner it resembles the 1834 tales. The title in the first edition is 'Sentiment!', perhaps in error.

2. *Letters*, I 54; and compare the reference to 'an extraordinary idea for a story of a very singular kind' in a letter to Catherine Hogarth, undated but soon after 20 Nov. (*Mr. and Mrs. Charles Dickens*, ed. W. Dexter, 1935, p. 36).

3. These memoranda include one other heading for which Dickens subsequently wrote a sketch—'The Prisoners' Van'. The others (The Cook's Shop and Bedlam, Banking-Houses, Fancy Lounges, Covent Garden, Hospitals, and Lodging-Houses) were never used. (This is probably the earliest reference to literary memoranda of any kind.)

Minns and his Cousin', the most thoroughly revised of all the tales, in a way that shows Dickens's dissatisfaction with his earliest publication. The rejection of all these might then be attributed to lack of time; for the dropping of 'Love and Oysters',[1] 'Seven Dials', and 'The Old Bailey'[2] it is difficult to see a reason, unless the last-named was felt to be superseded by 'A Visit to Newgate'.

No tale or sketch which does appear in the first collection was revised so thoroughly as those mentioned above; but not one was reprinted exactly as originally published. To begin with, they were rearranged and the original series broken up. The grouping as 'Scenes', 'Characters', 'Tales' was not yet made,[3] but the six *Evening Chronicle* sketches which had dealt with 'Our Parish' were brought together, and opened the first volume. Except for sketches which close this volume, and probably owe their position to their late date of composition, the order seems unplanned; there are two early tales, two *Morning Chronicle* 'Street Sketches', seven *Evening Chronicle* 'Sketches of London', three *Bell's Life* 'Scenes and Characters', and the newly written 'A Visit to Newgate'. There is no juxtaposition of sketches alike in subject matter; if there is any principle at work it is rather the emphasizing of variety. The second volume is slightly less miscellaneous in character, since 'tales' predominate (five old and two new), the other contents being two 'Street Sketches', four 'Sketches of London', and one 'Scenes and Characters'.

One form of revision, then, was simply mechanical: the removal of the original 'series' heading, and where necessary, as in the 'Parish' sketches, the provision of a new title. Almost equally formal was the re-paragraphing; the newspaper column was usually broken into only a few paragraphs. It is possible that this affected the original calculation of material to be included, and dictated some of the cuts.

The material omitted from the sketches and tales would almost make a small volume on its own, and it is extraordinary that no attempt has been made to recover it for modern readers. It is not

1. Later entitled 'Misplaced Attachment of Mr. John Dounce'. It is a slightly *risqué* story, but that may not have been the reason for its omission, since Dickens did not tone it down (except for the title) until the monthly parts edition of 1837–39.

2. Later entitled 'Criminal Courts'.

3. These headings apparently first appeared in 1839, the first volume edition which combined the two series; the order was that of the 'monthly parts' edition of Nov. 1837–June 1839. (Hatton and Cleaver's account of the parts does not mention the sub-headings there.)

of course all of equal interest; but no one who has read it would willingly lose the first half of the sketch of 'The Prisoners' Van', a passage not only exceptionally racy and vivid, but providing the best early example of Dickens's trick (to be elaborated in *Oliver Twist*) of dealing with low life in a detached and whimsical style. This is the beginning of the omitted section:

> We have a most extraordinary partiality for lounging about the streets. Whenever we have an hour or two to spare, there is nothing we enjoy more than a little amateur vagrancy—walking up one street and down another, and staring into shop windows, and gazing about as if, instead of being on intimate terms with every shop and house in Holborn, the Strand, Fleet-street and Cheapside, the whole were an unknown region to our wandering mind. We revel in a crowd of any kind—a street "row" is our delight—even a woman in a fit is by no means to be despised, especially in a fourth-rate street, where all the female inhabitants run out of their houses, and discharge large jugs of cold water over the patient, as if she were dying of spontaneous combustion, and wanted putting out. Then a drunken man—what can be more charming than a regular drunken man, who sits in a door-way for half an hour, holding a dialogue with the crowd, of which his portion is generally limited to repeated inquiries of "I say—I'm all right, an't I?" and then suddenly gets up, without any ostensible cause or inducement, and runs down the street with tremendous swiftness for a hundred yards or so, when he falls into another doorway, where the first feeble words he imperfectly articulates to the policeman who lifts him up are "Let's av—drop—somethin' to drink?"—we say again, can anything be more charming than this sort of thing? And what, we ask, can be expected but popular discontent, when Temperance Societies interfere with the amusements of the people?

This may be suspected as an omission dictated by space;[1] 'The Prisoners' Van' did not appear until 29 November 1835, and by that date the manuscript had already left Cruikshank's hands and printing had begun.[2] The only critical reasons one could suggest are that the passage is a long introduction to the real subject of the sketch, and perhaps impairs its unity; and that the self-portrait with which it opens might be thought too revealing.

Few omissions were as drastic as this, and some were of more or less 'formal' introductions and conclusions; recalling a pre-

1. The whole passage is three times as long as what is quoted here.
2. *Letters*, I 53–4.

vious promise to his readers, wishing them a merry Christmas, suggesting the subject of the next sketch, and such-like journalistic patter.[1] But even these sometimes involve the omission of characteristic sentiments; as in the omission of the last paragraph of 'Astley's', obviously removed because of its relation to a later sketch, 'Private Theatres', and perhaps felt to be superseded by that sketch.

> It is to us matter of positive wonder and astonishment that the infectious disease commonly known by the name of "stage-struck," has never been eradicated, unless people really believe that the privilege of wearing velvet and feathers for an hour or two at night, is sufficient compensation for a life of wretchedness and misery. It is stranger still, that the denizens of attorneys' offices, merchants' counting-houses, haberdashers' shops, and coal sheds, should squander their own resources to enrich some wily vagabond by paying—actually paying, and dearly too—to make unmitigated and unqualified asses of themselves at a Private Theatre. Private theatres, so far as we know, are peculiar to London; they flourish just now, for we have half a dozen at our fingers' ends. We will take an early opportunity of introducing our readers to the Managers of one or two, and of sketching the interior of a Private Theatre, both before the curtain and behind it.

The original closing paragraph often 'opens out' in this way; the end of 'London Recreations' touches on less harmless recreations than the gardening and frequentation of tea-gardens dealt with in the body of the sketch—such as standing in vaults drinking bad spirits, knocking at doors and running away, leaning against posts at street corners; it concludes with a militant statement of tolerance:

> Whatever be the class, or whatever the recreation, so long as it does not render a man absurd himself, or offensive to others, we hope it will never be interfered with, either by a misdirected feeling of propriety on the one hand, or detestable cant on the other.

Setting this beside other changes, one is tempted to wonder whether discretion sometimes dictated the omission of a closing paragraph; Boz as a journalist liked a strong curtain-line, some-

1. E.g. the omitted closing paragraphs of 'Our Parish', I, II, and III; 'Thoughts about People'; 'Greenwich Fair'; 'Brokers' and Marine Store Shops'; 'The Pawnbroker's Shop'; 'A Christmas Dinner'; 'The Boarding-House' (ch. i). But the apology at the end of 'The River' survives into the first collected edition, to be removed only in 1839.

times with a political flavour. The original form of the conclusion of 'Thoughts about People' is much more clearly partisan than the revised version of 1836. Here is part of the omitted passage:

> . . . we see no reason why the same gentleman of enlarged and comprehensive views who proposes to Parliament a measure for preserving the amusements of the upper classes of society, and abolishing those of the lower, may not with equal wisdom preserve the former more completely, and mark the distinction between the two more effectually, by bringing in a Bill "to limit to certain members of the hereditary peerage of this country and their families, the privilege of making fools of themselves as often and as egregiously as to them shall seem meet". Precedent is a great thing in these cases, and Heaven knows he will have precedent enough to plead.

When Dickens recast the conclusion of this sketch[1] he suggested a similar social criticism, but in a much more urbane manner:

> We may smile at such people as these [the London apprentices in their Sunday best], but they can never excite our anger. . . And if they do display a little occasional foolery in their own proper persons, it is surely more tolerable than the precocious puppyism of the Quadrant, the whiskered dandyism of Regent-street and Pall-mall, or gallantry in its dotage any where.[2]

Here we have a typical instance of the modification of the journalistic manner of the original sketches—not only in the substitution of the bland smile of the periodical essayist for the glare of the propagandist, but in the removal of a too ephemeral allusion; for the original reference was to the notorious 'Sunday' bill[3] persistently introduced in several successive sessions by Sir Andrew Agnew, the 'Lord's-Day-Bill Baronet' referred to in another sketch.[4]

The sketches containing specifically 'political' allusions—'The House', 'Bellamy's', and 'The Parlour'—were passed over, no doubt deliberately, when Dickens made his selection for the

1. He also omitted the promise of subsequent sketches on the same subject.

2. 1836, p. 95. In the 1850 edition the criticism was perhaps a little further softened by the addition (before 'And if') of 'Besides, they are always the faint reflections of higher lights' and the change of 'of' to 'in' before 'the Quadrant' and 'Regent-street'.

3. Attacked by Dickens in his pamphlet *Sunday under three Heads*, written some time after Apr. 1836 when the bill was re-introduced, and published in June under the name of 'Timothy Sparks'.

4. 'Bellamy's', *Evening Chronicle*, 11 Apr. 1835 (see 'A Parliamentary Sketch' in Second Series), published two weeks before 'Thoughts about People'.

First Series, and revised with particular care for the Second Series, as we shall see. But Dickens was alert to remove incidental topicalities in other sketches. The Irish orator from Exeter Hall, mentioned at the end of 'The Ladies' Societies' ('Our Parish' VI), was presented to the *Evening Chronicle* readers of 1835 as 'Mr. Somebody O'Something, a celebrated Catholic renegade and Protestant bigot'; in the first edition of 1836 he became 'Mr. Mortimer O'Silly-one', later 'a celebrated oratorical pedlar', and in the monthly parts edition 'a celebrated orator . . . an Irishman'.[1] In the tales, he removed, for example, the references to 'the Duke of Wellington waiting for a *peal*', 'Mr. Barnett's "Salamanders" ', and the 'individual to whose eager appetite [at 'the Edinburgh dinner'] we find allusion made in *The Morning Chronicle* of a few days since'.[2] Apart from the topicality of this, Dickens (or Hogarth) may have decided that it was improper to refer in his sketches to the journal which employed him; he also removed a reference to the 'clock at *The Chronicle* office' in 'Thoughts about People'.

The change in the name of one of the characters in the revised tale 'Mrs. Joseph Porter' shows Dickens avoiding a different kind of particularity; 'Mr. Harfield' in the *Monthly Magazine* version was the name of an actual friend and *Morning Chronicle* colleague.[3] In changing it to 'Harleigh', Dickens perhaps substituted another allusion, this time a friendly private joke; at the time when he was revising the *Sketches* for publication, he was in constant touch with John Pritt Harley, the actor and stage-manager for whom he was writing his farce *The Strange Gentleman.* He also removed two names, 'the Stubbs', the Halfpennys' from the list of the 'rank and fashion' of Clapham who attended the amateur theatricals; perhaps these were recognizable as real people in

1. The reference was to the Reverend Mortimer O'Sullivan, an Irish controversialist, who had come to England on a deputation from the Irish Protestant clergy; he had described their condition at meetings in Exeter Hall on 20 June and 11 July, and had also been 'going about this country like a showman . . . addressing [meetings] in the most bombastic, frothy, nonsensical style' (*Morning Chronicle*, 2 July).

2. 'The Steam Excursion'. Dickens was reporting the banquet given to Earl Grey at Edinburgh for the *Morning Chronicle* in Sept. 1834 (see *The Dickensian*, Dec. 1934, pp. 5–10), and the tale appeared in Oct. Johnson, I 96, quotes from his report what is clearly the passage referred to, but is unaware of the reference in the original version of the tale.

3. *Letters*, I 34 [1834]; see also I 63. The tale (published in Jan. 1834) is supposed to reflect Dickens's amateur production of *Clari* at Bentinck Street on 27 Apr. 1833; it may also bear some relation to his burlesque *O'Thello*, written about this time.

Clapton?[1] The only other change of name in a tale—from 'Bagshaw' to 'Budden' in 'Mr. Minns and his Cousin' (the revised 'Dinner at Poplar Walk' collected in the Second Series)—was evidently made to avoid the appearance of plagiarism, since 'Claudius Bagshaw' was the name of the hero in John Poole's story, 'Preparations for Pleasure'.[2]

Another type of revision of substance partly dictated by the transition from newspaper to book was the removal of the (very occasional) touches of indelicacy and profanity; Boz's column in the newspaper would probably be read only by men, but a book which wished to pass through the 'needle's eye' into 'families' must be more circumspect. Dickens modified a reference to pregnancy in 'The Four Sisters' ('Our Parish', chapter iii) by the omission of the bracketed words in the following sentence:

> . . . a circumstance of the most gratifying description [Coming events cast their shadows before, and events like that at] which [we hint with becoming delicacy and diffidence] *will* happen occasionally in the best regulated families [—indeed the best regulated are usually supposed to be the most subject to such occurrences]

And he removed the phrase 'or half undressed' from the picture of the dancing revellers at the end of 'Greenwich Fair'. But he seems hardly to have begun altering 'God' to 'G—' or 'gum' or 'Heaven', or 'damned' to 'd—d', until the collection of the Second Series a year later;[3] one wonders whether this was in response to criticism of the First Series,[4] or the result of his growing consciousness of himself as a widely popular author, after the success of *Pickwick*. The revision in the Second Series, and the further revision of both series for the monthly parts edition, is thorough, and hardly an oath escaped in the end.

Of course Dickens's revision was also sometimes stylistic—even

1. Marianne Leigh, the girl who made mischief between Dickens and Maria Beadnell, and annoyed him on the evening of the theatricals, lived at Clapton; her mother is supposed to be represented in the malicious Mrs Joseph Porter.

2. *New Monthly Magazine*, Oct. 1829; republished in *Sketches and Recollections* (1835). The general situation and several details of Poole's story are also recalled in 'The Steam Excursion'; and one of Poole's minor characters is named 'Frederick Snodgrass' (see K. Tillotson, *The Dickensian*, Mar. 1956, pp. 69–70).

3. One of the very few examples in the First Series is in the last paragraph but one of 'Miss Evans and the Eagle'. The *Bell's Life* version reads 'You and your friend be damned!', which becomes 'd—d' in 1836, and 'hanged' in the monthly parts.

4. No objection to the oaths has been found in any reviews, but the most influential criticism is not necessarily printed.

at this early stage, when he was often revising sketches written only a month or so before. He had written often in great haste ('a day's time is a handsome allowance for me—much less than I frequently had when I was writing for The Chronicle')[1] and in looking over the sketches he saw several places in which punctuation and expression could be improved. This revision was not at all systematic; but here and there the style is formalized by the removal of colloquialisms such as '–n't' from the narration or description; a few grammatical solecisms are detected, and awkward repetitions smoothed away. Very occasionally there is a change that suggests a more critical view of his own humour: in 'The Bloomsbury Christening', for instance, he noticed that he had spoilt an epigrammatic phrase 'He was never happy but when he was miserable' by adding the facetious 'pardon the contradiction', and removed it. But there is very little of this kind of revision compared with what is found a year later; it is worth mentioning only because it indicates the lines of later revision.

Not surprisingly—in view of the amount of work required from Cruikshank, Dickens's reporting engagements out of town,[2] and the habitual dilatoriness of Macrone—the collected *Sketches* were not ready in time for Christmas, as had been hoped;[3] but by 7 January 1836 Dickens was able to say 'the greater part, if not the whole of the book, is worked off';[4] and two days later it was advertised in the *Morning Chronicle* as 'nearly ready'.

It was published on 6 February; there was some unexplained delay in sending out review copies, but it had a good send-off with 'Hogarth's beautiful notice' in the *Morning Chronicle* on 11 February;[5] the subscription was 'an excellent one',[6] the reviews numerous and favourable; by 24 March the agreed payment of £150 had been made, and by the end of the month Dickens was able to refer to 'the great success of my book, and the

1. *Letters*, I 47.

2. During one such absence the proofs were read by George Hogarth (*Letters*, I 57).

3. *Letters*, I 54.

4. *Letters*, I 61. At this eleventh hour Macrone appears to have suggested some change in the title. But the *Morning Chronicle* advertisement gives the title in its full final form.

Some difficulty with Cruikshank at this stage seems to be implied by the advertisement of the *Sketches* (*Athenæum*, 6 Feb.) which specifies '20 illustrations' instead of the correct number of 16.

5. *Letters*, I 65. There was also a 'puff' in the issue of 2 Feb.

6. *Letters*, I 66.

name it has established for me among the publishers'.[1] Meanwhile *Pickwick* was begun[2]—though its success was not to supersede that of the *Sketches* for some months to come—and a real three-volume novel was in contemplation; and though the series of 'Scenes and Characters' in *Bell's Life* had been concluded, Dickens seemed to have found a new vehicle for his tales in Charles Whitehead's *Library of Fiction*. The success of the *Sketches* had many consequences, but the only one which concerns us here is the collecting of a Second Series.

III

The letters suggest that this began early in the summer; perhaps as soon as the success of the First Series was assured.[3] Cruikshank was at work at least by July, and in August Dickens told Macrone of a projected new series in the *Carlton Chronicle* which he proposed to call 'Leaves from an unpublished Volume by Boz'.[4] Two volumes were planned, and an advertisement to this effect appeared early in October,[5] but it must already have been clear that Dickens's other commitments (*Pickwick*, his farce and his opera, reporting for the *Morning Chronicle*, and the two novels promised to Bentley) would prevent him from writing enough new sketches to fill them;[6] and in November came the quarrel

1. *Letters*, I 68 (letter to his uncle Thomas Barrow announcing his forthcoming marriage).

2. See below, p. 62.

3. Johnson (I 149) quotes from an unpublished letter of 30 July, in which Dickens says he is revising the proof sheets of the second edition and 'preparing another series which must be published before Christmas'.

The second edition of the First Series is advertised in the *Athenæum* on 30 July; this is the first appearance in print of the author's name ('Mr. Charles Dickens' Sketches by Boz'), much earlier than has been generally supposed. A similar advertisement appeared on 13 Aug.; subsequent advertisements in Aug. and Sept. omit Dickens's name, perhaps at his insistence. The first published volume with Dickens's own name was *Pickwick Papers*, in Nov. 1837, where the dedication is signed; *Oliver Twist* (Johnson, I 223) was therefore merely the first to have his name on the title-page.

4. *Letters*, I 77. The first sketch, 'The Hospital Patient', appeared three days later, with the heading as given in the letter, plus the words 'which will be torn out once a fortnight'; but no other followed, perhaps because the 'Carlton Club' was not as 'liberal' as Dickens had expected. Its unauthorized printing of three sketches formerly published elsewhere, in the issues of 17 Sept., 8 Oct., and 15 Oct., indicates that there had been some trouble; Dickens protested against the piracy in a letter to Easthope, owner of the *Morning Chronicle*, on 1 Nov. (*Letters*, I 87).

5. *Athenæum*, 8 Oct., as 'Mr Charles Dickens' New Work'.

6. Some of the tales intended for the collection may instead have been included in *Pickwick*; see below, p. 73.

with Macrone over the Bentley agreements. So the Second Series consisted of a single volume, advertised as such on 3 December[1] and published on 17 December, just in time for the Christmas season in 1836.

This time there was no problem of selection. Emboldened by the success of the First Series, Dickens simply swept up all the items published in 1833–5 but omitted from the collection of February 1836. These are (in chronological order) one tale, 'A Dinner at Poplar Walk'; one 'Street Sketch', 'The Old Bailey'; two 'Sketches in London': 'The House' and 'Bellamy's'; six 'Scenes and Characters': 'Seven Dials', 'Making a Night of It', 'Love and Oysters', 'Some Account of an Omnibus Cad', 'The Vocal Dressmaker', and 'The Parlour'. To these he added the two last 'Scenes and Characters', published early in 1836: 'The New Year' and 'The Streets at Night'; and two isolated sketches: 'A Little Talk about Spring, and the Sweeps'[2] and 'The Hospital Patient'. The general heading of the latter in the *Carlton Chronicle* shows that it was written with the new collection in mind; and it is probable that the newly-published sketches, 'Our Next-door Neighbours' and 'The Drunkard's Death', which are similarly grim in tone, were also intended for this projected series in the *Carlton Chronicle*. Also designed for the new volume were the four which appeared as 'Sketches by "Boz". New Series' in the *Morning Chronicle* in the autumn: 'Meditations in Monmouth-Street', 'Scotland Yard', 'Doctors' Commons', and 'Vauxhall-Gardens by Day'.[3] (This series also should have continued, but was checked by Dickens's quarrel with the proprietors.) The only periodical item which Dickens omitted was 'The Tuggs's at Ramsgate',[4] presumably because of its length. In the Preface to the new volume (dated from 'Furnival's Inn, December 17, 1836'), Dickens was sufficiently explicit about the chronological range of its contents:

> Some of these Sketches were written before the appearance of the former series, and the remainder have been added at different periods since that time.

1. The *Athenæum* advertisements give 'In a few days', 3 Dec.; 'nearly ready', 10 Dec., the latter with Dickens's name.

2. *Library of Fiction*, June 1836; the title was changed to 'The First of May'.

3. 24 Sept., 4, 11, 26 Oct. All were reprinted in the *Evening Chronicle* and the last three also printed elsewhere (see Hatton and Cleaver, 102–3, and *Letters*, I 87); an interesting testimony to the enhanced value of the author's signature.

4. *Library of Fiction*, Apr. 1836.

But this is perhaps deliberately vague about the proportion of new work in the collection, and contains no hint of the amount of revision.

All of the previously published sketches underwent some alteration, but especially the earlier work. The earliest of all, 'A Dinner at Poplar Walk', had not only a new title, 'Mr. Minns and his Cousin', and a new surname for its hero, but three or four paragraphs entirely rewritten[1] with minor changes in substance, such as the omission of some of the cousin's garrulity and the tiresome behaviour of the boy Alick at the end, and the addition of the will. On the whole the motive seems to have been simply literary improvement, and there is nothing to regret except for one simile ('Minns . . . looked as merry as a farthing rushlight in a fog') and a detail of the pageboy's outfit ('with a parsley-and-butter border').

The omission of personal allusions and political or other topical references, already noted above, is most fully illustrated in the revision of 'The House' and 'Bellamy's'.[2] These are unusual in their direct use of material gathered by Dickens as a gallery reporter; he had already apologized for their allusiveness in the *Chronicle*, and the appearance of 'Bellamy's' was twice postponed, which perhaps suggests editorial doubts. They were run into one long sketch, under the title of 'A Parliamentary Sketch—with a few portraits'.[3] It is the individual portraits that are modified; one, the 'elderly man with the bald head and thin face . . . who has lived for two-thirds of his whole existence exactly one minute and a quarter's walk from Blackfriars'-bridge', is removed altogether. The portrait of the 'ferocious-looking gentleman' (Colonel Sibthorp) is toned down by the omission of such phrases as 'a brain slightly damaged', and perhaps made less easily identifiable by the omission of 'You must often have seen him in the box-lobbies of the theatres during the vacation.' The description of the 'awkward and ungainly-looking man' is considerably shortened, and the reference to his 'awkward scrape with his consti-

1. The whole text of the original version is accessible to modern readers in F. J. H. Darton's *Dickens, Positively the First Appearance* (1933), pp. 51–68, with some comments on pp. 73–7.

2. W. J. Carlton in 'Portraits in "A Parliamentary Sketch"', *The Dickensian*, June 1954, quotes some of the omitted matter and discusses the whole sketch; he identifies several 'portraits', but not the 'awkward and ungainly-looking man' or the 'young Member'.

3. This became 'A Parliamentary Sketch' in the monthly parts.

tuents . . . at the commencement of the present session' is left out; the identifying traits of the 'young Member' talking to '"Jane", the Hebe of Bellamy's'—his 'large quantity of hair', his near relation 'to the noble leader of a "section" of the House' are similarly omitted, along with his flirtatiousness and his consumption of brandy-and-water. Throughout, the motive is probably as much caution as the wish to eliminate ephemeral matter; much of the original matter, as Mr Carlton says,

> would almost certainly be deemed libellous to-day, and it would be surprising if [it] did not provoke a protest from some readers of the *Evening Chronicle*.

But enough salt remains to make the sketch one of the liveliest in the whole collection, whether we recognize the originals or not.[1]

Similar instances of 'political and topical' revision are found in other sketches. The legal dignitaries in 'Doctors' Commons' were evidently also portraits, and the suppressed details about the 'doctor of civil law'—'an ecclesiastical dignitary in the cinque ports, and a not very distant relation to a commissioner of lunacy'—must have made the identification immediately obvious to contemporaries.[2] The 'radiating sentence' with which the red-faced man in 'The Parlour Orator' banged out of the room 'in which such adjectives as "dastardly", "oppressive", "violent", and "sanguinary", formed the most conspicuous words', was originally much longer; he spoke of '"dastardly Whigs", "sanguinary Tories", "Mr. Roebuck", "depreciation of the currency", and "voluntary principle".' In the same sketch the greengrocer's reply 'I got no good out of the twenty million' to the accusation 'you *are* a slave', was evidently thought too allusive, and so was provided with a gloss 'that was paid for 'mancipation'.

The conclusion of this sketch was originally a good deal more

1. The *Spectator*, reviewing the Second Series (24 Dec. 1836, pp. 1234–5), said that no one who had ever seen the originals could fail to recognize them.

2. He was identified by Henry Jenner (*T.L.S.*, 22 Oct. 1931, p. 820; cf. *The Dickensian*, Dec. 1931, p. 5) with Dr Joseph Phillimore, Regius Professor of Civil Law at Oxford and at that time also Judge of the Court of Admiralty of the Cinque Ports. His brother, William Phillimore, was Chief Commissioner in Lunacy (*The Family of Phillimore*, Devizes, 1922). Mr Jenner regarded the descriptions as 'so recognizable as to be really actionably libellous'. He also identified 'the very fat and red-faced gentleman' with Sir Herbert Jenner-Fust, Dean of the Arches.

The case of 'Bumple against Sludberry' was drawn from an actual case reported by Dickens (W. J. Carlton, *Charles Dickens, Shorthand Writer*, 1926, ch. iv).

indignant in tone than the two paragraphs which were substituted and it is partly the indignation of one who is sated with official oratory:

> "Great ass," thought we,—"a very common character and in no degree exaggerated. Empty headed bullies, who by their ignorance and presumption bring into contempt whatever cause they are connected with: equally mischievous in any assembly from the highest to the lowest, and disgusting in all. There is a red-faced man in every 'parlour'."

In that context, 'parlour' almost achieves the status of a pun on 'parliament'.

There is also a more challenging tone in the superseded last paragraph of the 'Omnibus Cad', with its emphasis on the futility of imprisonment:

> You may confine his body between four stone walls, or between four brick walls and a stone coping, which is much the same in effect—he cares not—you may cramp his body by confinement, or to prevent his body's getting the cramp, you may exercise his legs upon the mill—he defies your tyranny; he appeals from your oppressive enactments to the Paddington committee; and flies back to his profession with an ardour which persecution and involuntary abstinence have in no wise diminished. Like many other great men, Mr. Barker is a rigid predestinarian, or to advert once again to his own pointed and eloquent form of speech, he reasons thus:— "If I am to get into trouble for this 'ere consarn, I may as vell get into trouble for somethink as for nothink,"—and acting upon this logical mode of reasoning, he sacrifices at the altar of philosophy any little scruples he might otherwise entertain, and gets into trouble with great ease and coolness, getting out of it as well as he can; and losing no opportunity of getting into it again.

Two minor changes elsewhere illustrate the rebellious or impertinent attitude to those in high places of the earlier Boz:

> We never saw a green so drunk, a lord so quarrelsome (except in the house of peers after dinner)[1]

where 'except' is slightly softened, to 'no: not even'. In 'The Old Bailey' ('Criminal Courts') the following sentence was cut out:

> We never can help thinking that a full-dressed Lord Mayor looks like a South Sea idol, on which grateful devotees have hung a

1. 'A Little Talk about Spring, and the Sweeps', *Library of Fiction*, June 1836 ('The First of May'). In the Second Series 'green' becomes ' "Green" ',

variety of gorgeous ornaments without the slightest regard to the general effect of the whole.

Two sketches were shorn of their long introductory paragraphs: 'The Parlour' began with a general account of different types of parlour, and its unity is improved by the concentration on the 'Orator'; and 'Scotland Yard' began with a general lament over the changes in the London scene, of which this is the first half:

> If our recollection serves us, we have more than once hinted, confidentially, to our readers that we entertain a strong partiality for the queer little old streets which yet remain in some parts of London, and that we infinitely prefer them to the modern innovations, the wide streets with broad pavements, which are every day springing up around us. The old Exeter 'Change, for instance, and the narrow and dirty part of the Strand immediately adjoining, we were warmly attached to. The death of the elephant was a great shock to us; we knew him well; and having enjoyed the honour of his intimate acquaintance for some years, felt grieved—deeply grieved—that in a paroxysm of insanity he should have so far forgotten all his estimable and companionable qualities as to exhibit a sanguinary desire to scrunch his faithful valet, and pulverize even Mrs. Cross herself, who for a long period had evinced towards him that pure and touching attachment which woman alone can feel.

The detail about the elephant was perhaps thought too topical to perpetuate.

Oaths were occasionally but still not consistently removed. For example, for the curse 'Flare up!' used by the boy at the end of 'Criminal Courts' a circumlocution in the Bill Sikes manner is substituted, though the same imprecation survives (with inverted commas added) in 'Making a Night of It'. There are many minor changes of expression, but the only one of interest is the substitution of 'we' for 'I' throughout 'The Hospital Patient', to bring it into line with the other sketches.

At about the same time as the planning of the Second Series, Dickens was preparing the second edition of the First Series; he added a new Preface, and either then or in the third edition[1] he made further small changes on the lines of those already noted in the first edition. Again he was on the watch for unsuitable collo-

1. No copy of the second edition is at present available; there is none in the British Museum, the Bodleian, Cambridge University Library, National Library of Scotland, nor in the Forster collection.

quialisms, and certain kinds of facetiousness. The old gardener in 'London Recreations' was described as 'digging, and sweeping, and cutting, and messing about'; for the last two words, Dickens substituted 'planting'. For the apprentices' 'oh-no-we-never-mention-'ems' in 'Thoughts about People' he substituted 'summer trousers'. Some exuberance of simile in 'The Boarding-House' was reduced; in 'He was as empty headed as the great bell of St. Paul's, and had about as long a tongue', Dickens cut out the last seven words; Mrs Bloss's watch was compared to 'a small tea-cup' instead of a breakfast-cup.[1] A few topicalities were removed from 'Horatio Sparkins': 'to see St. George and the Dragon' becomes 'to the theatre', and 'he talks like a second Pelham' is cut out, perhaps in deference to Bulwer.[2]

IV

The most minute and careful revision was applied to the first combined edition of the two series for the monthly parts published (after much controversy)[3] by Chapman and Hall from November 1837 to June 1839, and as a single volume, uniform with *Pickwick*, in May 1839.

One item, 'The Tuggs's at Ramsgate', was collected for the first time, and the sketches were put in the order which survives in modern editions. They are grouped as follows: 'Seven Sketches from our Parish' (the six of the First Series, with 'Our Next-door Neighbour' rather incongruously tacked on); twenty-five

1. The latter comparison disappeared altogether in the monthly parts, along with others in the sentence; see below, p. 58.

2. 1839 has 'he talks like an oracle'. (This is one of many instances which suggest that the revision for 1839 was based on the first edition, not the second or third.)

3. See Forster, II 1; *Letters*, I 110–11; Johnson, 183–5, 208–9. Chapman and Hall's edition had probably been under consideration since their purchase of the copyright from Macrone in mid-June, and this would allow time for revision, even with Dickens's commitments to *Pickwick*, *Oliver Twist*, and *Bentley's*. It was first advertised in the Sept. number of *Pickwick*, as 'revised by the author', and again in Oct.; the *Athenæum* advertisement (21 Oct.) and the title-page lack this phrase, calling it simply 'New Edition'. Thirteen additional illustrations were provided by Cruikshank, to make up the two plates to each number, as in *Pickwick*; the text, however, is usually shorter (24 pp. each in Nos. I–XVIII, 56 pp. in No. XIX, and 38 pp. in No. XX), and the end of a number never coincides with the end of a sketch.

The pink cover was used possibly at Dickens's wish to distinguish it from *Pickwick*, as it was not a new work; he had especially objected to Macrone's project of monthly parts in 'just the same form' (*Letters*, I 110). The cover was originally drawn by Cruikshank for Macrone's projected edition; see *The Dickensian*, June 1937, p. 175.

'Scenes'; twelve 'Characters'; and twelve 'Tales'. Within the groups there is some system in the order: six pieces on recreations and entertainments, for example, now fall into a natural sequence.

The whole series was further revised, not excepting the tales and sketches that had been specially written for the previous collections; these therefore are changes that cannot be attributed simply to the shift from periodical to book. By the autumn of 1837 Dickens was established as a popular 'family' author, and also as the editor of a periodical himself; he had a keener sense of his audience and of his responsibilities towards it; he was rising socially, and possibly especially sensitive to imputations of vulgarity.[1] And by this time he had the benefit of Forster's advice.[2]

Sometimes the impression of the writer's personality is modified; in 'The New Year' he takes out 'quaffing our grog' and omits the original conclusion, in which he had dismissed 'all gloomy reflections' with the words

> We were happy and merry in the last [year], and will be, please God, in this. So as we are alone, and can neither dance it in, nor sing it in, here goes our glass to our lips, and a hearty welcome to the year one thousand eight hundred and thirty-seven, say we.

He is now more particular about anything verging on indelicacy. The speculation, at the appearance of the prisoners' van, 'upon the possibility of the Duke of Cumberland being brought up on a warrant for assaulting the Princess Victoria', is omitted; the aphrodisiac effect of the oysters upon Mr John Dounce is toned down by two cautious alterations.[3] Not only is most of the strong language modified or removed,[4] but also slang expressions (in the

1. The reviews of the First Series can hardly have influenced Dickens in this direction; in about twenty notices, many of them long ones, there are hardly any unfavourable comments of any kind, and only one objection to 'sheer vulgarity' (in the *Atlas*, 21 Feb., p. 123). The *Examiner*'s notice (28 Feb., pp. 132–3) found 'too much' of the 'caricature of Cockneyism'; the *Court Journal* (20 Feb., p. 123) found some sketches 'coarse, it is true, but very real. The subjects of "Boz" generally preclude refinement.' The *Observer* (8 May, p. 3) noted that 'The vernacular idiom is given in all its truth and richness, yet free from grossness'. But the *Quarterly*'s comment, in its generally favourable article on *Pickwick* (Oct. 1837, pp. 484–518), that 'Mr. Dickens may well afford to disregard the imputation of vulgarity' suggests that there was more criticism of this kind than survives in print.

2. Forster does not mention the *Sketches* in this connexion, but states clearly (II i) that his help with proofs began in June 1837.

3. Perhaps in deference to the *Athenæum*'s review of the Second Series (31 Dec. 1836, p. 916): 'Mr. John Dounce is one of the best papers, but is a little too broad to suit our pages.'

4. E.g. 'God' to 'Heaven', 'by G—d' to 'by gum', 'God bless you' to 'Bless you';

narrative) such as 'goes of gin', 'regular good ones, and never a bit the worse for it', 'come-up-to-the-scratch kind of manner' and even simple colloquialisms like ''em' and 'wasn't'.[1] There is some cutting of humorous similes;[2] the stout Mrs Bloss no longer 'looked like a pin-cushion on castors', nor does the man in 'Early Coaches' start up in bed 'as if . . . rehearsing the tent-scene in *Richard*'. Two of these cuts fall into a special category:

> which certainly was 'rayther warm', as the child said when it fell in the fire.[3]
>
> ev'ry one to his liking, as the man said when he pisoned hisself.[4]

Dickens evidently came to feel that this locution should be the monopoly of Sam Weller; and with a similar protectiveness towards a later-born character, he altered the name 'Fitz Winkle' in 'Public Dinners' to 'Fitz Binkle'. One or two of his more elaborate puns are also removed; Mr Calton in 'The Boarding-House' is habitually compared to a 'knocker', and on his last appearance he has to pay damages for breach of promise 'because he had declined to *ring* the *belle*'. In the same tale, the simile for Mrs Bloss's watch, already modified,[5] disappears, with two others in the same paragraph, 'a chain like a gilt street-door chain' and 'stones about the size of half-crowns'.

Dickens no longer assumes his readers' easy familiarity with London inns. In 'Mr. John Dounce' a reference to 'the Rainbow' in 1835 becomes 'the Rainbow in Fleet-street' in 1836, and 'the Rainbow Tavern in Fleet-street' in 1837; and 'the Albion' in 'Making a Night of It' is similarly glossed with 'in Little Russell-street'. A few references to passing events that had survived the first revision, and had become more out-of-date with the further passage of time, were altered; Mr Potter is no longer looking for

---

'damn' to 'hate', 'confound', 'damning' to 'execrating', 'a d—d sight' to 'a deal', 'damned odd' to 'odd'. At the end of 'Private Theatres' the Shakespearean 'bloody officer' becomes 'bleeding officer'; an early appearance of a well-known schoolboy joke.

1. This kind of revision is fairly consistent, and also that of ''Tis 'or 'It's' to 'It is'.

2. Cf. p. 56 above.

3. 'London Recreations' (*Evening Chronicle*, 17 Mar. 1835); this therefore is Dickens's earliest Wellerism.

4. 'The Great Winglebury Duel'. The *Quarterly* (p. 515) had quoted this passage and remarked on the family likeness.

5. See above, p. 56.

the comet but for the moon, and the comparisons 'like Ward in Gustavus' and 'with all the dignity of a minor Manners Sutton'[1] are omitted. One of the drawing-room ballads sung at the Bloomsbury christening-party—'Can I believe Love's Wreath will pain?'[2]—goes out, and several names of newspapers; it is a loss that John Evenson's reading of the *Examiner* no longer survives to define his radicalism.[3] An added footnote in 'A Visit to Newgate' explains that conditions have changed since the sketch was first published; on the other hand, another footnote complimenting Ainsworth on his portrayal of Dick Turpin in *Rookwood*, introduced since the first edition, is removed.[4] The hinted prospect of further stories about Mrs Tibbs's boarding-house goes out, since the tally of Dickens's early stories was now complete,[5] and the collection would not be further enlarged.

V

The final clean-up was made for the cheap edition of 1850, which carries the apologetic Preface quoted at the beginning of this essay. Here the language was further softened, even 'cursedly' and 'the deuce' and the mere reference to imprecations and kicks in 'The Pawnbroker's Shop', being expurgated; 'taken to prigging' in 'Criminal Courts' becomes 'got into trouble'; the 'legs' of the young lady in 'The Dancing Academy' become 'ankles'; an added phrase in 'A Parliamentary Sketch' makes it clear that Jane's 'friskings and rompings . . . in the passage' 'are very innocent'; one more reference to the effect of oysters on gallantry was detached; in 'The Boarding-House', Mrs Bloss's 'two grain calomel pill' becomes 'a pill', and Mrs Tibbs no longer distributes 'all the *et ceteras*' as well as 'towels and soap'. The tales received particular attention; the harshness of their humour, especially towards women, is sometimes softened, and once again some lively comparisons are cut out. Horatio Sparkins formerly 'looked as handsomely miserable as a Hamlet sliding upon a bit

1. 'The Boarding-House'; 'The Steam Excursion'.
2. We have not yet succeeded in tracing this song.
3. 'The Boarding-House'; 1839 substitutes 'a Sunday paper'.
4. *Rookwood* was as popular as ever, but Dickens's view of it had changed.
5. An American reprint of 1839 (Philadelphia 1842) adds 'The Public Life of Mr. Tulrumble' and 'The Pantomime of Life' from *Bentley's*, which Dickens never collected.

of orange-peel'; Teresa blushed 'like a full-blown peony'; the Miss Tauntons in 'The Steam Excursion'

> advanced to the table, with that ballet sort of step which some young ladies seem to think so fascinating—something between a skip and a canter.

Perhaps that particular affectation had gone out of fashion; and it is probably a loss of topicality that deprives us of the comparison of the draper's price-figures:

> a seven with a little three-farthings in the corner, something like the aquatic animalculae disclosed by the gas microscope,[1] "perfectly invisible to the naked eye".

It is these small cuts that are typical of the 1850 revision; but a few are more extensive, and suggest some change of sentiment or social attitude. Dickens's work for Miss Coutts's Ragged School is surely reflected in the change of 'irreclaimable wretches' to 'creatures of neglect' in the description of the juvenile delinquents of 'A Visit to Newgate'. In 'The First of May' the closing phrase, 'How has May-day decayed!' was formerly expanded into a condemnation of the 'profligate and vicious customs', the 'degradation and discontent', that had replaced the 'merry sports' of the past. The revision of the close of 'Gin-shops' shows the substitution of practical social reform for ironic defiance:

> Gin-drinking is a great vice in England, but poverty is [1850, 'wretchedness and dirt are'] a greater; and until you can cure it [1850, 'improve the homes of the poor'] . . . gin-shops will increase in number and splendour. If Temperance Societies could suggest an antidote against hunger and distress [1850, 'would suggest', 'hunger, filth, and foul air'] . . . gin-palaces would be numbered among the things that were. Until then, their decrease may be despaired of. [1850 omit 'Until . . . of'.]

And one minute but significant change also comes in a 'curtain-line'; a family Christmas dinner, Dickens says, does more

> to awaken the sympathies of every member of the party in behalf of his neighbour, and to perpetuate their good feeling during the ensuing year, than all the homilies that have ever been written, by all the Divines that have ever lived.

1. 'Horatio Sparkins'; the words 'something . . . microscope' are omitted in 1850. The gas microscope had been a popular public exhibit of the 1830s, and contributed a point to one of Sam Weller's famous ripostes to Sergeant Buzfuz.

In 1850, whether from conviction, or from caution prompted by Forster, Dickens altered this to read:

> than half the homilies that have ever been written, by half the Divines that have ever lived.

This account of Dickens's revisions is by no means exhaustive, and has been almost confined to points of substance; but it is enough to show that the suppression of the original versions in modern editions brings some loss of understanding, both of Dickens's methods and of the very nature of the original sketches, which critics have followed Dickens rather than Forster in underrating. The establishment of a critical text of the *Sketches by Boz* is surely a prerequisite for a true estimate of these 'first sprightly runnings of his genius'.

CHAPTER III

From Sketches to Novel: *Pickwick Papers* (1836-7)

I

In a letter of 31 March 1836, Dickens speaks of 'the great success of my book, and the name it has established for me among the publishers . . .' One immediate consequence of the *Sketches by Boz*, published on 6 February 1836, was the well-known offer from Chapman and Hall[1] on 10 February:

> I was a young man of three-and-twenty, when the present publishers, attracted by some pieces I was at that time writing in the Morning Chronicle newspaper (of which one series had lately been collected . . .), waited upon me to propose a something that should be published in shilling numbers. . . The idea propounded to me was that the monthly something should be a vehicle for certain plates to be executed by MR SEYMOUR; and there was a notion . . . that a "NIMROD club", the members of which were to go out shooting, fishing, and so forth, and getting themselves into difficulties through their want of dexterity, would be the best means of introducing these.[2]

The terms offered for providing the letterpress for Seymour's plates were £14 a month for an instalment of about twelve thousand words. 'The emolument', wrote Dickens, 'is too tempting to resist'.[3] At the same time, it must have seemed to cut across

1. Chapman (Forster, I v) gave a slightly different account, explaining that he and his partner William Hall were attracted by the *Monthly Magazine* stories, and wished to enlist the writer as a contributor to their new periodical the *Library of Fiction*, edited by Charles Whitehead (his first story there, 'The Tuggs's at Ramsgate', appeared at the end of March), and that having opened this connexion, they naturally applied to him for *Pickwick*. For a summary of most of the evidence, see W. Dexter and J. W. T. Ley, *The Origin of Pickwick*, 1936.

2. Preface to 1847 edition of *Pickwick Papers*.

3. *Letters*, I 65.

his plans, which were apparently to use such leisure as he had from his full-time reporting for further sketch-writing, and, above all, for the three-volume novel already in his mind. The Preface to *Sketches by Boz* refers to that publication as a 'pilot balloon'; there was already a real balloon designed for launching if it succeeded—the 'proposed novel' referred to as early as 1834,[1] but now presumably re-forming in his mind as *Gabriel Vardon, the Locksmith of London.*[2] Such a design at least helps to explain the implied wish to 'resist' the 'tempting' emolument; and also the remark (ironic by then) in the 1847 Preface to *Pickwick*:

> My friends told me it was a low, cheap form of publication, by which I should ruin all my rising hopes . . .[3]

The 'friends', one supposes, were the only two established novelists whom Dickens already knew—Harrison Ainsworth and Edward Bulwer, both with respectable three-volume novels to their credit; perhaps the editors among his acquaintance, Laman Blanchard, Douglas Jerrold, and William Jerdan, may have added their arguments. Dickens's 'rising hopes' early in 1836 were literary rather than journalistic; he was working his way out of journalism, with the collection and revision of his *Sketches*, his comedy and his burletta, and his plans for a novel; Chapman and Hall's proposal must have seemed to pull him back into hack work again. For his position was only that of a salaried partner in the proposed monthly enterprise: the artist was already commissioned, and the subject more or less prescribed; four of Seymour's plates were to be illustrated by twenty-six pages of text, and the anticipated circulation of the 'serial' was about four hundred copies. The shilling number, so soon to be transformed in public estimation, had then no status: even two years later, in 1838, the *Edinburgh Review* noted the paradox of the form of Dickens's novels—that of 'literary *ephemerae* . . . the lightest kind of light reading'.[4] When the proposal was made to Dickens, he associated the form only with

> a dim recollection of certain interminable novels in that form, which used, some five-and-twenty years ago, to be carried about

1. *Letters*, I 29: 'I shall cut my proposed novel up into little magazine sketches'.
2. See below, p. 76.
3. The corrected proof (in the Forster collection) shows that Dickens originally wrote 'Everybody' for 'My friends'.
4. Oct. 1838; p. 76.

> the country by pedlars, and over some of which I remember to have shed innumerable tears, before I served my apprenticeship to Life;[1]

an association which perhaps affected his choice of a picaresque fiction, with reminiscences of his favourite Smollett. The artist's plan of plates illustrating the comic misadventures of a Nimrod Club of Cockney sportsmen[2] was of course derived rather from the popular series in annuals (such as Cruikshank's *Comic Almanack*) and monthly magazines (such as the *New Sporting Magazine*, in which Surtees's *Jorrocks* series had recently appeared, and the *New Monthly*, where John Poole had a series called 'A Cockney's Rural Sports'); and from the publication in numbers, in the previous decade, of Pierce Egan's *Life in London* ('Tom and Jerry'), with illustrations by Cruikshank and others.

It is clear that Seymour was the initiator of the plan, and was seen from the start as the dominant partner; and although Dickens at once demanded and was conceded certain modifications so as to give him a 'freer range of English scenes and people', Seymour might conceivably have maintained his position had he lived. But his sudden death decisively shifted the emphasis; first, it 'brought about a quick decision' to reduce the plates from four to two and increase the text to thirty-two pages;[3] and then, by the substitution of a very young artist, Hablôt K. Browne, who was virtually Dickens's own choice, ensured the dominance of the author. By the third number the external pattern of *Pickwick* was established; all that was wanting was success. His 'rising hopes' had not, as his friends prophesied, been ruined by *Pick-*

1. Preface to Cheap edition, 1847. In his autobiographical fragment Dickens, according to Forster, had named the 'cheap series of novelists then in course of publication' which his father bought and in which he, like David Copperfield, first met the eighteenth-century classics. The series has not been identified, but probably resembled Cooke's *British Novelists*, referred to by Hazlitt, and published in sixpenny numbers in 1792.

There had been a recent revival of the method for the reprinting of popular successes; see M. Sadleir, *XIX Century Fiction* (1951), II 94ff.

2. The plan survives in Seymour's cover-design, which is not very appropriate to *Pickwick* as we have it, but evidently represents Seymour's own intentions before Dickens's views were 'deferred to'. Seymour had illustrated Richard Penn's *Maxims and Hints for an Angler, and Miseries of Fishing* (1833); the frontispiece shows a fat spectacled man fishing, and the 'maxims' are presented as 'extracts from the Common Place Book of the Houghton Fishing Club'.

3. The 'Address from the Publishers' in No. III (dated 30 May) claimed that the change was made 'on a suggestion which has been made to them from various influential quarters' and pointed out that it entailed 'considerable expense, which nothing but a large circulation would justify them in incurring'—a cunningly ambiguous phrase.

wick; but they had certainly not been stimulated, with the circulation of the 'monthly something' still in the region of five hundred copies, and very few press notices. He must still have felt doubtful about this 'low, cheap form of publication' which he had consented to adopt simply because 'the emolument'[1] was 'too tempting to resist'; which he had adopted, moreover, without regarding it as other than one of several journalistic sidelines, for after two numbers of *Pickwick* had appeared, he signed a contract with Macrone, the publisher of *Boz*, to supply for £200 a three-volume novel to be completed by the following November.[2] The coincidence of events is suggestive; he was still seeing *Pickwick* as journalism, as distinct from a real novel, which he saw as a considered work 'compact in three separate and indiwidual wollumes'—the one form that he was never to use for the first publication of a novel.[3]

As we know, Dickens was to learn how to reconcile the foresight and planning which a novel required with writing in numbers; but he began *Pickwick* before he had learnt it, and before he even knew that the lesson was relevant. Looking back from ten years' experience, he wrote that:

> no ingenuity of plot was attempted, or even at that time considered very feasible by the author in connexion with the desultory mode of publication adopted.

—here recalling what he had written in the 1837 Preface:

> it was necessary—or it appeared so to the author—that every number should be, to a certain extent, complete in itself, and yet that the whole twenty numbers, when collected, should form one tolerably harmonious whole, each leading to the other by a gentle and not unnatural progress of adventure.
>
> It is obvious that in a work published with a view to such considerations, no artfully interwoven or ingeniously complicated plot can with reason be expected.

The qualifying clauses in the first sentence suggest that he was already changing his mind. And by 1847 he had come to realize that 'experience and study' had now taught him something in that respect, and to wish that the separate papers had been

1. This was raised to £16 when the amount of text was increased, after being reduced to 10 guineas in May.

2. See below, p. 76.

3. *Oliver Twist* and *Great Expectations* were published in this form after serial publication.

strung together on a stronger thread of general interest; still, what they are, they were designed to be.

Plotting and planning, even had Dickens thought it 'feasible', was in any case virtually ruled out by the exigencies of the calendar. *Pickwick* is unique among Dickens's novels, not in being written from month to month 'almost as the periodical occasion arose'—all his novels were so written—but in being *begun* in response to an external demand, instead of gradually taking shape in his mind. There was no preliminary period of imaginative incubation, such as is found even for the other early novels. Between contract and first instalment for *Oliver Twist*, six months elapsed; for *Nicholas Nickleby*, four months (partly spent in visiting Yorkshire); and for *Barnaby Rudge* the quite extraordinary period of at least five years. For later novels the period of preparation is well documented by reference in letters ('vague thoughts', 'agonies of plotting and contriving'), and sometimes by such evidence as the preliminary design of *Dombey and Son* and *The Chimes*; and from 1846 on, he usually began publication with a few numbers in hand. Improvisation thereafter was within the limits of a foreseen plan, which might be modified in detail, but not radically. But for *Pickwick* the time-table is: Chapman and Hall's offer, 10 February; its final acceptance, 16 February; writing begins, 18 February; first number promised to the publishers early in March; second number by the end of March; Number I on sale 31 March.

How it was done is a matter largely of inference. No complete manuscript, no number plans, no proof sheets, very few letters to Forster (whom Dickens did not meet until December 1836) are available here.[1] It may be assumed that as publication proceeded, Dickens watched the sales, that he noticed that they began to rise in July with the introduction of Sam Weller; certainly he took notice of William Jerdan's advice to 'develop' this character 'to the utmost';[2] and the soaring success, from the fifth number on, buoyed him up on a rising wave of confidence, doubled, after

1. The series of notes to Catherine Hogarth in Feb. and Mar. is undated, and the dating supplied by the late Walter Dexter (in *Mr. and Mrs. Charles Dickens: his Letters to her*, 1935, and again, with some changes in dating, in the few extracts also given in *Letters*) is difficult to accept. For example, the remark that 'the sheets are a weary length—I had no idea there was so much in them' seems likely, in its suggestion of inexperience, to refer to the writing of No. I in late Feb. or early Mar., and there is nothing in this or other letters to contradict such dating; but Dexter dated it '[18 March]', without query or explanation, and subsequent writers on Dickens have so accepted it.

2. *Autobiography* (1852), IV 364.

the eleventh number, by the simultaneous success of *Oliver Twist* as a serial in *Bentley's Miscellany.* The peculiar advantage of hand-to-mouth writing—its immediate sensitiveness to public response—must have been disclosed to him in the course of *Pickwick.* But how he began, as an unknown author in an unprecedented form, with merely the experience of his sketch and story writing behind him, can be seen only by looking closely at the early numbers themselves. (As the object is to show the improvised nature of the early instalments, in contrast to the emerging unity of the novel, detailed commentary is not carried further than Number V, chapters xii–xiv.)

II

The first number (chapters i–ii, and the first two pages of chapter iii) is essentially a single 'sketch' combined with the first part of a farcical episode such as we find in the *Monthly Magazine* tales. The 'sketch' is the Pickwickians' meeting in chapter i, supposed to be taken from the Transactions of the Club. Besides its obvious expository function, it has an evident satirical purpose, for the oration and debate 'bear a strong affinity to the discussions of other celebrated bodies'. It is the reporter who is speaking, with recollections of Parliament and political meetings and innumerable other public meetings in mind; and with more than a side-glance, in the Theory of Tittlebats, at the proceedings of the recently established British Association[1] (already a target in Cruikshank's *Comic Almanack* of 1835); the chapter is virtually a further variant on the committee meeting in 'The Steam Excursion' of 1834.[2] From his earliest to his latest writings Dickens loved to set his characters speechifying; 'The Election for Beadle' already foreshadows the humours of the United Metropolitan Improved Hot Muffin and Crumpet Baking and Punctual Delivery Company in *Nicholas Nickleby* and the Mudfog Association for the Advancement of Everything, and John Willet at the Maypole may be seen taking shape in 'The Parlour

1. The notice in the *Bath Herald* called this number 'a squib directed against the British Association' (*The Dickensian,* June 1936, p. 216).

2. 'He had the highest esteem for Mr. Percy Noakes as an individual, but he did consider that he ought not to be intrusted with these immense powers (oh, oh!) He believed that in the proposed capacity [as organizer of a picnic] Mr. Percy Noakes would not act fairly, impartially, or honourably; but he begged it to be distinctly understood that he said this, without the slightest personal disrespect'—that is, in a Pickwickian sense. (*Sketches by Boz,* First Series.)

Orator'. When Dickens is writing under pressure, the guying of public debate is the humorous device that he most readily turns to; deflating the pomposities of the self-intoxicated orator, amateur and professional, was his revenge for the years of enforced listening to speech-making recorded in *David Copperfield*:

> Night after night, I record predictions that never come to pass, professions that are never fulfilled, explanations that are only meant to mystify. I wallow in words.[1]

The first chapter also prepares for the travels of the four Pickwickians, which begin accordingly in the second, with the journey to Rochester, the meeting with Jingle,[2] and the first stage of the embroilment with Dr Slammer. Tracy Tupman's ambition to cut a dash in company and his amorous bent, the empty pretensions of Mr Winkle's claims to sportsmanship, are illustrated in the manner of 'humours'; the whole episode is from stock, clearly recalling the duel in *The Rivals*. Dickens expected Jingle to make 'a decided hit'; but there is nothing as yet to suggest that he is more than a transient character; and the desultory form of the papers is confirmed by the appearance, at the end of the number, of 'dismal Jemmy', who prepares to tell a tale. Thus the conclusion of the farcical episode is left in suspense, and the third chapter is interrupted for a month at the foot of its second page.

In the second number (chapters iii–v) the interrelation is still loose; the grim 'Stroller's Tale' is first narrated, with no other apparent purpose than to exhibit Boz's versatility[3] and his independence of Seymour's designs; its impact is nullified by the immediate return of the farce. Chapter iv introduces an entirely new episode with the field-day at Fort Pitt and a new group of characters with the Wardle party; which results in the invitation to Manor Farm, and the humours of the journey with the horse and trap.[4]

1. Ch. xliii.

2. Dickens had written thus far, the equivalent of eight printed pages, by 21 Feb. (*Letters*, I 67; the date is confirmed by the letters to Chapman and Hall in the same week.)

3. Compare such a sketch as 'The Black Veil' (*Sketches by Boz*, First Series). It is possible that this, like other intercalated tales, was originally designed for separate publication. Dickens was working under considerable pressure, for the MS. of No. II was in the publishers' hands by 29 Mar. (Dexter and Ley, op. cit., p. 43), presumably to allow time for his honeymoon (2–?14 Apr.) and for the four illustrations, of which Seymour had done three before his death on 19 Apr.

4. The review in the *Sun* (2 May) describes it as 'the second number of an entertaining, miscellaneous collection of tales, anecdotes, etc., collected and arranged by Boz'.

The third number (chapters vi–viii), more obviously a miscellany than any, inaugurates a new amorous adventure for Mr Tupman, provides sporting humour with Mr Winkle's shooting and the cricket match, and some more comic oratory; it also includes a set of verses, 'The Ivy Green', known to have been written independently,[1] and the second intercalated 'grim' story, 'The Convict's Return'. The characters remain in the flat, the situations stock; though the farce is diversified and enlivened by means of minor characters like the Fat Boy. But this number also suggests some planning ahead, through the recurrence of Jingle, now cast as a rival to Tupman; and the number ends on a note of suspense:

> The host was in high spirits, for he had satisfied himself that there was no ground for the charge against Mr. Tupman. So was Mr. Tupman, for Mr. Jingle had told him that his affair would soon be brought to a crisis. So was Mr. Pickwick, for he was seldom otherwise. . . So were Mr. Jingle and Miss Wardle, for reasons of sufficient importance in this eventful history, to be narrated in another chapter.

This simple type of number-ending is Dickens's favourite in *Pickwick.*

The fourth number (chapters ix–xi) makes no marked departure from the pattern. The elopement of Jingle and Miss Wardle, his pursuit, exposure, and buying-off apparently complete the second farcical episode, and the retreat of the disconsolate Tupman sets the Pickwickians on their travels again; the self-contained incident of 'Bill Stumps his Mark' reminds us of the antiquarian researches of the Club, and there is the usual dose of the macabre in 'The Madman's Manuscript'. The only anticipation of the next number is the prospect of the election at Eatanswill, 'a scene so interesting to every Englishman'. Thus far there is no reason why the sales of *Pickwick* should at this point have shown a spectacular rise; this must be partly attributed[2] to the appearance of a particularly racy though apparently transient minor character in the exposure scene—the Boots at the White Hart, Sam Weller. It is unlikely that his full possibilities were as yet foreseen. Writing to a friend, Dickens draws attention to him

1. F. G. Kitton, *The Poems and Verses of Charles Dickens* (1903), p. 35.

2. This is the explanation usually given, but in any case three or four months seems about the right time for a new publication, unusual in form, to make its impact.

simply as a 'specimen of London life'[1]—a true-to-life Cockney 'character', that is, of the order of 'the Omnibus Cad' in the *Sketches*. Nothing of his future relation to Mr Pickwick is as yet suggested; but the characteristic anecdote of his father, and still more, the skilful use of his observations so as to show the whole Jingle incident from a fresh and unexpected point of view, seem to promise a more than merely episodic function. Perhaps Dickens had vague designs for him as the stock comic servant in the eighteenth-century tradition, sharpened up with Cockney humour and with verbal reminiscences of Simm Spatterdash in Beazley's popular comedy.[2] Whatever he foresaw, he at once responded to Jerdan's suggestion to 'develop' this character 'to the utmost', not only by ever-resourceful comic invention of detail, but by integrating the character with the plot and themes of the novel.

The 'development' of Sam in subsequent numbers gives a new depth and a new motive force to *Pickwick*; henceforward it is built, not simply upon events, but upon the deepening relation between him and his master. Much weight, in criticism of *Pickwick*, is commonly given to Dickens's well-known account of its beginnings—'My views being deferred to, I thought of Mr. Pickwick'; but Pickwick is not 'thought of' as a character distinct in kind from the other Pickwickians until he is connected with Sam Weller. Until then, he is simply the benevolent butt, the fat man who loses his hat and is upset in a postchaise, differentiated from the amorous Tupman and the would-be sporting Winkle only by being less clearly ticketed with a single 'humour'; with Sam, he becomes that most fruitful of all comic archetypes, the innocent at large, with a touch of the chivalrous crusader. Not only Smollett, but Cervantes, was Dickens's model here, as several contemporary reviewers recognized.[3]

Chapter xii, which opens the fifth number and includes Mr Pickwick's engagement of Sam as his servant, is crucial in another way too: and this, no doubt, is what Dickens had in mind

1. *Letters*, I 73.

2. *The Boarding House*, 1811. Simm is a cheeky servant who acts as a go-between in the 'love'-plot; the only specific resemblance is in his use of 'Wellerisms' ('as the — said'), which Dickens had already adopted in his *Sketches* (see above, p. 58). The review in the *Westminster Review*, July 1837, referring to 'those imaginary speeches . . . after the fashion of Cockney wags', suggests that they were taken from life.

3. E.g. *Edinburgh Review*, Oct. 1838: 'the modern Quixote and Sancho of Cockaigne'.

in its descriptive title, 'A very important Proceeding on the part of Mr. Pickwick; no less an epoch in his Life than in this History'. The importance of Mrs Bardell's misunderstanding of Mr Pickwick's intentions, which dawns upon the reader in the sixth number with the letter from Dodson and Fogg, is here proclaimed; and this supplies a plot-interest which continues to the end of the novel. Thus, a quarter of the way through its course, *Pickwick* discovers its shape, with the emergence of Sam and the beginning of the action of Bardell v. Pickwick.

The new plot-material sprang directly from a recent journalistic experience. Dickens wrote the fifth number in July; on 22 June, as a reporter on the *Morning Chronicle*, he had attended the Norton-Melbourne case, his report occupying twenty-six columns of the paper next day. He saw the possibilities of the trial, not only the prosecuting counsel's comments on the formal notes of Lord Melbourne[1] and the browbeating of witnesses,[2] but more soberly, as material for satiric exposure of social corruption, for it was a flagrantly deliberate attempt to damage the character of innocent persons. Dickens's treatment is serious as well as comic, producing what the *Edinburgh Review* was to call

> one of the most acute and pointed satires upon the state and administration of English law that ever appeared in the light and lively dress of fiction.[3]

It is the earliest and one of the most successful instances of Dickens's use of topical appeal in his novels and an excellent

1. ' "I will call about half past 4. Yours, Melbourne" . . . The style and form of these notes, Gentlemen, seems to import much more than they contain. Cautiously, I admit, they are worded; there are no professions of love . . . but still they are not the letters of an ordinary acquaintance'. The final speech for the defence ridiculed the argument, quoting the notes again; 'Are Lord Melbourne's declarations very violent? Are his protestations exceedingly warm? (*Laughter*).' The *Quarterly Review* (Oct. 1837) quotes Buzfuz on 'Chops and tomata-sauce' as 'a fair specimen of Mr. Dickens's tact in stimulating the reader's attention by little sly allusions to contemporary events'.

2. Compare also the exchange between Mr Thesiger and Sir William Follett in the examination of a lady's maid, obviously the source of the little judge's flat contradiction of Mr Winkle:

> *Witness:* I have often known Lord Melbourne there but I could never get a look at him. *Sir William Follett:* What? *Mr Thesiger:* She said she had often known Lord Melbourne there but could never get a look at him. *Sir William Follett:* No, she did not.

3. Oct. 1838, p. 80; and compare Charles Buller's review in *Westminster Review*, July 1837. F. G. Kitton, in his notes to the Autograph edition (1903), says that Dickens was helped in his account of the trial by Talfourd, who revised the proof.

example of how he selected and reassembled facts[1] (for Justice Gaselee and Serjeant Bompas, notoriously the models for Stareleigh and Buzfuz, did not appear in the case) and transformed them by exaggeration and invention into a timeless comic fantasy. Nor is the immortal Trial merely a star episode; it is one of the key scenes of the novel, in displaying the main characters, especially Pickwick, Winkle, and the Wellers, at their most characteristic. It appeared in the twelfth number, in March 1837; but Dickens had surely had it in mind for several months before.

III

This is the clearest instance of foresight and planning. But alongside the Bardell–Pickwick plot and the deepening relation of master and servant, the looser, more miscellaneous pattern proceeds as before; adventures at Eatanswill, Ipswich, Bath; the shooting party, the skating scene, the medical students' party, with inset tales and verses, diversify the numbers. As it grew into a novel, *Pickwick* did not lose its character as a miscellany, with a 'free range of English scenes and people', nor its loosely picaresque form. The *Athenæum*, reviewing the first nine numbers, summed up their ingredients as—

> two pounds of Smollett, three ounces of Sterne, a handful of Hook, a dash of a grammatical Pierce Egan—[2]

rightly recognizing the basis of the mixture as Smollett, though with a significant difference—'Smollett without his coarseness'.[3] Dickens had also in mind such periodical series as the De Coverley papers—on the whole the nearest precedent offered by the eighteenth century for the serial novel. *Pickwick* remains to the

1. Other *crim. con.* trials may be recalled; in *Birch v. Neale* (Court of Common Pleas, 25 June 1835) a good deal is made to depend on what the servants can see through the cracks of a bedroom door. Charles Philips, the Irish barrister, was notorious for his pleadings in such cases, and was 'a great practical patron of the brow-beating system' (James Grant, *Portraits of Public Characters*, 2 vols., 1841, I 212; and see *Edinburgh Review*, Oct. 1815 and Nov. 1817).

2. 3 Dec. 1836; compare *New Monthly Magazine* (Sept. 1836): 'his spirit is akin to that of our Fieldings and Smolletts'.

3. But not all readers agreed. Lockhart told Ainsworth that he thought *Pickwick* ' "all very well—but" with one of his usual laughs—"damned low!" ' (S. M. Ellis, *William Harrison Ainsworth and his Friends*, 1911, I 336) and two members of a circulating Book Society opposed the notion to take in the numbers because 'they considered the work vulgar' (MS. notes in a British Museum copy of first edition).

end more strictly 'periodical' than any of his later novels. The high proportion of inset tales seems to show that he pursued, perhaps in a crude form, the principle of variety within a single number; the episodes are farcical, the inset story macabre. (In the Fleet numbers, where the main content is more serious, no such tales occur.) A more practical and economical motive may have contributed. Dickens had written many short tales when he began *Pickwick*; very likely he had some in his desk and used them to eke out his numbers.[1] Seven of the nine stories occur in the first half of the novel; they are almost completely disconnected from their contexts, related casually by unimportant people, and seldom making any impact on their hearers. In one case the immediate source in recent experience is evident; Dickens visited Bedlam in June 1836 (he had planned a 'sketch' on the subject and was also probably already thinking of *Barnaby Rudge*) and in the July number inserted 'The Madman's Manuscript'.

The 'journalistic' nature of *Pickwick* is also evident in one curious and unique feature: the consistent relevance of the numbers to the time of year in which they appeared, so that, for example, the cricket match falls in the June number, the shooting scene in October, and the skating scene in February. Some numbers are slightly retrospective in dating; Christmas at Dingley Dell is in the January number, the September number opens with a description of August, Sam Weller writes his Valentine in the March number, and the final (November) number opens with Mr Pickwick going to Gray's Inn 'in the healthy light of an October morning'. Dickens appears to have imagined his readers asking themselves on the first of the month, What have the Pickwickians been doing since we saw them last? and to have reported accordingly. The duration of the action matches the nineteen months of publication, running from May (1827) to October (1828), parallel with the serial appearances from April 1836 to November 1837. The law terms are observed, and when, after the trial, Mr Pickwick is told that 'they can issue execution just

1. Bibliography seems to confirm this in one instance; the story of Prince Bladud in the thirteenth (Apr.) number was set up separately with a blank space before and after. Dickens might well be pressed for time just then, having recently begun the editing of *Bentley's* and the writing of *Oliver Twist*; and February, as he often ruefully notes, is a short month.

He reverted to the practice only once in a later novel; the second number of *Nicholas Nickleby* contains two tales, whose presence is explained by a letter to Forster: 'I . . . have yet five slips to finish, and don't know what to put in them for I have reached the point I meant to leave off with' (*Letters*, I 162).

two months hence', the necessary interval is occupied with the visit to Bath in the next two numbers. This exact correspondence is not observed in any later novel, though isolated instances of 'seasonal relevance' can be found, such as Little Nell's death in January; and the pointed reference to the date in chapter xiii of *Barnaby Rudge*, published on 4 April:

> It was, in fact, the twenty-fifth of March, which, as most people know to their cost, is, and has been time out of mind, one of those unpleasant epochs termed quarter-days.[1]

But the novels after *Pickwick* were each worlds of their own, not tied to the reader's calendar.

The other external circumstance which may have affected the direction of *Pickwick* was the writing of *Oliver Twist*, which overlapped with it after the first nine numbers. Its success may have emboldened Dickens to introduce a more serious kind of social satire into *Pickwick*. Just after the new serial had begun to appear comes the Trial; it had been running for three months when Mr Pickwick enters the Fleet prison. 'The next Pickwick', he wrote to Forster, 'will bang all the others';[2] he was right; the sales rose to forty thousand.

The interlocking of the first three novels is indeed made clear by a remark in the Preface to *Nicholas Nickleby*. He says he had had the evils of the Yorkshire schools in his mind for many years; and 'at last, having an audience, resolved to write about them'.[3] 'Having an audience': this was assured to Dickens, and for his lifetime, after the fifth number of *Pickwick*; and 'having an audience', he resolved to expose the corruptions of the law, the plight of the pauper child, the evils of prison, school, and workhouse. But, having captured that audience by his power as an entertainer, he never abused his position:

> the rascalities of those Yorkshire schoolmasters *cannot* easily be exaggerated, and I have kept down the strong truth and thrown as much comicality over it as I could, rather than disgust the reader with its fouler aspects.[4]

So Stiggins, Bumble, and Squeers remain comic characters, and

1. See also the description of Chancery Lane in the hot days of a long vacation, in *Bleak House*, No. VI (ch. xix), published in August 1852, and of late autumn weather in No. IX (ch. xxix), published in November.

2. *Letters*, I 124.

3. Preface to *Nicholas Nickleby*, Cheap edition, 1848.

4. *Letters*, I 185.

the trial of Bardell v. Pickwick shows no trace of the revolting coarseness of the testimony of the suborned witnesses in the Norton-Melbourne trial. He was first a creator and entertainer:

> The author's object in this work, was to place before the reader a constant succession of characters and incidents; to paint them in as vivid colours as he could command; and to render them, at the same time, life-like and amusing.

Thus the opening of the 1837 Preface to *Pickwick*. But looking back ten years later he saw something more:

> I have found it curious and interesting, looking over the sheets of this reprint, to mark what important social improvements have taken place about us, almost imperceptibly, ever since they were originally written. The license of Counsel, and the degree to which Juries are ingeniously bewildered, are yet susceptible of moderation; while an improvement in the mode of conducting Parliamentary Elections (especially for counties) is still within the bounds of possibility. But legal reforms have pared the claws of Messrs. Dodson and Fogg; . . . the laws relating to imprisonment for debt are altered; and the Fleet Prison is pulled down!

Forster's words were true in more senses than one:

> The book itself, in teaching him what his power was, made him more conscious of what would be expected from its use; and this never afterwards quitted him.[1]

*

Dickens had discovered his power; he had also discovered his medium in the monthly number.

> My friends told me it was a low, cheap form of publication, by which I should ruin all my rising hopes; and how right my friends turned out to be, everybody now knows.

Other experiments in form were still to be made; but with *Pickwick*, Dickens embarked upon his lifelong love-affair with his reading public; which, when all is said, is by far the most interesting love-affair of his life.

1. Forster, II i.

CHAPTER IV

Barnaby Rudge: The First Projected Novel

I

BARNABY RUDGE, though it is now one of the least read of Dickens's novels, deserves special attention on account of two unusual features: the length of time which Dickens had it in mind, and the particular kind of 'work' it involved, in research upon original sources. Also notable, though not unusual, is the way he makes his historical romance a tract for the times, relating it to some of the social and political preoccupations of the years of writing.

He had it in mind for at least five years. For it should have been his first published novel, instead of his fifth. Instead of coming out in the threepenny numbers of *Master Humphrey's Clock* in 1841, it should have appeared in all the traditional dignity of 'three compact indiwidual wollumes' at the end of 1836, when Mr Pickwick had progressed no farther than Ipswich. That, at least, was the agreement made in May with Macrone, publisher of *Sketches by Boz.*[1] What interfered was the soaring circulation of *Pickwick*; by August a contract for an outright payment of £200 and an edition of a thousand copies, welcome enough for the young beginner, could only seem derisory. The agreement was eventually cancelled and the projected novel (its title now changed from *Gabriel Vardon, the Locksmith of London* to *Barnaby Rudge, a tale of the Riots of '80*) transferred to Bentley.[2] In Septem-

1. *Letters,* I 71–2. The 'entire manuscript' was to be delivered 'on or before' 30 Nov. or 'as soon afterwards as I can possibly complete it'.

2. Dickens believed himself released from the Macrone agreement and on 22 Aug. agreed to provide two novels (unnamed) for Bentley. Macrone however wished to hold him to his contract and in Dec. was advertising *Gabriel Vardon*; the release was only obtained, on consideration of a reduction in the sum paid for the copy-

ber 1837 its delivery was promised by October 1838; but this was soon found incompatible with the claims of serial writing, and the next project, to run it as a monthly serial in *Bentley's Miscellany* in 1839,[1] also broke down. It was postponed again to January 1840 ('as a novel, and not in portions');[2] in the following July transferred to Chapman and Hall as a novel 'of matter sufficient for ten monthly numbers',[3] and finally appeared weekly in the *Clock*[4] from 13 February to 27 November, 1841. This complicated and harassing history has a more than biographical interest; the novel was affected by the change of form, and still more by its exceptionally long period of incubation. Dickens's persistence in his plan for 'a tale of the Riots of '80' is evidence of his tenacity of purpose and the grip of the original idea on his imagination; not, as has been suggested, of the grudging performance of a task. There were difficulties; being committed to the weekly appearances of the *Clock*, he had to begin with all his 'thoughts and interest hanging about'[5] the just-concluded *Old Curiosity Shop*; and to the last he was, as he told his readers, 'often cramped and confined in a very irksome degree' by the short weekly instalments.[6] But after 'warming up' in the middle chapters, he could write to Forster: 'I was always sure I could make a good thing of *Barnaby*, and I think you'll find that it comes out strong to the last word . . . I am in great heart and spirits with the story'.[7]

What then was the original idea which he had held in mind for so long? We know from the Preface that Dickens began with the object of writing about the Gordon Riots, which he believed to be new material for fiction,[8] 'presenting many very extraordinary

---

rights of the *Sketches*, in Jan. 1837. These and later agreements were published in *The Dickensian*, Sept. 1935, pp. 241–54 and June 1937, pp. 199–204, and the whole story of Dickens's publishing troubles for the four years 1836–40 was first clearly set out, with extracts from unpublished correspondence, by Johnson in *The Dickensian*, Dec. 1949, pp. 10–17, and Mar. 1950, pp. 76–83.

1. It is advertised in the first edition of *Oliver Twist* (published 9 Nov. 1838) as to be 'published forthwith, in *Bentley's Miscellany*', and again in the *Miscellany* itself, 1 Dec. 1838.

2. *Letters*, I 198; letter of 31 Jan. 1839. The payment on delivery of the manuscript was now to be £2,000.

3. *Letters*, I 263; the publishers had the option of publishing 'in fifteen smaller numbers'. The terms for six months' copyright were now £3,000.

4. Nos. 46–87. 5. *Letters*, I 297.

6. 'To the Readers . . .'; see below, p. 88. 7. *Letters*, I 345.

8. Thomas Gaspey's *The Mystery or, Forty Years Ago* (3 vols., 1820), in which three chapters are concerned with the riots, was possibly not known to him; yet he must have known the author as a member of the staff of the *Evening Chronicle*. James Grant, *The Great Metropolis* (first series, 2 vols., 1836), II 47–8, describes Gaspey

and remarkable features'. This means that in 1836 he set out to write a serious historical novel, and by his choice of subject challenged comparison with Scott. The storming of the Tolbooth in the opening chapters of *The Heart of Midlothian* is the literary inspiration of his central scene, as Madge Wildfire is of his central figure—who also recalls (especially in appearance) Davie Gellatley, the daft servant in *Waverley*.[1]

All this, however, is secondary to the direct inspiration of Newgate itself, both as place and symbol. Its exterior had been a familiar and awesome sight to Dickens as a schoolboy.[2] In 1835 he visited it, in order to write the sketch for the collected First Series of *Sketches by Boz*,[3] and was struck by the aspect and the imagined suffering of three condemned men, of whom two, he learnt, were afterwards executed, and one respited during His Majesty's pleasure. There is the germ of chapters lxxvi–lxxvii of *Barnaby*. His essay also emphasized the massiveness of the walls and gates, the hopelessness of escape; a perception closely connected with his triumphant letter of September 1841: 'I have just burnt into Newgate, and am going in the next number to tear the prisoners out by the hair of their heads.'[4] One may suspect that it was this incident in the riots that first fired his interest in the subject. In contemporary accounts, the burning of Newgate appears more terrifying than all the attacks upon Catholic chapels and property in its expression of the lawlessness of the mob; and to the next generation it carried the shadow of a far greater historical event, the fall of the Bastille. Dickens's imagination was also stirred by a rumoured scheme of violence still more terrifying—the release of the lunatics from Bedlam. This,

---

as also 'favourably known as the author of several novels, which he wrote some years ago'. Dickens's only known reference to him is in his Diary for 31 Jan. 1839: 'Gaspey. Chapter on Executioners' (*Letters*, I 191). The entry looks like a memorandum to read such a chapter, and it is natural to connect it with *Barnaby Rudge*, which is mentioned in a letter of the same date (*Letters*, I 198). The 'chapter' may be ch. vii of *The Mystery*, vol. I, in which 'Ned Dennis' appears, accompanied by the same kind of macabre jesting as in *Barnaby Rudge*, though this hardly seems to account for the plural, 'executioners'. Another general parallel in a novel of Gaspey's is found in *George Godfrey* (3 vols., 1828) where there is an execution scene (III i) in which one of the three condemned criminals is reprieved at the last moment.

1. This parallel was noticed as early as June 1841, in Patrick Robertson's speech at the Edinburgh banquet.

2. See the opening paragraph of 'The Old Bailey' (*Morning Chronicle*, 23 Oct. 1834), included in the Second Series of *Sketches by Boz* under the title 'Criminal Courts'.

3. 'A Visit to Newgate'; see above, pp. 40–1.

4. *Letters*, I 349.

along with the mad streak in Gordon's own character, contributed to his conception of Barnaby; at one time he had even thought of making good the rumour, and showing three Bedlamites as the unsuspected leaders of the rioters.[1] Forster's sober counsels deterred him, and indeed the ironic social point is better made by his actual choice of leaders—Hugh, the bastard of a fine gentleman and a gipsy hanged at Tyburn; Barnaby, the imbecile son of a murderer; and Dennis, the public hangman.

The two titles of the projected novel suggest that the outline of his main design respecting the riots was already formed in 1836. He may also have had it in mind on his visit to Bedlam 'for the new series' (of *Sketches by Boz*) and certainly on his second visit to Newgate in 1837.[2] The writing, however, is not known to have begun until the autumn of 1839; early in October, hard upon the conclusion of *Nickleby*, he was 'going . . . tooth and nail at Barnaby',[3] and by February 1840 two chapters[4] were written, substantially chapters i–iii of the published novel, which introduce the main characters and provide clear evidence of an elaborated plan for the whole. *Master Humphrey's Clock* and *The Old Curiosity Shop* then intervened and occupied him for the rest of the year. In January 1841 he revised and redivided the two opening chapters,[5] and began to write the fourth chapter;[6] but he soon lost the advantage of starting with material for two numbers in hand, and by April was 'getting on very slowly'.[7] But with the riots he wrote more rapidly, and by mid-September was again a few weeks in advance.[8] Although he still complained of lack of room ('Oh! If I only had him . . . in monthly numbers.')[9] the

1. Forster, II ix. Dickens refers to the rumour in ch. lxvii.

2. On 27 June 1837, with Macready, Forster, Cattermole, and 'Phiz' (*Diaries of W. C. Macready 1833–1851*, ed. William Toynbee, 2 vols., 1912, I 401–2). Chigwell was also perhaps in his mind as one of the settings; a picnic there 'last year' is described in his *Sketches of Young Gentlemen* (1838).

3. *Letters*, I 231, to Cruikshank, who was then expected to illustrate it.

4. *Letters*, I 249.

5. *Letters*, I 296. Ch. i originally ended with 'and galloped away', and ch. ii included the whole of what is now ch. iii. In revision, several passages were added, and some references to Barnaby as 'the idiot' were omitted. John Willet was called 'Peter Badge' for the first few pages.

6. He sent Cattermole '4 slips' on 30 Jan. (*Letters*, I 298); this was the beginning of No. III (48), published on 28 Feb.

7. *Letters*, I 317.

8. *Letters*, I 353 (18 Sept.): 'I have let all the prisoners out of Newgate, burnt down Lord Mansfield's, and played the very devil' (chs. lxv–lxvi, published 1 Oct.); see also the letters to Cattermole of 6 and 19 Aug. and 12 Sept.

9. *Letters*, I 343.

problem was less acute than in the earlier numbers, where he had committed himself to the careful laying-down of clues for the Haredale–Rudge murder-mystery part of the plot. This, much more appropriate to a three-volume novel than to short weekly instalments, set him a problem in exposition, and no doubt accounts for the anxiety shown in the letters of the early months.

The manuscript survives, but without the proof sheets; the considerable differences between manuscript and printed text show that much revision must have taken place in proof. Dickens's space was indeed small. With two exceptions,[1] each number consisted of two chapters, and twelve pages of print, in which the illustrations were inset.[2] Sixteen and a half of Dickens's quarto pages or 'slips' went to a number. Cutting in proof was frequently necessary, both for length and other reasons, and Forster's assistance was often sought:

> if there be anything here you object to, knock it out ruthlessly[3]

> Don't fail to erase anything that seems to you too strong[4]

> It was too bad of me to give you the trouble of cutting the number, but I knew so well you would do it in the right places.[5]

Nothing of particular interest has, however, been lost. The description of eighteenth-century London at the beginning of chapter iv originally included the following:

> receiving Houses for the sick, which are now blocked up to swarming labyrinths—hotbeds for the constant growth of all the worst diseases they receive—were then upon the very borders of the town. The Middlesex Hospital, and those at Westminster and Hyde Park Corner, were of this kind. Their several sites selected with a view to the healthiest and purest air, they were at that time in the outskirts; beyond them were florists' gardens, widespread fields, green lanes and country roads. Half a century appears but a little time for so much growth, but it is with cities as with human beings—once dropsical they rapidly increase in size, and in a short space become more overgrown and more unwieldy than in all their lives before.

1. No. I (*Master Humphrey's Clock*, No. 46), and No. VII (No. 52). The latter was a short number, as it closed vol. II of the *Clock* and included the frontispiece, title-page, and preface.

2. Dickens sometimes indicates in the manuscript where he wishes the illustration to come, and his instructions were usually followed.

3. *Letters*, I 309.

4. *Letters*, I 312; letter of 5 Apr., apparently referring to chs. xvii–xviii (published 18 Apr.) as just written.

5. *Letters*, I 317.

A passage which was possibly one of those 'knocked out' by Forster occurs in chapter xvii; it is a continuation of the stranger's threat, which ends in the text at 'if you betray me':

> 'By this right hand whose history you know and by this Devil's seal stamped upon me you remember when, I will!'
>
> He pulled his slouched hat from his brow, and pointing, as he spoke, to the gash upon his cheek, replaced it, and sat awaiting her decision.

Solomon Daisy's revelations in chapter xxxiii were delayed in the original, and Mr Willet's impatience was thus emphasized:

> They waited so long, and questioned him so often, without receiving any more satisfactory answer than a wild start, that Mr. Willet had entertained serious thoughts of [throttling him *deleted*] inserting a fork in his arm or leg by way of opening a vein, and had indeed begun to polish one of those instruments with his apron, and to look intently at the little man as if considering where to have him, when Solomon Daisy, with tears in his eyes, implored them to have patience for a minute longer and to fill his glass once more, to the end that he might rally his scattered spirits and be coherent in his speech.
>
> 'If he don't tell us now,' said John as he stirred the liquor and held it to his lips to take, 'if he don't tell us now in a quarter of a minute what's the matter, I shall do him a mischief. Mind that.'

But after the riots are reached there is much less revision,[1] and everything points to this part of the novel being written easily, by an author thoroughly familiar with his material: 'Many thanks for your kind offer', he writes to Charles Ollier, 'but I don't need the Trials'. He had made up his mind about his reading of Lord George Gordon's character and does not appear to have made any concessions to Forster's objections here.[2]

His favourable view was emphasized in the closing chapter, where he related the circumstances of Gordon's death in Newgate, five years after the riots.

> The prisoners bemoaned his loss, and missed him; for though his means were not large his charity was great, and in bestowing alms among them he considered the necessities of all alike, and knew no distinction of sect or creed. There are wise men in the highways of

1. In one or two places, however, it is clear that the manuscript itself is a fair copy.

2. *Letters*, I 324; Forster had just read chs. xxxv–xxxvi, and thought 'some points . . . stated much too favourably'; the letter (3 June 1841) gives Dickens's defence.

> the world who may learn something, even from this poor crazy Lord who died in Newgate.

The general moral of the story is made explicit in the Preface, written in November 1841:

> those shameful tumults, while they reflect indelible disgrace upon the time in which they occurred, and all who had act or part in them, teach a good lesson. That what we falsely call a religious cry is easily raised by men who have no religion, and who in their daily practice set at nought the commonest principles of right and wrong; that it is begotten of intolerance and persecution; that it is senseless, besotted, inveterate, and unmerciful; all History teaches us. But perhaps we do not know it in our hearts too well, to profit by even so humble and familiar an example as the "No Popery" riots of Seventeen Hundred and Eighty.

But this was only one of the many lessons for the times to be drawn from Dickens's tale.

II

The five years' delay between design and publication had increased the novel's topicality. At any time in the 'thirties and 'forties, it would have suggested (as most historical novels did) 'new foes with an old face', for the revolution that never happened seemed always imminent. But the events of 1836–41 made the novel almost journalistically apt. The Poor Law riots, the Chartist risings at Devizes, Birmingham, and Sheffield, the mass meetings on Kersal Moor and Kennington Common, and most pointed of all, the Newport rising of 1839 with its attempt to release Chartist prisoners—all these, with their aftermath of trials, convictions, and petitions against the punishment of death, gave special point in 1841 to 'a tale of the Riots of '80'. The imperfections of the historical parallel, the vital difference between agitation directed to limited and specific ends and the madness of the underworld let loose, were less obvious then than now. What most often repeats itself in history is the fear that history will do so. Dickens was responding not to enlightened historical analysis, but to the average man's horror of looted chapels and distilleries, armed robbery in the streets, prisons and mansions ablaze—sights imprinted ineffaceably upon the memories of many living individuals, and the family memories of thousands more.

There were other topical parallels. 'It is a common but dangerous error', wrote Thomas Hood,[1] rebuking Dickens for a too charitable view of Gordon, 'to attribute all moral to mental obliquities'. The question of criminal responsibility and degrees of insanity had been newly raised by the 1840 trial of Edward Oxford, who shot at the Queen and was found guilty but insane.[2] (Three years later the M'Naghten rules were framed.) Dickens recognized that in the popular mind madness, crime, and revolutionary agitation ran into and coloured each other; but he saw the need for discrimination, and suggests it by his emphasis on Gordon's abnormality and the reprieve of Barnaby. These questions are also related to the growing pressure of capital punishment, and especially of public executions, upon the conscience of the thoughtful; Courvoisier's execution (which Dickens witnessed)[3] and Thackeray's harrowing account of it in 'Going to See a Man Hanged'[4] are also part of the contemporary context of *Barnaby*.

In his Preface Dickens gives most emphasis to the dangers of the unscrupulous exploiting of Protestant bigotry, and the timely relevance of this warning is less likely to be grasped by modern readers. But his contemporaries were well aware of the Protestant Association, newly founded in 1839, with local branches for 'operatives', great meetings in Exeter Hall, and petitions to the government against favours supposedly shown to Catholics, especially in education. Though violent only in language, and dissociating itself emphatically from social agitation, it gave grounds, not least by its defence of the Association of 1779–80,[5] for fears of another 'false religious cry'. The unexpected religious animus in the novel also expresses Dickens's general dislike of puritanism, whether in Little Bethel or the 'Protestant Manual'; as a defender of the humble, he strikes a blow for the domestic happiness of Mrs Nubbles and of Gabriel Varden. In Mrs Varden (and Mr Chester) he must have had his eye especially on the Evangelicals; Crabb Robinson noted in his diary that 'Dickens will lose popularity with the saints, for he too faithfully exposes

1. *Athenæum*, 22 Jan. 1842.

2. Dickens regarded him not as mad, but 'brimful of conceit, and a desire to become, even at the cost of the gallows (the only cost within his reach) the talk of the town', and saw in such cases a further argument against capital punishment (letter to the *Daily News*, 9 Mar. 1846; *Miscellaneous Papers*, ed. B. W. Matz, 1914, p. 27).

3. With Maclise and Henry Burnett, his brother-in-law; see F. G. Kitton, *Charles Dickens by Pen and Pencil* (1889–90), pp. 142–3.

4. *Fraser's Magazine*, Aug. 1840.

5. *Protestant Magazine*, Jan. 1840.

cant'.[1] Thomas Hood, in his review, comparing 1841 with 1780, saw 'the same—nay, a worse fanatical demon abroad . . . a Zeal-of-the-Land Busy' attacking 'Art, Science, Literature, the Drama and all other public amusements'; which itself would explain Dickens's bias in making all his 'Protestants' objectionable. Ten years later he would have had other axes to grind, and the writer of the *Child's History of England* would hardly have drawn the Catholics Langdale and Haredale sympathetically: indeed, 1841 was only just in time. During that year the waves from Oxford (Tract 90 was published in March) were to reach London; early in 1842 Dickens's friends in *Punch* were attacking the 'Pussyites'.[2]

III

Barnaby, then, is related to the events and mood of the exact years of its writing and publication. Further, as a novel of recent history, history at the ideal distance of 'sixty years since',[3] it drew support from the memories, oral[4] and written, of men living or recently dead. One passage (at the end of chapter lxv) suggests that Dickens had talked to eyewitnesses, and he is likely to have read many recently published reminiscences—those, for instance, of Frederick Reynolds the actor (1827) and Henry Angelo (1828).[5] He would read too the published letters of Dr Johnson, Horace Walpole, and Crabbe; and if he wanted general inspiration for description of mob violence, there was Carlyle's *French Revolution* (1837), 'that wonderful book'. But his main sources were undoubtedly the brilliantly written *Narrative* of 'William Vincent' (Thomas Holcroft),[6] Robert Watson's *Life of Lord George Gordon* (1795), and the reports in the newspapers.[7]

1. *Books and their Writers*, ed. Edith Morley (3 vols., 1938), p. 599.
2. 'Punch's Pencillings', no. xxxii (vol. II, p. 109). Dickens himself satirized ritualism in his article on Oxford in the *Examiner* (3 June 1843); see *Miscellaneous Papers*, p. 97, and below, p. 180.
3. See the defence in *Waverley*, ch. i.
4. 'It is a matter of pride with some of our old citizens, to remember the Great Riots of '80 . . . they seem to recall every particular of the tumult' (*Athenæum*, 22 Jan. 1842).
5. Reynolds lived till 1839 and Angelo till 1841.
6. See the Bibliography in J. P. de Castro, *The Gordon Riots* (1926), for this and other contemporary pamphlets. Dickens owned copies of Holcroft's *Narrative* and of Watson's *Life*; the latter was annotated by him (see F. G. Kitton, notes to Autograph edition, III 336).
7. Several are named in ch. xxxix: 'the *St. James's Chronicle*, the *Herald, Chronicle*, or *Public Advertiser*'. Dickens presumably had access to the files of the *Morning*

Dickens's use of his historical sources, which has never received the detailed consideration it deserves, can only be summarized here. What is most remarkable in his powerful narrative of the riots (chapters xxxvi–lxxiii) is the way he combines fidelity to fact with the doings of his fictitious characters. He adds, but never falsifies. The main events of eight days (2 June to 9 June) are all brought in, with accurate particulars of time and place; almost every action ascribed to the mob in London or to unnamed individuals is factual, down to such telling anecdotes as the burning of the canary-birds and the young man hanged in Bishopsgate. *The Thunderer* and *England in Blood* really existed, some released convicts did return voluntarily to the jail, and the attack on the Bank was led by a man on 'a brewer's horse . . . caparisoned with fetters'. The break into Newgate and the burning of Langdale's distillery are described often in the very words of contemporary accounts. No rioters are known to have gone as far as Chigwell, but several country mansions were threatened, and the mob's attempt 'to burn the Warren' (i.e. the Woolwich Arsenal) probably gave Mr Haredale's house its name. 'The Boot' was an actual inn, in Lamb's Conduit Fields. General Conway, Sir John Fielding, Lord Mansfield, Akerman the keeper of Newgate, and the Lord Mayor acted or suffered just as Dickens describes. The appearance, manner, and after-history of Gordon, and some of his words (as in the warrant of protection conveyed to Gabriel Varden) are faithfully given, and Dickens's interpretation of his character and actions, if coloured by Robert Watson's *Life*, represents at least a legitimate reading of the evidence.

For the actions and motives of other characters, fact and fiction are mingled in varying proportions. At one end of the scale is Mr Langdale, historic except for his dealings with the invented characters; at the other, Gabriel Varden, whose valiant refusal to break the lock of Newgate is based on a mere hint—the resistance

---

Chronicle; he also had a reader's ticket for the British Museum, and F. G. Kitton recorded in 1891 that 'Dr. Bullen, of the Museum, remembers having seen Dickens in the Reading-room, where he used to go for the purpose of consulting the newspapers about the London Riots in 1780, when he was writing "Barnaby Rudge"' (*Charles Dickens by Pen and Pencil: Supplement*, p. 15).

A good short account of the riots was published in 1837 by Charles Knight, as chs. ii–iii of *Sketches of Popular Tumults*, in the series 'Contributions to Political Knowledge'. It is interesting evidence of current interest in the events of 1780, but can hardly be regarded as a source, though it may possibly have led Dickens to such pamphlet-sources as Holcroft's *Narrative* and the anonymous *Fanaticism and Treason*, which it quotes freely.

of a Moravian blacksmith, urged under threats to strike off the prisoners' irons. Dickens may have noticed that idiots, gipsies, apprentices, and a 'one-armed man' were among the rioters; and he surely caught hints for Miggs and Sim from a description of 'debating societies' with 'female orators' and the 'apprentice' who spent the night 'in rehearsing harangues' and 'wasted the day (the property of his master)' in dreams of political power.[1] In two characters, Gashford and Dennis, the interweaving of fact and fiction is especially curious, and in the former case still a matter of conjecture. Something is borrowed from the career of the secretary Robert Watson[2] (whose suicide was fully reported in 1838) and the treachery of James Fisher; but Gashford exists mainly as an ingenious means of connecting Dickens's sympathetic interpretation of Gordon with his view of the riots. His plot and his picture alike require a cold-blooded villain manœuvring in the dark, and the presence of such an agent is a plausible reading of events. With Dennis he worked more imaginatively. The presence of 'Edward Dennis, the public hangman' among the rioters convicted of helping to burn a private house, was sufficient basis:[3] Dickens's sense of ironic fitness extended Dennis's activities to the burning of Newgate, had him hanged instead of respited, and elaborated his craftsman's pride in his calling in a way both diverting and horrible. In him Dickens continues the studies of evil begun in Sikes and Quilp. But Dennis, though a grotesque, is less of a bogey-man than Quilp, and more closely related to the themes of the novel. He embodies Dickens's open concern with the social horror of hanging and his less conscious obsession with the man about to be hanged; and he also derives something from literary tradition—from the first chapter of Charles Whitehead's *Autobiography of Jack Ketch*, and, more generally, from the irony of *Jonathan Wild*.

Dickens's complex intentions are fulfilled in the almost allegorical juxtaposition of Dennis, Hugh, and Barnaby, and their discriminated attitudes to violence and death. Through Hugh

1. *Fanaticism and Treason* (anon.; 1780), p. 22. This is also obviously topical. Sim may be compared with 'a journeyman carpenter' who took the chair at meetings of a Radical Association in Marylebone (James Grant, *The Great Metropolis*, second series, 1837, I 91ff).

2. Watson has been claimed as the original of Gashford (*The Dickensian*, June 1933, pp. 175ff).

3. Thomas Gaspey's novel, if he knew it, provided a precedent for fictional treatment.

and Barnaby the fictitious and historical parts of the novel are firmly related; and they, perhaps alone of the invented characters, gain in interest under the pressure of public events. Dickens's slow approach to his historical subject, though it has many advantages, brings certain difficulties. The first third of the novel is all fiction: the Haredale–Rudge murder-mystery and Mr Chester's intrigues, diversified with the domestic comedy of the Willet and the Varden households, are set out in a leisurely way without much 'period' colouring and with hardly a hint of history to come. Then, after a silent lapse of five years, the tide of history advances, slowly at first, then with increasing force, involving all the characters; as it recedes, the mystery is resolved, and the nemesis, tragic and comic, fulfilled. Although the mystery-plot could be detached (as was done in two dramatic versions, presented before publication was complete),[1] it loses thereby much of its interest, for Dickens's integration of the two main lines of narrative, which, as we realize later, he is quietly preparing throughout the early chapters, is excellently managed. By reserving the history till later he conveys the irony of the common assumption that private lives are immune from public events, an irony pointed by his presentation of the same scene under two different lights; the snugness of the Maypole makes us share John Willet's sense of its devastation as an almost personal insult, while we also enjoy the nicely contrived nemesis by which 'history' converts the innkeeper from invincible stupidity to imbecile stupor, and from petty tyranny to submissiveness. But the change in tempo in the middle chapters is exacting, and the rush of events in what Dickens called 'the thick of the story' made him chafe, as we have seen, at his 'want' of 'elbow-room'.[2]

IV

Dickens's experience in the writing of *Barnaby* fixed his preference for the 'monthly number' as a form of publication. The period of experiment was over. He had introduced the new plan

> hoping that to shorten the intervals of communication between

1. One, by Charles Selby and Charles Melville, was acted at the Lyceum on 28 June 1841, another at the New Strand in August. The former, which Dickens saw (*Letters*, I 339), was published in August. (A third version, including the riots, was put on at the Adelphi in December.)

2. *Letters*, I 353 (when writing chs. lxv–lxvi).

himself and his readers would be to bind more closely [their] pleasant relations.[1]

The disadvantages had proved too great. In October 1841 he published his manifesto, which because of its clear statement of the drawbacks of the weekly part (and its inaccessibility to modern readers)[2] deserves reproducing in full:

TO THE
READERS OF "MASTER HUMPHREY'S CLOCK".

DEAR FRIENDS,

NEXT November, we shall have finished the Tale, on which we are at present engaged; and shall have travelled together through Twenty Monthly Parts, and Eighty-seven Weekly Numbers. It is my design, when we have gone so far, to close this work. Let me tell you why.

I should not regard the anxiety, the close confinement, or the constant attention, inseparable from the weekly form of publication (for to commune with you, in any form, is to me a labour of love), if I had found it advantageous to the conduct of my stories, the elucidation of my meaning, or the gradual development of my characters. But I have not done so. I have often felt cramped and confined in a very irksome and harassing degree, by the space in which I have been constrained to move. I have wanted you to know more at once than I could tell you; and it has frequently been of the greatest importance to my cherished intention, that you should do so. I have been sometimes strongly tempted (and have been at some pains to resist the temptation) to hurry incidents on, lest they should appear to you who waited from week to week, and had not, like me, the result and purpose in your minds, too long delayed. In a word, I have found this form of publication most anxious, perplexing, and difficult. I cannot bear these jerking confidences which are no sooner begun than ended, and no sooner ended than begun again.

Many passages in a tale of any length, depend materially for their interest on the intimate relation they bear to what has gone before, or to what is to follow. I sometimes found it difficult when I issued thirty-two closely-printed pages once a month, to sustain in your mind this needful connexion; in the present form of publication it is often, especially in the first half of a story, quite impossible to preserve it sufficiently through the current numbers. And although in my progress I am gradually able to set you right, and to show you what my meaning has been, and to work it out, I see no reason why

1. Preface to *Master Humphrey's Clock*, vol. 1 (Sept. 1840).
2. It is reprinted only in the National edition (vol. XXXIII, pp. 342–4).

you should ever be wrong when I have it in my power, by resorting to a better means of communication between us, to prevent it.

Considerations of immediate profit and advantage, ought, in such a case, to be of secondary importance. *They* would lead me, at all hazards, to hold my present course. But, for the reasons I have just now mentioned, I have, after long consideration, and with especial reference to the next new Tale I bear in my mind, arrived at the conclusion that it will be better to abandon this scheme of publication, in favour of our old and well-tried plan, which has only twelve gaps in a year, instead of fifty-two.

Therefore, my intention is to close this story (with the limits of which I am, of course, by this time acquainted), and this work, within, or at about, the period I have mentioned. I should add, that for the general convenience of subscribers, another volume of collected numbers will not be published, until the whole is brought to a conclusion.

Taking advantage of the respite which the close of this work will afford me, I have decided, in January next, to pay a visit to America. The pleasure I anticipate from this realization of a wish I have long entertained, and long hoped to gratify, is subdued by the reflection that it must separate us for a longer time than other circumstances would have rendered necessary.

On the First of November, eighteen hundred and forty-two, I purpose, if it please God, to commence my new book in monthly parts, under the old green cover, in the old size and form, and at the old price.[1]

I look forward to addressing a few more words to you, in reference to this latter theme, before I close the task on which I am now engaged. If there be any among the numerous readers of Master Humphrey's Clock who are, at first, dissatisfied with the prospect of this change—and it is not unnatural almost to hope there may be some—I trust they will, at no very distant day, find reason to agree with

ITS AUTHOR.

SEPTEMBER 1841.

1. *Martin Chuzzlewit* in fact began publication in Jan. 1843.

CHAPTER V

Dombey and Son: Design and Execution

I

WHEN the first instalment of *Dombey and Son* appeared on 30 September 1846 in the familiar green covers, Dickens was embarking once more upon his favourite form of publication. Since the early numbers of *Pickwick* he had been paying increasing attention to problems of structure, as previous essays have shown. In the Preface to his latest novel, *Martin Chuzzlewit* (1844), he had claimed that he had from time to time 'put a strong constraint' upon himself and had kept 'a steadier eye upon the general purpose and design'. This and other statements indicate his belief that there was no insuperable obstacle to writing, barely ahead of its publication in monthly instalments complete in themselves, a novel with a well-defined purpose worked out by such an 'artfully interwoven or ingeniously complicated'[1] plot as he had once felt that he must eschew. In *Dombey and Son*, when for the first time he planned each instalment on paper before he began writing, he went a great way towards realizing the intention he had so clearly formulated. It may, in fact, be said that with *Dombey and Son* he began a new chapter in his work.

Apart from the text itself, the available sources of evidence for 'the strength of his mastery over his first design' and the degree of consistency with which he maintained his purpose, fall under five heads:[2] (1) the title, (2) the cover-design, (3) the letters (especially the letter to Forster on 25 July 1846,[3] accompanying

1. See above, p. 65.
2. No 'master plan' survives, and there is no reason to suppose that such a plan was set on paper.
3. Forster, VI ii.

the first four chapters), (4) the manuscript, including the number plans, (5) the proofsheets. An examination of (1) and (2) and the letters of the three months preceding publication will throw light on the nature of that 'first design' at a stage when the writing of the novel had barely begun.

It is impossible to say just when the design took shape, but it was evidently growing in the author's mind for six months before he put pen to paper. 'A new book in shilling numbers' was in his thoughts at the end of January 1846; between then and his departure for Switzerland at the end of May he was clearing the decks for action. In March the publishers were approached; in mid-April the first announcement appeared in the press—'A New English Story, By Mr. Dickens, to be published in Twenty Monthly Parts, price 1s. each, is now in preparation'; and on 18 May the author committed himself also to a date—'No. 1 will be published on the First of October'.[1] Such open self-commitment would nowadays imply some pre-existent writing of the novel; for Dickens it was enough that 'the characters . . . were growing in his mind'. Not until he was well settled at Lausanne, at the end of June, did he 'plunge straight over head and ears into the story . . . BEGAN DOMBEY'.[2]

Forster had been, as usual, his sole confidant over the unwritten book, though he has unfortunately not extended much of his confidence to us. To him the word 'Dombey' must have already carried a whole train of associations; the title had undoubtedly been decided on some time before. No hesitance over it, and no alternative forms (as for *Copperfield*, *Bleak House*, and *Little Dorrit*) are recorded; but Dickens showed what store he set by it in emphasizing the need for secrecy, 'the very name getting out would be ruinous' (18 July),[3] and to another correspondent 'the name shall not pass these lips, until the bills proclaim it' (9 July).[4] The bills proclaimed it at the end of August:

> Dealings with the Firm of Dombey and Son, Wholesale, Retail, and for Exportation.

Immediately after the announcement of the title, Dickens wrote to Mitton, 'I think it is an odd one, and therefore a good one'.[5] It was the most provocative he had yet devised. The need for

1. This information, not given by any of Dickens's editors or bibliographers, is all available in Forster's *Life*, the *Letters*, and the contemporary press.

2. Forster, v ii. 3. Forster, v iii. 4. *Letters*, I 766. 5. *Letters*, I 783.

secrecy is clear; in contrast to titles of Dickens's earlier novels, this is to some extent declarative of purpose and defines a new field of operations. (A 'business' novel, from Boz?) Titles were a special problem for the serial-writer, since no title could be modified to suit a subsequent change of intention: yet readers must be attracted. Hitherto Dickens had played for safety, usually with the 'life and adventures' type of title; but in this, the first of his novels to be thoroughly designed in advance, he could risk committing himself more deeply. The title promised the fortunes of a firm; while the author's name (although the famous words were as yet unwritten) guaranteed 'the firm of Human Interest Brothers, with a rather large connexion in the fancy goods line'. The title also indicated an increased concern with contemporary life. And possibly the particular collocation 'Dombey *and Son*' suggested the history of a relation between two characters as distinct from the 'life and adventures' of one, and that a relation in two fields, business and domestic. Deliberately, too, the title exploits the serial-writer's special privilege of misleading as well as capturing attention. The evidence of correspondence shows that the whole design of Mr Dombey's history as a parent had been worked out before the title was announced; and the first number was already written, emphatically concluding with Walter Gay's toast, 'So here's to Dombey—and Son—and Daughter!' The title kept a bigger secret than it disclosed.

Meanwhile, during August, Dickens must have been instructing his illustrator Hablôt K. Browne about the cover-design, which was to appear on the first number and be repeated for each monthly instalment; for early in September he approved it as 'very good; perhaps with a little too much in it'.[1] This also was a new departure in the extent to which it foreshadowed the story, though its general method bears an evident relation to the cover of *Chuzzlewit*. Dickens spoke of the *Dombey* cover later as 'shadowing out [the] drift and bearing' of the story,[2] and his choice of phrase is a useful pointer. Previous commentators[3] have interpreted the cover over-literally and have therefore found consistency or inconsistency according to what they thought they saw. The story in its development shows a *general* consistency with the

1. Forster, VI ii.

2. In a letter of 29 Oct. 1846 on *The Battle of Life*, his current Christmas book (Forster, V vi).

3. E.g., Kentley Bromhill, *The Dickensian*, Sept. 1942, pp. 219f; F. G. Kitton, *The Novels of Charles Dickens* (London, 1897), p. 103.

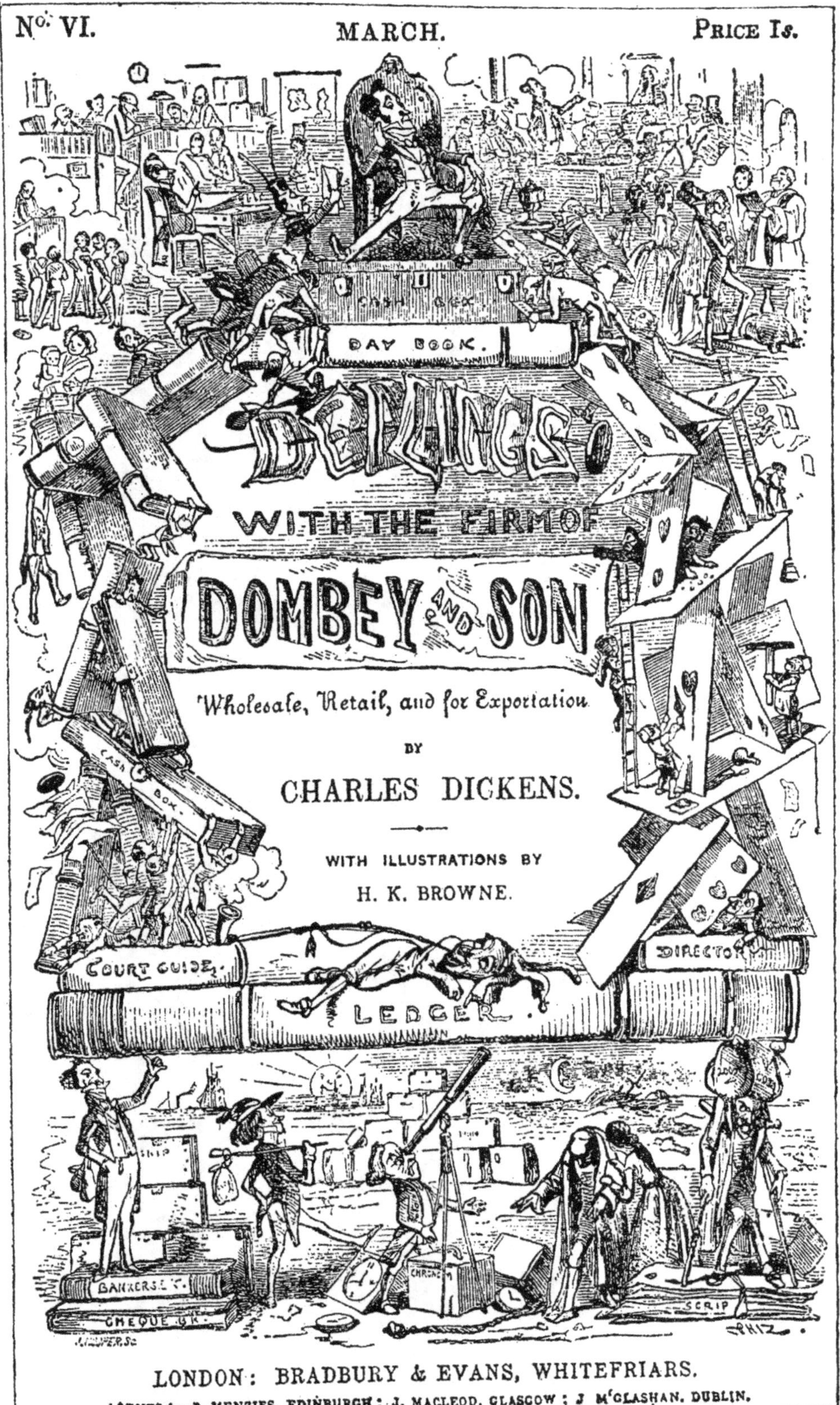

No. VI.
MARCH.
PRICE 1s.
CASH BOX
DAY BOOK.
WITH THE FIRM OF
DOMBEY AND SON
Wholesale, Retail, and for Exportation
BY
CHARLES DICKENS.
WITH ILLUSTRATIONS BY
H. K. BROWNE.
CASH BOX
COURT GUIDE
DIRECTOR
LEDGER
SCRIP
CHEQUE BK
PHIZ
LONDON: BRADBURY & EVANS, WHITEFRIARS.
AGENTS:—J. MENZIES, EDINBURGH; J. MACLEOD, GLASGOW; J. M'GLASHAN, DUBLIN.

cover, within the elastic limits of a semi-allegorical or 'shadowing' method. The cover-design of *Chuzzlewit* is built up on a system of simple contrasts; roses on the left balance thorns on the right, dream balances nightmare and riches poverty. But there is no narrative line running through these disconnected symbols. In the *Dombey* cover there is such a line, which also suggests part of the moral curve of the narrative. The line of prosperity and promise runs upwards from the left of the centre, through the precariously balanced ledgers, to where the hero sits enthroned in an office chair on the platform of a cash box, and down through the tumbling house of cards on the right. The allegorical scenes at the foot emphasize the turn of Fortune's wheel. Hopeful youth sets out to seek its fortune, with a background of rising sun, smooth-sailing ships, and calm sea; at the other side is the evening of life—a broken-down figure set against a night sky, shipwreck, and storm. At one side, 'rising' Mr Dombey lightly balances his wealth on brow and thumb; on the other, 'fallen' Mr Dombey, old and crippled, is nearly crushed by the descending money bags. At the top are more realistic scenes, in general illustration of his seemingly secure prosperity: his hopeful heir (baby with nurse, and boys' classroom); his power in the office; his distinction in public life (a House of Commons scene);[1] and the new turn in his social and domestic fortunes (bridegroom at a society wedding, with a military witness). The figure of Mr Dombey dominates the whole. Other characters are there only to substantiate his background, and the little goblin-like creatures among the ledgers and cards are as impersonal as the decorations on Doyle's *Punch* cover. The figure at the bottom centre certainly bears some relation to the Wooden Midshipman (not, as has been thought, to Sol Gills),[2] but its significance in the 'drift and bearing' surely rests rather on the surrounding symbols of Time, and the blind confidence in the future implied by the closed eye at the telescope. The whole method is allegorical; if readers of the first number tried to 'look at the end' by scanning the cover they would find little to help them.[3] It would need

1. See below, p. 103, n. 1.

2. There is no likeness to Sol as he is shown in the plate to ch. ix. But it is conceivable that Browne, when doing the cover, had confused the descriptions of shop-emblem and shop-owner in ch. iv.

3. The *Athenæum* reviewer of Nos. I–II (31 Oct. 1846) disclaimed prediction, but commented with some acuteness:

The title-page reveals something of the prominent idea, in whatever forms em-

exceptional discernment even to detect the despised little daughter of chapter i in the young female figure who gently attends the fallen hero. This may have been where Dickens found 'a little too much in' the cover, if by this remark he meant that it was too revealing and not merely too crowded. Secrets are kept—notably the death of Paul. The only specific event predicted is the second marriage; and this is hardly a close secret, since it is already prepared for (though with a false lead as to candidate) in Mrs Dombey's death and its aftermath. The cover does what Dickens wanted; it 'shadows out the drift and bearing' of the whole, not disclosing secrets, not committing the author, but still picturesquely confirming and enlarging the promise of the title, and clearly showing the existence of a ruling general design for the unwritten story. The novel's centre is the head of a great firm, its main concern is the intertwining of his domestic and his business life (the falling cards are hearts and diamonds), and to this is added the overshadowing, menacing moral—that Pride of Wealth must have a Fall.

Dickens's early letters to Forster confirm this intention, but, since they are private, add more detail of its projected execution. Before the letters begin, conversation with Forster had established one part of the intention; the novel 'was to do with Pride what its predecessor [*Martin Chuzzlewit*] had done with Selfishness',[1] and this presumably is the 'leading idea' of the letter of 12 July.[2] The letters themselves survive only in the extracts Forster selected. But the main document in the case, the letter of 25 July, is probably given with little omission, for Forster printed it in 1873 partly to rehabilitate Dickens as a serious designer, to counter criticisms (such as Taine's) that Paul's death and Mr Dombey's final relenting were improvised as adventitious aids to interest. This important letter, somewhat similar to the letter of 18 October 1844 sent with the first part of *The Chimes*, is our substitute for a 'master plan'. In it the design is seen from another angle; the emphasis is almost wholly on the family situation, the dynamic relation between Dombey and Son and Daughter.

---

bodied, which is intended to be wrought out by the plastic hand of Mr. Dickens in this new work;—and the first chapter confirms the revelation. His hero . . . is to personate one of those representatives of a long commercial line in whose contracted and exclusive minds selfishness takes the quality of reflecting the single figure of its own commercial importance on all the objects which surround it.

1. Forster, VI ii. 2. Forster, V iii.

Florence here takes the prominent place deliberately and ironically withheld from her in title and picture.[1]

> I will now go on to give you an outline of my immediate intentions in reference to *Dombey*. I design to show Mr. D. with that one idea of the Son taking firmer and firmer possession of him, and swelling and bloating his pride to a prodigious extent. As the boy begins to grow up, I shall show him quite impatient for his getting on, and urging his masters to set him great tasks, and the like. But the natural affection of the boy will turn towards the despised sister; and I purpose showing her learning all sorts of things, of her own application and determination, to assist him in his lessons: and helping him always. When the boy is about ten years old (in the fourth number), he will be taken ill, and will die; and when he is ill, and when he is dying, I mean to make him turn always for refuge to the sister still, and keep the stern affection of the father at a distance. So Mr. Dombey—for all his greatness, and for all his devotion to the child—will find himself at arms' length from him even then; and will see that his love and confidence are all bestowed upon his sister, whom Mr. Dombey has used—and so has the boy himself too, for that matter—as a mere convenience and handle to him. The death of the boy is a death-blow, of course, to all the father's schemes and cherished hopes; and 'Dombey and Son,' as Miss Tox will say at the end of the number, 'is a Daughter after all.' . . . From that time, I purpose changing his feeling of indifference and uneasiness towards his daughter into a positive hatred. For he will always remember how the boy had his arm round her neck when he was dying, and whispered to her, and would take things only from her hand, and never thought of him. . . At the same time I shall change *her* feeling towards *him* for one of a greater desire to love him, and to be loved by him; engendered in her compassion for his loss, and her love for the dead boy whom, in his way, he loved so well too. So I mean to carry the story on, through all the branches and off-shoots and meanderings that come up; and through the decay and downfall of the house, and the bankruptcy of Dombey, and all the rest of it; when his only staff and treasure, and his unknown Good Genius always, will be this rejected daughter, who will come out better

1. It is accorded to her in the frontispiece to the first edition, which first appeared as one of the plates in the concluding double number. This is another semi-allegorical composition, summarizing the novel in retrospect, when the need for keeping secrets is past. Florence occupies the centre, seated on a sea-beach beside Paul's wheel-chair. Above, an angel points upwards to a heavenly choir; and below, a rough sea beats against the shore. Besides taking precedence over Paul in the central scene, Florence also appears in most of the surrounding scenes—at the two deathbeds, with Polly, with Edith, struck down by Mr Dombey, welcoming the literally shipwrecked Walter, and rescuing her symbolically shipwrecked father.

> than any son at last, and whose love for him, when discovered and understood, will be his bitterest reproach. For the struggle with himself, which goes on in all such obstinate natures, will have ended then; and the sense of his injustice, which you may be sure has never quitted him, will have at last a gentler office than that of only making him more harshly unjust.

This forecasts the main development up to about the seventh number ('positive hatred' is clearest in chapter xx), and the references to the downfall of the firm and the redemptive power of Florence's persistent love reach forward to the close. (The prediction is fulfilled, save for the hinted active rôle for Florence.) The heart of the design is now exposed: the theme is the opposition of pride and love, with Mr Dombey as the meeting-point. The novel is thus to be a new departure for Dickens—a novel founded upon a relation, and upon a character's inner conflict.

The letter goes on to mention only two minor characters, Susan Nipper and Polly Toodle (who are to 'go over' to Florence, 'like everybody else'). Dickens sums up his outline as 'the stock of the soup', to which 'all kinds of things will be added'. It was 'stock' in the sense that it would not change;[1] doubts and deliberations affected other persons—notably Walter Gay—but not Mr Dombey, Paul, and Florence.

The 'stock', the main design, already posed a problem to which Dickens perhaps did not yet penetrate: the interweaving of Dombey's domestic and business fortunes. This interweaving is achieved, partly by chapter headings, in the first few numbers, but it wears thin after Paul's death, and Carker, who had probably been designed as the canker of both office and family, becomes much more prominent in the latter capacity.

II

So far as Paul's death the way lay clear ahead and the number plans record little that can be interpreted as hesitation. Proofs and letters to Forster show that the chief difficulty was to find space for all that needed saying. Paul, the 'Boy born, to die' (in the words of the first number plan) was originally to die at the

1. This is interestingly confirmed by an entry in the diary of the Hon. Mrs Watson, who records on 12 Sept. 'a Soiree at Mr. Dickens to hear him read the first number. . . The career of Dombey, Son, and Daughter are settled, but I think none of the others'. (*The Dickensian*, Dec. 1950, p. 18.)

end of Number IV, but the pace in the first two numbers was so leisurely that Forster was asked,[1] while III was being planned, whether Paul should not be killed in V. Even this respite was not sufficient, for each of the first four numbers proved to be overwritten by amounts varying from one page to six. When faced with the need of extensive cuts at proof stage, Dickens was accustomed to economize at the expense of the comedy. The luxuriant growth of fancy displayed in Mrs Chick and Major Bagstock was accordingly pruned;[2] but passages of greater significance were removed as well. One of them, describing Mr Dombey's destruction of a letter written by his dead wife, was retrieved by Forster[3] who regarded it as evidence 'thus early . . . of the struggle with itself that such pride must always go through'. Less ambiguous are Mr Dombey's comments (chapter i) when Florence disregards his invitation to 'go and look at [her] pretty brother':

> 'Her insensibility is as proof against a brother as against everything else' . . . and he seemed so confirmed in a previous opinion by the discovery, as to be quite glad of it,

and the 'expression of positive pain—pain that was suffering to him; that he could not conceal, and was ashamed to show' which appeared in Mr Dombey's face (chapter xi) as he confided to Mrs Pipchin that Paul had concentrated too much of his childish affection on his sister. Perhaps nothing essential to our understanding of the novel's purpose was lost by cuts such as these, but the book as we now have it is weaker by some distinct loss of emphasis.

Restrictions of space were also felt in other ways. The third number plan (chapters viii–x) shows that Miss Tox was to have

1. Forster, VI ii.

2. Readers who enjoy the partnership of Mrs Chick and Miss Tox will regret that Dickens could find no room for the following passage (deleted in proof from ch. viii), in which Mrs Chick once more insinuates Miss Tox's claims on Mr Dombey's serious consideration:

'My dear Paul,' returned Mrs. Chick, 'with your usual discrimination, which I am weak enough to envy you, every time I am in your company; and so I think is Miss Tox—'

'Oh my dear!' said Miss Tox, softly, 'how could it be otherwise. Presumptuous as it is to aspire to such a level; still, if the bird of night may—but I'll not trouble Mr. Dombey with the sentiment. It merely relates to the Bulbul.'

Mr. Dombey bent his head in stately recognition of the Bulbul as an old-established body.

3. Forster, VI ii.

given a party at which 'Her uncle the Magistrate' (a character who never appeared, though already named in chapter v to impress Towlinson and the cabman) and 'The Major' were to have been present and would have been introduced, we may safely assume, to Mr Dombey. Carker was also to appear in this number, and the 'Offices in the City' were to have been described, for it was time for the firm to take a larger share of the reader's attention. But there was no room in Number III and the two scenes were marked in the plan 'To stand over'. The party was never to take place; Major Bagstock, however, characteristically introduced himself to Mr Dombey at Brighton later in this number (chapter x). Thus the irony of Miss Tox presenting the man who was to undermine her position in the Dombey household was necessarily dropped; but the change seems to square with the general intention of reducing Miss Tox from her prominence in the opening numbers. A description of the counting-house was deferred till the next number, and meanwhile the glimpse of Dombey and Son in a business transaction is supplied by the loan of money to 'pay out' the broker at the Little Midshipman's. 'You will consider that it is done by Master Paul', says Mr Dombey, as he hands the note to Walter. This is his effective answer at the end of the number to the question, so simple yet so powerful in irony, which Paul had asked at the beginning, 'Papa! What's money ... what can it do?'

Restricted though he was for space, Dickens might have had room for the scenes marked 'to stand over' if he had fully determined what to do with Walter Gay. The notion of showing Walter 'gradually and naturally trailing away . . . into negligence, idleness, dissipation, dishonesty, and ruin'[1] required an appropriate setting of characters. We know that Florence was to have been 'always at the bottom of it', and we may suspect that Carker the Junior would also have played an important part. 'The strangest man, Mr. Carker the junior is', Walter is made to remark to Florence, as he conducts her (chapter vi) to his uncle's shop;

> 'If you could understand what an extraordinary interest he takes in me, and yet how he shuns and avoids me; and what a low place he

1. From the close of the letter of 25 July. Forster, so often a check to Dickens's gloomier notions, represents himself as responsible for discouraging Dickens from this plan, 'for reasons that need not be dwelt on here' (VI ii); one may guess that they were connected with sales, perhaps also with the danger of too close portrayal of some actual person.

holds in our office, and how he is never advanced, and never complains, though year after year he sees young men passed over his head . . . you would be as much puzzled about him as I am.'

The passage was removed in proof after Dickens had decided to reserve Walter for a happier future, but it remains to motivate a character who is unnecessary to the story as it developed. We may be sure that Carker the Junior's 'extraordinary interest' in Walter Gay was an interest in a young man who was to fall as he had fallen.

Dickens told Forster that he could also 'bring out Solomon Gills and Captain Cuttle well, through such a history' of deterioration as Walter's might have been. Cuttle remains an important figure in Walter's happier fate. But Gills, whose heart seems made to be broken, had no place in Dickens's revised intentions. He could only duplicate Cuttle's rôle, so he is cleared off at an early opportunity. 'Uncle Sol to die?' Dickens inquires in the eighth number plan (chapters xxiii–xxv); but though he immediately relents ('No, run away, to look after Walter'), he can find no use for him until the eighteenth number (chapter lvi) when he returns to crown the happiness of Walter and Florence.

But these are blemishes in an otherwise faultless exposition. Our attention is mainly directed to 'that one idea of the Son taking firmer and firmer possession of [Mr Dombey], and swelling and bloating his pride to a prodigious extent'. The theme of Pride is not merely developed in the father's regard for his son, in the 'family humbug' of Mrs Chick, and in the use of honest and dishonest toadies, Tox and Bagstock, but is expounded with remarkable thoroughness in Mr Dombey's treatment of his social inferiors, Polly Toodle and her son. He would make the relations between Paul and his wet nurse 'a mere matter of bargain and sale. . . It is not at all in this bargain that you need become attached to my child, or that my child need become attached to you. I don't expect or desire anything of the kind. Quite the reverse'. Dickens, we may be sure, has already determined upon an affectionate relationship between Paul and Polly even though he may not have foreseen the incident where Paul summons his old nurse to comfort him on his death bed, or the still later scene when all Mr Dombey's dependants have left his house and Polly returns to look after him. So closely are we bound together, Dickens implies, despite what a sense of class can do to separate us. Polly's immediate recompense for her services was to have her eldest son nominated to a vacancy in the Charitable Grinders' School, where Mr Dombey was assured that he would be taught to know his position and conduct himself properly. Again we may safely infer that Dickens relished the retribution in store for Mr Dombey, though he might not then have decided precisely how Rob the Grinder would assist Mr Dombey's enemy. But he shows that he was keeping Rob's development in sight by placing in Mrs Chick's mouth the solemn and ironic rebuke:

> 'If it was *my* ungrateful case . . . and I had *your* reflections, Richards, I should feel as if the Charitable Grinders' dress would blight my child, and the education choke him.'

A reader need not be particularly shrewd to suspect that Pride of such a kind will have a fall. He might forecast Mr Dombey's bankruptcy and expect that in some way Paul would disappoint his father. But Paul's death was intended as 'a great surprise', and Dickens thought his friend Mrs Marcet was clever to have guessed it when he read the first number to her.[1] In Number II it is clearly enough forecast in the chill of the christening and the ominous conclusion of chapter v: but already in Number I, the distinction drawn by Susan Nipper—'Miss Floy being a permanency, Master Paul a temporary'—carries ironic overtones.[2]

In the same sentence in which Dickens told Forster of the 'great surprise', he spoke of 'a new and peculiar sort of interest, involving the necessity of a little bit of delicate treatment'.[3] It is possible that he was looking ahead to Paul's final illness in Number V (chapter xiv) and the decision recorded in the number plan that 'His illness [should be] only expressed in the child's own feelings—Not otherwise described'. It is reasonable to suppose that it was the novelty of this treatment that brought tears to the eyes of so many readers.[4]

Meanwhile the 'neglected daughter' motif of the plan has been steadily developed throughout the first number, though its im-

1. Forster, v v.

2. But the secret is not betrayed, since the words could be read with Susan's own meaning—the necessary impermanence of the suckling period and so of the wet-nurse.

3. Forster, v iii.

4. It was also in keeping with Dickens's decision to take the child's point of view so far as possible, notably in the Brighton scenes both at Mrs Pipchin's boarding-house and at Dr Blimber's academy. This also was 'a new and peculiar sort of interest', and its success no doubt prompted the extension of this treatment in his next novel, *David Copperfield*.

portance is not realized until we reach the last chapter (chapter iv). That was the chapter which Dickens at one point thought of removing when he discovered that the number was too long. The alternative was to substitute a shorter version of what later became chapter vii (where Major Bagstock is introduced as Miss Tox's neighbour in Princess's Place). It is altogether fortunate that this was not done, for pleasing as chapter vii is it does not open up such possibilities in the development of character and theme as chapter iv. Here is our first glimpse of the firm of Dombey and Son, seen from the point of view of a promising young recruit; and (though Dickens was still undecided whether to disappoint Walter's prospects) here is the young 'Sir Richard Whittington [who] married his master's daughter'. Sol Gills and Captain Cuttle admit that 'the Son's a little in our way, at present', but the chapter and the number end with the toast 'So here's to Dombey—and Son—and Daughter!' Thus the importance of 'Dombey and Daughter' is emphasized from the very beginning; and lest we should overlook it, that toast is echoed at the end of Number V (chapter xvi), which concludes the first movement of the novel:

> 'Dear me, dear me! To think,' said Miss Tox, bursting out afresh that night, as if her heart were broken, 'that Dombey and Son should be a Daughter after all!'[1]

III

The plan of Number VI begins with an important memorandum for the second movement of the novel, 'Great point of the No. to throw the interest of Paul, at once on Florence'[2] and accordingly the whole of Number VI (chapters xvii–xix) is devoted to this. Chapter xviii, originally intended to open the number (but moved, presumably to avoid two successive Cuttle chapters), is given the half-misleading title 'Father and Daugh-

1. The sentence is dropped from all editions after 1858, except the two reprints of the first edition (Macmillan, 1892–5, and Glasgow, n.d.). See K. Tillotson, 'A Lost Sentence in *Dombey and Son*', *The Dickensian*, Mar. 1951, pp. 81f.

2. Jeffrey's complimentary letter of 31 Jan. 1847 must have been in one respect disquieting: 'After reaching this climax in the fifth number, what are you to do with the fifteen that are to follow?' (Lord Cockburn, *Life of Lord Jeffrey*, 1852, II 407). After receiving it, Dickens wrote to Forster: 'To transfer to Florence, instantly, all the previous interest, is what I am aiming at. For that, all sorts of other points must be thrown aside in this number.' (VI ii.)

ter'. The two should be drawn together by Paul's death; instead there is first cold neglect, then open repudiation of the child's timid advance. The latter is kept subdued, by a cautious memorandum

> not to make too much of the scene with the father, or it may be too painful.

Accordingly, some suspense remains; there is no open break. This is important to the other aspect of Florence's status—she is now the possible 'heir' to the firm, and the interest is also 'thrown' on her by hints of the webs being spun round her. Though this is not shown as part of Mr Dombey's consciousness, and indeed is never really explicit, it is henceforth a vital contribution to the course of the narrative, and a means of foreshadowing its close. Number VI, in which to all appearances Florence's fortunes are steeply declining (Paul dead, Walter going abroad, her father slighting her), contains also a clear hint of how the firm is to be perpetuated—she asks Walter to be a brother to her, and he sails in the *Son and Heir*. And—a brilliant stroke of economy—Captain Cuttle artlessly reveals his fairy-tale hopes to Carker, who now dawns on the reader as Walter's rival:

> 'There's a son gone; pretty little creatur. Ain't there?'
> 'Yes, there's a son gone,' said the acquiescent Carker.
> 'Pass the word, and there's another ready for you.'
> (chapter xvii)

When Carker thinks (in the next chapter) of 'some obstacle removed' he has Walter as well as Paul in mind. All this is unemphasized, but carefully planted; it is followed up in the next two numbers by Carker's setting his spy on Florence's visits to Sol Gills (chapter xxii) and his seeking her out at the Skettleses (chapter xxiv).

But the situation has the triplicity of fairy-tale; the 'king's fair daughter under a spell' has three suitors—Fairy Prince, Demon King, and Fool. Number VI also re-introduces Mr Toots, whose visit with the gift of Diogenes does most to 'throw the interest on Florence', while also maintaining the link with Paul and Blimber's Academy. And by closing the number with the symbolic incident of Toots's meeting with Carker on Mr Dombey's doorstep, and Diogenes' instinctive bite, Dickens emphasizes the reassuring effect of the protective squire. Mr Toots makes no appearance in the original plan, and never figures prominently in the number plans; but he is perhaps the most tasty of the 'all kinds of things' that were 'added to' the stock of the soup.

Florence is again the centre of Number VIII (chapters xxiii–xxv). On one of her few excursions into the world, her visit to the Skettleses (of whom surely more was meant to be made),[1] she observes and overhears things that sharpen her sense of deprivation; and her desirability as a match is reiterated. The three suitors are not forgotten; Toots rows past Fulham, Carker pays his sinister call, and brings bad news of the *Son and Heir*. With her prominence fairly established, Dickens can devote himself to the more dynamic relationship of Mr Dombey, Edith Granger, and Carker (Numbers VII and IX). Since the early stages of the plan say nothing of the second marriage, we may guess that it grew under Dickens's hand, partly from its intrinsic interest (and especially the possibilities he finds in Edith), partly from the unforeseen limitations of Florence as a plot-producing character. Her silent presence modifies all events, and much revolves round her; but her rôle is to feel and inspire (in all save her father) admiration and affection and to suffer from his neglect. Her very virtues, as well as her age and social status, preclude her from taking any initiative.

The second marriage is the real storm-centre of the novel. Mr Dombey's courtship is presented as we should expect—in the shape of a business deal. He is ready to buy a wife with 'blood' and accomplishments, to grace his house and provide him with another son (and, as one symbolic piece of description suggests, to stand between him and his daughter).[2] He meets a woman who is prepared to be bought: this is how the notes for Number VII prepare for Mrs Skewton and Edith Granger:

> The mother and daughter. The mother, and her cant about 'heart', and nature— Daughter who has been put through her paces, before countless marrying men, like a horse for sale— Proud and weary of her degradation, but going on, for it's too late now, to try to turn back.

The social implications do not escape Dickens;[3] and he develops

1. The snobbish and ambitious Sir Barnet was an M.P., and the cover shows Mr Dombey speaking in the House. Parliament does have its share in the novel, but only through the faded reminiscences of Cousin Feenix.

2. Near the end of ch. xx ('He saw her image . . . what was there he could interpose between himself and it?').

3. It was at just this time (1846–7) that he was corresponding with Miss Burdett-Coutts about her scheme for establishing a home for fallen women.

them ironically by providing a counterpart to Edith in Alice Marwood, introduced in Number XI (chapter xxxiii) but prepared for as early as Number II, when Good Mrs Brown, the kidnapper of Florence, speaks of 'a gal of my own—beyond seas now—that was proud of her hair'. The difference in social status is as nothing to the identity of the situation; Dickens evidently asked, like his contemporary Florence Nightingale,

> The woman who has sold herself for an establishment, in what is she superior to those one may not name?[1]

Carker is connected with both; he has been the agent of Alice's degradation (another social point is made when she nevertheless refuses to take his money) and schemes to be that of Edith's; her recognition that he can read her thoroughly is the climax of Number IX[2] (chapters xxvi–xxviii), whose business was, in the words of the plan:

> To bring on the marriage gradually—connect Carker with Edith, before the wedding, and get in Florence.

Florence is 'got in' (chapter xxviii) by the scene in which Edith treats her with affection, and the complex of relationships is thus completed. We shall see how Edith's sole escape from 'degradation' is through her affection for Florence, which proves no escape since it turns Mr Dombey more against them both; how it leads him in his sultan-like pride to use Carker as his emissary, thus allowing Carker to strengthen his hold upon Edith. The situation is wonderfully planned for its ultimate purpose—the 'fall' and late enlightenment of Mr Dombey. But though the main design is still kept in view, the 'thickening' of the situation here raised some problems for Dickens, and he was driven to unforeseen economies among characters who could not directly contribute to it. Florence's protectors and 'reflectors' (Nipper, Toots, Cuttle) must of course remain; but Mrs Chick will have to give way, though in a superbly comic scene (chapter xxix). Major Bagstock and Mrs Skewton, having served their purpose by contriving the marriage, will not reap their expected reward,[3]

1. In 'Cassandra', written about 1852, and first published as Appendix to Ray Strachey's *The Cause* (1928), p. 412.

2. Singled out for emphasis in the plan, 'First interview between Carker and Edith. Very important'.

3. The shift in emphasis comes in the plan for ch. xxxi, where the Major is deleted as proposed speechmaker at the wedding in favour of Cousin Feenix. This is

which the Major's words promise in chapter xxvi: 'Cleopatra the peerless, and her Antony Bagstock . . . sharing the elegance and wealth of Edith Dombey's establishment'.

More important still, there will be no room for the firm, until Mr Morfin appears in Number XVII (chapter liii; after waiting in the wings since Number XIII, when he first appears in the number plans, 'to stand over') and 'shadows forth Mr Dombey's ruin'. This shrinking of the firm is perhaps the one considerable modification of the main design; the letter to Forster had hinted at an almost symmetrical rise-and-fall line for the firm's fortunes; in the event, the 'decay and downfall of the house', and the 'bankruptcy of Dombey' are not only deferred until very late (to the closing double number) but occur in an unchronicled year, just before chapter lviii ('After a Lapse'). The moral shape of the novel, however, is not really affected; the pervasive suggestion remains that a family cannot be run on business lines; Mr Dombey's fall still begins from the story's mid-point, his second marriage; the hastener of the catastrophe is still the 'trusty agent', 'Mr. Carker the Manager'.

IV

The converging lines that lead towards both catastrophe and resolution first stand out clearly in Number XIII (chapters xxxix–xli). The number caused trouble in the writing—it 'requires to be so carefully done';[1] for it must mark clearly (though not coarsely) the breakdown of the marriage. The climax of the big central chapter, 'Domestic Relations', is a show-down between the two whom we now see as 'mighty opposites' in pride, Mr Dombey and Edith; its setting is 'her own apartment', which he will not see again until 'a very different occasion'—one of many indications that her flight with Carker was already designed. The catastrophe is also prepared for by further isolation of the four main characters; Mrs Skewton is to die, Mrs Pipchin to be installed as housekeeper (which will mean the routing of her old enemy Nipper, and thus leave Florence unprotected). All this is calculated in the notes: as is also the confronting of the two base mothers and their proud degraded daughters, which, contrived

more plausible, and also prepares for Cousin Feenix's final vindication of the family honour.

1. Forster, VI i (19 Sept. 1847).

and theatrical though it is, again foreshadows Edith's fate.

This is the half-way point; it is time not only to provide for the future, but to round back upon the past. Themes of the first movement reappear: Mrs Skewton is taken in her fatal illness to Brighton, Blimber's Academy is revisited, and voices in the waves are heard once more.

Chapter xli was a calm before storm; events now hurry to the catastrophe, the flight of Edith and Carker, which first appears in the plans in the note on chapter xlv (Number XIV). The rôle devised for Edith is that of an unwilling adulteress, still claiming the reader's sympathy in her resistance to a doubly intolerable situation, and meeting her final defeat only when her one refuge —her love for Florence—is turned into a weapon against them both. 'She . . . relenting by force' is the note for chapter xlv;[1] a little later he wrote to Forster, 'Of course she hates Carker . . . I have relied on it very much for the effect of her death'.[2] He was then writing the chapters just before the elopement; his change of plan for Edith was late, but he was unconsciously prepared for it. For in engaging the reader's sympathies he had entrapped his own, and so was ready to welcome one influential reader's incredulity at Edith's guilt, as an excuse to swerve from his course. But this was later; when he was leading up to and describing the elopement he still designed Edith for guilt, and consequently a repentant deathbed—we may guess, with Florence at her bedside, matching Harriet, whose main function is to attend at Alice's and to forgive.[3] The reader would not suspect the change of plan; Dickens's hold on his main design conceals the swerve of his intention. This is an 'offshoot', if not a 'meandering'; the fall of pride and its redemption are unaffected by it.

From the opening of Number XIV the pace quickens in both plot and counterplot. The 'headline' note in the plan is 'Carker employed as go-between to reduce proud Edith'; and this manœuvre is accelerated by the riding accident, which immobilizes Mr Dombey in the downstairs apartments and gains Carker unhampered admission to Edith. It also gives an opportunity for Nipper to speak her mind, Paulina-like, so that a good reason is

1. Before proofs showed that a cut was necessary, the chapter ended by emphasizing her despair: 'If he has spoken truth, she is lost to me, and I have no hope left'.

2. Forster, vi ii.

3. Foreshadowed in Alice's 'I'll thank you when I die' at the end of ch. xxxiv.

supplied for her banishment; and with Mr Toots as appointed escort, a consolation prize is prepared for the faithful squire; not the rose, but something that grows near it. The finer threads in the pattern are never forgotten. Susan Nipper's explosion is a double preparation for Florence's flight; it isolates her, and also, through its substance, seems a casting-up of accounts, preparing for the final reckoning. And it follows Florence's first doubts of her father (chapter xliii).

All was ready for Number XV (chapters xlvi–xlviii). But in the original plan 'The Thunderbolt' would have fallen last, making the number conclude with Florence's stricken flight, but not its destination and consolation. The serial reader would then have remained in horrified suspense through December 1847. But as the chapter was written first, Dickens had time to change his mind; 'to leave a pleasanter impression on the reader' (had he perhaps the Christmas season in mind?) he pushed this chapter back into the middle place, and added the chapter (xlviii) which shows Florence safely under Captain Cuttle's protection, with mystified but not mystifying hints from Toots of 'a person' awaiting him round the corner. (The note is 'Preparation for Walter'.) The first chapter (xlvi)[1] was ostensibly a 'counterplot' chapter, opening with Carker's diligence at business and closing with his vengeful vision of Edith; it nevertheless prepares ingeniously for his defeat, for he is recognized by Good Mrs Brown, and is warned that his brother is watching Mr Dombey's interests. We may observe that Dickens had not yet decided to use Edith herself as a means of Carker's defeat, for diligence at business suggested to the Stock Exchange 'that Jem was going to marry a rich widow'; and, for contrast with Edith in her degradation, Alice once more appears refusing to touch any money which Carker has to bestow. The views of the Stock Exchange can be interpreted ironically in the light of what is to come; but there are no ironic overtones in the last long paragraph of this chapter, which summarizes the 'slow and sure degrees' by which Edith was to become Carker's mistress and was thus to obtain

> the dark retaliation [i.e., upon Mr. Dombey], whose faintest

1. The letter of 19 Nov. 1847 seems to suggest that as originally planned the first chapters (when 'The Thunderbolt' came last) were to be 'light'. But Forster is here perplexing, for he refers to the writing of the 'fourteenth' number, which was already published. It is late even for the writing of No. XV; perhaps date and not reference is mistaken.

> shadow seen once and shuddered at, and never seen again, would have been sufficient stain upon her soul.

Number XVII is now prepared for, and the intervening Number XVI (chapters xlix–li) can be mainly devoted to the idyll of Florence and Walter; the solitary general note is 'Return of Walter', and this dominates the number. Dickens had privately prepared for the betrothal in a way which reveals his care over detail, and the peculiar problems of the serial-writer. Before writing chapter xlvii, he went over earlier numbers from VI onwards working out Florence's age, and satisfied himself that she could be 'almost seventeen'. Her age is then specified in that chapter, with a reference to her diminished hopes of her father's love and to 'the change from childhood to womanhood'.[1] It was necessary to 'bring on' Florence's marriage, partly to remove her from the scene of action and partly so that the third generation might arrive in time for the reconciliation. But while it is suitable for the balance of interest[2] that the actual wedding should be deferred till Number XVIII (chapter lvii) this involves Dickens in another time-problem: what to do with the year which nature dictates, when he has only five chapters left. The closing chapter of Number XVI is another 'pause', a quiet preparation for the final rush of events around Mr Dombey, Carker, and Edith. In 'Mr. Dombey and the World' the full irony of the proud man's exposure is brought out, by presenting him in his humiliation through a series of choruses; as the memoranda summarize it:

> The Major & Cousin Feenix / The clerks—the city—Perch / Miss Tox / The servants.

The dominant theme of Number XVII (chapters lii–liv) is pursuit; the notes reiterate it—'pervading the number'—and each of the three chapters is built up to a 'pursuit-ending, quick and fierce'. Mr Morfin, at last justifying his dim existence, tells the good Carkers about their brother, 'shadowing forth Mr. Dombey's ruin', and incidentally revealing Dickens's modification of his first design:

1. Dickens also in these notes works out the duration of the second marriage, which he puts at exactly two years; which is longer, perhaps, than accords with the reader's impression (for by this calendar eighteen months must elapse from ch. xl to ch. xlvii) but is not contradicted by any of the time-indications.

2. No. XVII is the only number in the whole novel in which Florence neither appears nor is mentioned.

> The distractions of death, courtship, marriage, and domestic unhappiness, have left us no head but your brother for this long, long time.

That is, for nearly three years, and three-quarters of the novel, Mr Dombey has neglected Dombey and Son, and Dickens has let private life overrun his 'business' novel. The situation has its own irony, but the cover and the letter to Forster are evidence that it was not what was originally intended.

Number XVII concludes with the great chapter of Edith's repudiation of Carker at Dijon; here the change of plan already noted[1] was devised only three weeks before the number went to press. On 21 December 1847 Dickens wrote to Forster:

> Note from Jeffrey this morning who won't believe (positively refuses) that Edith is Carker's mistress. [Jeffrey had read chapter xlvii, published at the beginning of the month.] What do you think of a kind of inverted Maid's Tragedy, and a tremendous scene of her undeceiving Carker, and giving him to know that she never meant that?[2]

Forster agreed, and it went down in the notes—'Edith <u>not</u> his mistress'. Jeffrey's protest provided occasion rather than cause; the change chimed with Dickens's own view of Edith, who 'hates Carker in the most deadly degree', and whose revenge is only thus completed. The change also lightened his task in the closing numbers; the business of the self-explanation, repentance, and death of an Edith guilty in fact as well as appearance could hardly have been enclosed in the shambling amiabilities of Cousin Feenix, and must have left a lingering shadow on Florence's happiness. The diagrammatic equivalence between Alice and Edith, already overemphasized by the revelation of their cousinship in chapter lviii, would have been too starkly obtruded. And, not least in importance, by this change of plan Carker's isolation in evil is sustained to his end.

The first chapter of Number XVIII, with its brilliantly half-revealing title 'Rob the Grinder loses his place', not only wipes out Carker; by concentrating upon the progress of his flight, swift yet protracted, it emphasizes one of the big transitions in the narrative, even as Mr Dombey's railway journey to Leamington had done. The same devices are even repeated—the whirling thoughts

1. See p. 106 above. 2. Forster, VI ii. Jeffrey's note has not survived.

that accompany the wheels, the symbolically intended railway junction. But this journey makes a full stop; with it the only irredeemable evil in the novel's world is abolished—not merely destroyed, but torn to fragments.

V

There could be no doubt in either author's or reader's mind about the general content of the closing chapters (lviii–lxii, in the final 'double number', XIX–XX). The main action must fulfil itself in the undermining of Mr Dombey's pride from within and his reconciliation with Florence, and there must be news of all the other characters, as satisfactory as their conditions and deserts allow, leading to a final fireside or sunset glow. There was, however, the problem of time: for that reconciliation to carry conviction, time must not only pass but be felt to pass, and it must be the time of heart-throbs as well as clocks and calendars. Mr Dombey has been unseen, save for oblique glimpses, for several chapters; we are behindhand even with events, still more with his response to them. He is now to be seen at close quarters after a year has passed; but not at once. The first chapter (lviii) seems leisurely and quiet, but is packed with useful information. Its purpose is to expound the changed situation, both by narrative and dialogue, to give Mr Dombey his final prominence, first through choric commentary from Mr Perch, Major Bagstock, and Mrs Chick, then more fully through the conversation of Harriet and Mr Morfin, which also ties in many other loose ends. (Dickens's instinct for economy leads him, while he has Harriet in hand, to dispose of her consoling visit to Alice's repentant deathbed, though she is not an obvious confidante for Good Mrs Brown's revelation of family history.) Turning from the world and the firm to the 'great house in the long dull street' (chapter lix), the approach to Mr Dombey is still gradual, through the chorus of the 'kitchen council',[1] the sale, the refrain 'the house is a ruin and the rats fly from it', and the glimpse of Toodle and Tox, ghosts of past loyalty lurking in the shadows. A bare five pages are devoted to Mr Dombey himself, but so thorough has been the preparation, and so concentrated and searching is the

1. From Dickens's running title added in the edition of 1867. The intention was calculated; in the number plan for X he notes 'carry on the servants as a sort of odd chorus to the story', and he had indeed already initiated this in earlier chapters.

light shed upon him as he roams the memory-haunted house, that the picture of his fallen pride seems to dominate the entire number. The main design is at last fulfilled,

> for the struggle within himself, which goes on in all such obstinate natures, will have ended then,

and so intense is our sense of his retributive suffering that the almost theatrically opportune return of Florence can be accepted as morally earned. Miss Tox's last comment, with its echo ('So Dombey and Son, as I observed upon a certain sad occasion, is really a daughter after all!') draws a concluding line under the climax. The notes in the plan include 'q^y order of chapters'; but there is no doubt that chapter lix is rightly placed.[1] The stage is now left clear for the final grouping of the other characters, whom Dickens's plan conscientiously lists for a final round-up, with ticks added when they had been disposed of. Not one was forgotten,[2] not even Master Bitherstone and Miss Pankey, though the Skettleses and the last glimpse of Miss Tox were inserted only at proof stage. The return to Brighton (chapter lx) helps to link the final chapters to the close of the first movement, and again enforces the sense of passing time, and of changelessness in change. The detail of Mr Bunsby's wedding is at first sight surprising in its amplitude; but apart from the attraction of one broadly comic scene at the close, it makes an adequate last appearance for that somewhat petted character Captain Cuttle. There is no one for him to marry, so we must be shown by means of this awful warning how glad he is to have escaped marriage.

But throughout the 'matrimonial' winding-up the epilogue of Florence and her father is kept before us; the movement of chapter lx is traced in the notes, with a final lead back to the central figures:

> Open with Blimber's—lead to Bunsby, through the Captain, & end with Susan and Florence.

Mr Dombey's illness (predicted on the cover) is persuasively used to emphasize his change of heart, and is also an excuse to

1. Possibly the original intention was to include a Florence-chapter; the first note is 'The birth of Florence's child and her relenting towards her father', then 'The scene in his own room'.

2. At least of the humans; and the dog Diogenes was remembered a week before publication. Dickens wrote to Forster (VI ii; 25 Mar. 1848) asking for him to be inserted in proof, and a brief addition stands on the last page of the proof sheet: 'and an old dog is generally in their company'.

'distance' him, so that even our glimpse of him in recovery, improbably clinking glasses with Captain Cuttle (like Scrooge at the Cratchits'), does not seem incongruous.

One item on the agenda of the plan was doubtful; the note shows an unexpected hesitation over the meeting between Edith and Florence:

> Edith—q^y Edith and Florence—certainly, Edith and Cousin Feenix. Yes, all three.

Edith has her just place; shadowed herself,[1] but removing the one remaining shadow on Florence. The substance and style of their speeches could be predicted; but the scene draws a surprising extra vitality from the rôle of Cousin Feenix. His gentility is at last revealed as the genuine article (Edith is to reveal the truth 'not for the honour of the family . . . but because it *is* wrong, and not right'), and his oratory is for the first time effectual; but he retains all his native absurdity, and while ministering to the mood of the epilogue he is not subdued (as is Nipper) into a mere contributor to the chorus.

Echoes reverberate in the closing number; incidents and scenes are recalled, themes reappear, dominant images and even words are repeated.[2] But one echo planned for the conclusion of the final chapter was removed in proof:

> End with the sea—carrying through, what the waves were always saying, and the invisible country far away.[3]

That popular sentiment which added an apocryphal wildness to the waves in a drawing-room song might have preferred it so.

1. The gradations of poetic justice are delicate; her destination is the south of Italy, whereas little Em'ly must go to Australia.

2. E.g., Miss Tox's comment, quoted above, and 'Let him remember it in that room, years to come'; the latter also the caption of an illustration.

3. In correcting proof Dickens had to reduce his number by seven lines, yet wished to find room for Skettles and Miss Tox. It was the last two paragraphs he chose to sacrifice. They read as follows:

> The voices in the waves speak low to him of Florence, day and night—plainest when he, his blooming daughter, and her husband, walk beside them in the evening, or sit at an open window, listening to their roar. They speak to him of Florence and his altered heart; of Florence and their ceaseless murmuring to her of the love, eternal and illimitable, extending still, beyond the sea, beyond the sky, to the invisible country far away.
>
> Never from the mighty sea may voices rise too late, to come between us and the unseen region on the other shore! Better, far better, that they whispered of that region in our childish ears, and the swift river hurried us away!

But the conclusion is comparatively restrained, and comes no nearer that echo than a last 'long shot' of the sea-beach in autumn, and a natural grandfatherly recollection of the other Paul. It is with the two Florences that Dickens ends; mindful in valediction of his main design.

CHAPTER VI

David Copperfield Month by Month

THE last number of *Dombey and Son* was published in April 1848, and before the year was out Dickens was brooding upon his next novel *David Copperfield.* As for *Dombey*, no master plan survives, and there is no reason to suppose that such a plan was set on paper. Other evidence bearing upon the nature of his first design is slight, and when compared with what survives about the design of *Dombey*[1] is disappointing. It is true that on one page of the manuscript are written as many as seventeen draft titles, but all are variants upon a single pattern. What began as 'Mag's Diversions: Being the personal history, experiences, and observations of Mr. Thomas Mag the Younger, of Blunderstone House' ended as 'The Personal History and Experience of David Copperfield the Younger'. After promising so much in the title of *Dombey*, he would seem to be returning to the noncommittal type of *The Life and Adventures of Nicholas Nickleby*: even 'Mag's Diversions', an old saying like 'the deuce and all', was no more compromising than *As You Like It.* The cover-design of the monthly numbers, which had foreshadowed the drift of *Dombey*, tells no secrets here. It shows indeed that the story will begin in earliest childhood, but that is no more than the first number itself reveals. Forster, it is true, found the 'unity of drift or purpose . . . apparent always', and added, in explanation:

> By the course of the events we learn the value of self-denial and patience, quiet endurance of unavoidable ills, strenuous effort against ills remediable; and everything in the fortunes of the actors warns us, to strengthen our generous emotions and to guard the purities of home.[2]

1. See above, pp. 90–6. 2. Forster, VI vii.

This is well said; but it is said after the event. Of the seminal period Forster could afterwards recall only his suggestion in 1848 that Dickens should write his next book in the first person—a suggestion 'which he took at once very gravely . . . though as yet not dreaming of any public use of his early personal trials',[1] and that when his sixth son was born in January 1849 he decided to call him Henry Fielding 'in a kind of homage to the style of work he was now so bent on beginning'.[2] All this amounts to little. Substantial evidence of a commanding purpose at the outset must be found, if at all, inside the book and in the number plans, which are now published *in extenso* for the first time.[3]

Number I: May 1849
Chapters i–iii: written in April 1849

The plans of the first numbers of *David Copperfield* and *Little Dorrit* were removed from their manuscripts by Forster. He had facsimiles of them made and used these in his *Life of Dickens* to show in *Dorrit* 'the labour and pains' and in *Copperfield* 'the lightness and confidence of handling'. The plans were never restored, and have disappeared with the rest of Forster's manuscript. This would not have mattered so much if Forster had reproduced the plans in their entirety; but his purpose of contrast was served by a two-thirds facsimile of each, and this truncated specimen (printed on pp. 116–17) is all that now survives.

1. Ibid., VI vi. But the successful adoption of the child's point of view in *Dombey and Son* (see p. 100, n. 4) had awoken an interest in his own childhood which had led him to write some chapters of an autobiography probably in 1847. 1847 was also the year of publication of an impressive novel written in the first person, *Jane Eyre*. See Tillotson, *Novels of the Eighteen-Forties* (Oxford, 1954), pp. 114, 192, 260.

2. Forster, VI vi.

3. Though it is impossible to convey in print all that the number plans reveal, in their manuscript form, of hesitation and decision, of haste and excitement, and of afterthought squeezed into what might seem the least inconvenient space unfilled, our transcription is as exact as it is practicable to make it. A line in the manuscript is invariably represented by a line of type, and in position it matches as closely as possible an entry on the half-sheet of paper facing it. Capitalization and underlining have been preserved. Erasures, where legible, are printed within angle-brackets. Compare frontispiece, and see pp. 25–9.

Lobsters & Crawfish

The people living on the Barge.

Mr Hasden
Murdle Murdstone
Murden

The progress of his mother's second courtship

Brooks of Sheffield
Goes to Peggotty's

The first number is a charming and lavish piece of exposition. Apart from the rich possibilities latent in the Peggottys and Betsey Trotwood, Dickens had provided himself in this number with three possible themes for future development. The first, though the least important, is the mystery of Betsey Trotwood's husband. That this mystery was no casual embellishment of his preliminary sketch of her character, but was intended for future use, the number plan seems to confirm, for the note 'Her old wrongs' may have served to keep in mind something for later use.

The second theme is David's relations with Mr Murdstone, whose well-chosen name is determined after three attempts. It is likely that Mr Murdstone's harsh treatment of David was already foreseen, if not the form which that treatment was to take, for the reader receives more than one covert warning. The autobiographical mode of writing is employed with notable irony when David and Peggotty discuss the subject of marriage and when David relates the tiff between Peggotty and Mrs Copperfield after Mr Murdstone's visit. The unwitting David is made to convey, without expressly stating, that Mrs Copperfield has been too easily won by flattery, and that Peggotty has good reason to disapprove the coming marriage. After this it is not altogether surprising that the first number should end with a flutter of ominous excitement. David and Peggotty return from their visit to Yarmouth, but Mrs Copperfield is not at the door to greet them.

(Personal History and Adventures of David Copperfield—N° I)

chapter I.

I am born

Father dead—Gravestone outside the house
Young mother—Tendency to weakness and vanity
Miss Betsey—Her old wrongs Peggotty
Why rookery? Ham Peggotty
Morgan the Dr

chapter II.

I observe

The things that come out of the blank of his infancy on looking back.—child at church—
—The future father in law "at this minute I see him turn round in the garden with his damned black eyes"—&c

Peggotty with difficulty explains to David that he has 'got a Pa . . . A new one', and her agitation affects David too. The scene in the parlour when David is at last brought to his mother is described with an economy of words for which Dickens is not often credited:

> My mother dropped her work, and arose hurriedly, but timidly I thought.
>
> 'Now, Clara my dear,' said Mr. Murdstone. 'Recollect! controul yourself, always controul yourself! Davy boy, how do you do?'
>
> I gave him my hand. After a moment of suspense, I went and kissed my mother: she kissed me, patted me gently on the shoulder, and sat down again to her work. I could not look at her, I could not look at him, I knew quite well that he was looking at us both; and I turned to the window and looked out there, at some shrubs that were drooping their heads in the cold.

The agony to come is implied briefly but sufficiently. The drooping shrubs are an emblem of the cold which has invaded the home; and with another emblem, of the man who has come to ruin their domestic happiness, the number is concluded:

> My old dear bedroom was changed,[1] and I was to lie a long way off. I rambled downstairs to find anything that was like itself, so altered it all seemed; and roamed into the yard. I very soon started

1. He had formerly slept 'in a closet within my mother's room'.

back from there, for the empty dog-kennel was filled up with a great dog—deep-mouthed and black-haired like Him—and he was very angry at the sight of me, and sprung out to get at me.

The third theme is as ominous as the second: it is Little Em'ly's future. The manuscript shows that the scene at Yarmouth was elaborated in two respects after the draft of the first number was completed.

(1) As Dickens first conceived her, Mrs Gummidge had no character at all. It was only after completing chapter iii that he turned back and interpolated the long episode beginning 'I soon found out that Mrs. Gummidge did not always make herself so agreeable as she might have been expected to do, under the circumstances of her residence with Mr. Peggotty.' It is then that she becomes 'a lone lorn creetur', and thus helps to exemplify the forbearing character of Mr Peggotty.

(2) The second interpolation is more important. In the first draft Em'ly is no more than the little girl whom young David adored, though the sequel shows that even this first affair of David's undisciplined heart is of some importance. But on completing the chapter Dickens added the long passage, beginning '"You're quite a sailor, I suppose?" I said to Em'ly' and ending 'This may be premature. I have set it down too soon, perhaps. But let it stand.' In this passage is revealed Em'ly's wish 'to be a lady' so as to prevent Mr Peggotty and Ham from risking their lives at sea in stormy weather. She is afraid of the cruel sea for their sake, but not a whit for her own; and she demonstrates her fearlessness by running 'along a jagged timber which protruded from the place we stood upon, and overhung the deep water at some height, without the least defence'. She seemed to spring forward to her destruction; and David, recalling the scene, reflected 'there has been a time since . . . when I have asked myself the question, would it have been better for little Em'ly to have had the waters close above her head that morning in my sight; and when I have answered Yes, it would have been'.

This interpolated passage forecasts the part which Em'ly is to play. With his mind occupied by Miss Coutts's project for establishing a home for fallen women,[1] Dickens reverts to one of the themes of *Dombey and Son*, the repentant prostitute: someone, it is clear, will offer to make Em'ly a lady on speciously honourable

1. See below, p. 148.

terms, and she will fall in attempting to improve the lot of Mr Peggotty and Ham.[1]

Thus in the first number many incidents are already forecast. In one direction Dickens could see as far perhaps as Number V, where David comes to live with Betsey Trotwood; in another he might see as far as Number XVI (in which Mr Peggotty at last finds Em'ly in hiding), or even as far as the great storm in Number XVIII, though it is not at all likely that he yet knew all that he would meet on either road. The contemporary reader who recognized these two themes might have speculated upon their ultimate connexion. Since David himself could not have been cast for Em'ly's seducer, was he then to effect her rescue, perhaps even to marry her? Or was he, whose caul forecast immunity from drowning, to rescue her in a final storm which the interpolation so clearly promises? Much would depend upon the identity of the seducer. He was to be revealed in the next number, the plan of which is presented overleaf.

1. The interpolation of this important passage in the first draft of the number invites speculation. Did the theme first occur to Dickens after finishing the number, or had he already meditated it and set it aside for fuller treatment on a future occasion? The first number was evidently written in haste. Though publication was set for 1 May, it was not finished on 19 April (*Letters*, II 150). The opportunities of the story may therefore have been imperfectly recognized and have opened before him as he wrote. On the other hand, it should be noted that there are thirty sheets of manuscript in the first draft, which is rather more than his normal monthly stint. Proofs, however, would show him that he had more space at his disposal than the number of manuscript sheets had led him to believe, and he may have decided thereupon to broach this important theme at the earliest possible moment.

Number II: June 1849

Miss Murdstone
Their religion
Picture of all that, and its effect on Davy's life.
Cast off and getting sullen.
qy His books and reading?
His offence, and confinement upstairs. Child's remembrance of the latter.
Sent away

⟨I attend church.⟩

⟨hospitably received⟩
⟨I am received‸by Mr Peggotty⟩

The first number had ended with the reader's curiosity roused about David's relations with Mr Murdstone. Dickens decided to satisfy it immediately in the first chapter of Number II. The memoranda relate entirely to chapter iv and, with the summary, cover all the incidents in their order of narration, except Peggotty's visit to David in his confinement. It might be deduced that chapter iv required particular care and that the details of the journey to school and the boys' return could be improvised in the act of writing. The only memorandum bearing upon the journey is scored out, perhaps because a second visit to Mr

Chapters iv–vi: completed by 5 May 1849

experience
(Personal History and ⟨adventures⟩ of David Copperfield—No II.)

chapter IV.
I fall into disgrace

Progress of his mother's weakness under the Murdstones.
Miss Murdstone
Beat's him
Bites
Shut up and dismissed

chapter V.
—And am sent away from home.

The carrier & Peggotty.
Waiter—Glass of ale—chops—pudding—himself
journey
to be left till called for
School with the boys all at home
"Take care of him. He bites"

chapter VI.
I enlarge my circle of acquaintance.

Mr Creakle.
return of the boys
spending his money
Steerford
Steerforth.

Peggotty's barge would have conflicted with the impression of friendlessness in which David makes his way to Salem House. Though the bareness of the summary of chapter v contrasts with the lavishly fanciful expansion of the incidents in the text, it is enough to recall what is essential and, in the instance of 'the carrier and Peggotty', to keep in mind the one point for future development. But the summary of chapter vi is even more bare and brief; yet this is the chapter in which Steerforth is introduced, the foundations of whose character are laid with obvious care. How deftly Dickens suggests by the confiscation and disposal of David's pocket-money that Steerforth's actions are not in keeping with his heroic demeanour; and any reader who doubts that Steerforth is already reserved for a dark future need only turn to the description of him lying asleep and observe there the first anticipation of the final scene on Yarmouth sands in chapter lv:

> I . . . raised myself, I recollect, to look at him where he lay in the moonlight, with his handsome face turned up, and his head reclining easily on his arm. He was a person of great power in my eyes; that was of course the reason of my mind running on him. No veiled future dimly glanced upon him in the moonbeams.

Number III: July 1849

School. Master	
	<u>The</u> Afternoon
Steerforth	
	Peggotty's enquiries about school Tells her of Barkis
Goes home	Mother says she is not to leave her. It may not be for long.

Mother with a baby.
comes back, & receives news of her death.

again,
Goes home ∧ to the funeral.

⟨I enjoy one afternoon's holiday⟩

⟨The holidays are concentrated into one afternoon.⟩

⟨My holidays.⟩

He is, so far, the only possible seducer for Little Em'ly, and that he was already destined for this rôle may be guessed from a hint of the young libertine, undeveloped as yet, but casual and untrustworthy in his approaches to women:

> 'You haven't got a sister, have you?' said Steerforth, yawning.
> 'No,' I answered.
> 'That's a pity,' said Steerforth. 'If you had had one, I should think she would have been a pretty, timid, little, bright-eyed sort of girl. I should have liked to know her. Good night, young Copperfield.'

Chapters vii–ix: completed by 21 June 1849

(Personal History and Experience of David Copperfield—N° III.)

chapter VII.

My First half at Salem House.

School—His progress
Steerforth's character.
Traddles. D°
Mr Mell's poverty and mother, and dismissal.

Visit from ⟨Peggotty⟩ Mr Peggotty? Yes. And Steerforth
Summing up, & going home.

chapter VIII.

My holidays. Especially one happy Afternoon

The Afternoon. The baby
Peggotty & his mother.
The Murdstones—progress of their influence &c
Holding up the baby

chapter IX.

I have a memorable Birthday.

Mrs Creakle breaks it to him
His state of mind—childish incidental whimsicalities
The undertaker's, Mr Omer's
State of home, and recollection of funeral
Peggotty's narrative
close with the idea of his
mother as she was, with him
as he was, in her arms.

The confidence which Dickens felt in his story at this juncture is reflected in a letter to Forster dated 6 June 1849.[1] '*Copperfield* half done', he wrote; 'I feel, thank God, quite confident in the story. I have a move in it ready for this month; another for next; and another for the next.' It seems not unlikely that the first 'move' was the meeting of Mr Peggotty and Ham with Steerforth at Salem House in chapter vii. The number plan shows that Dickens had first chosen Peggotty as David's visitor. It was a natural choice to make; but it seems to have flashed across his mind—the form of the summary supports this—that if Mr Peggotty, a less likely visitor, came instead of his sister, the way lay open for a meeting between him and Steerforth, which might in turn give rise to a meeting between Steerforth and Em'ly. Steerforth himself is presented throughout with notable irony. Every adult reader recognizes how meanly he behaves; but David 'could not help thinking . . . what a noble fellow he was', and every unworthy action of his patron is given a suitably heroic and generous interpretation.

With Steerforth's character sufficiently shaped in chapter vii, Dickens could turn back to pursue the Murdstones' influence in the two remaining chapters. Once decided that David's mother shall die, it is obvious that her death must occur in the last chapter of the number. 'Get a clean pocket-handkerchief ready for the close of Copperfield N° 3;' he wrote to Lemon on 25 June; ' "simple and quiet, but very natural and touching."—*Evening Bore.*'[2] Manuscript and proof disclose some adjustment of emphasis in the pathos. The 'RAT-tat-tat' of Mr Joram's hammer on the coffin was an afterthought, and so was the first passage of repartee between Minnie Omer and her father.[3] A paragraph describing the morning of the funeral was deleted in proof. It read as follows:

> When the day came, I remember being awakened in the morning by the sharp strokes of a spade, and that I looked out of the window, and saw men working in the churchyard, underneath the tree, and went to bed and wept. I remember that I lay there, sobbing, until

1. The letter is misdated 6 June 1850 in the Nonesuch edition (II 218), and Forster (VI vi) is wrong in referring it to the second number which was already published.

2. *Letters*, II 157.

3. The passage beginning ' "Father!" said Minnie, playfully. "What a porpoise you do grow!" ' and ending 'Mr. Omer took me back into the parlor, breathing with some difficulty on the way.'

> Peggotty came up to help me dress myself, and that being in her black dress for the first time, she wrung her hands—a thing it turned my very blood to see her do—and gave way to her sorrow before me, for the only time in all my knowledge.

When proofs of Number III reached him, Dickens found that he had overstepped his monthly allowance of thirty-two pages by thirty-five lines of type. Something had to go, and this was one of the passages cut. Its omission involves a small but appreciable relaxing of tension.

(*Continued overleaf.*)

Number IV: August 1849

---

what I know so well

I become neglected and am provided for

I begin life on my <account> own account.

I go on with life, rather uncomfortably
on my own account and don't like it

I make a resolution

Though he had already made use of his unpublished autobiography in Number II, it is in this number that he relies most heavily on his past experiences. The memoranda are accordingly brief, amounting to little more than drafts of chapter titles, and the manuscript itself shows unusually few corrections. It was not a mere question of transcribing, however; 'I really think I have done it ingeniously,' he wrote to Forster on 10 July, 'and with a very complicated interweaving of truth and fiction.'[1]

A change which Dickens made in the colour of his ink while writing this number shows that the summaries of chapters xi and xii were made before chapter x was written, and that the items in the summary of chapter x were jotted down concurrently with the episodes to which they refer. They reveal little. He was not

1. *Letters*, II 160.

Chapters x–xii: written during the first fortnight of July 1849

(Personal History and Experience of David Copperfield—N° IV.)

chapter X.

I become neglected, and am provided for.

Go away with Peggotty—Barkis
Mr Peggotty's
Her marriage ride with the two children
neglect
Quinion.—arrangement
"Behold me" &c

chapter XI.

I begin life on my own account, and don't like it.

all the ⟨Murdstone and⟩ life at the warehouse
Murdstone and Grinby
M^r^ and Mrs Micawber—Prison—Insolvent Court

chapter XII.

Liking life on my own account no better, I form a great resolution.

The young man with the donkey cart

run away to Aunt Betsey

---

accustomed to sketch his characters in these plans, and accordingly 'M^r^ and Mrs Micawber' and 'the young man with the donkey cart' stand starkly with no indication of how they will develop under his hand. More surprising is to find no record of Em'ly's interest in the account which David and Mr Peggotty give of Steerforth.

(*Continued overleaf.*)

Number V: September 1849

Chatham—Canterbury sunshine
Tramps—pint of beer?

Your sister, Betsey Trotwood

Mr Dick's history? qy Yes, very briefly. by Miss Betsey

Donkies
Miss Murdstone comes on a donkey

Mr Dick and his memorial

His delusion

Introduction of the real heroine

Dickens was not fully persuaded of the advantages of dividing a long novel into books until later in his career. These divisions guide the reader; but the author may be presumed to be aware of them even though he does not mark them. Such a division comes at the end of Number IV: one movement of the novel ends with David running away to Aunt Betsey, and another begins in Number V with the introduction of fresh characters representing fresh contributions to the principal theme. His first duty to his readers was to resume the flight to Dover which the demands of the serial form had interrupted at so important yet so convenient a juncture. The prospect opening upon David—the new home and its inmates, the dismissal of the Murdstones, and the preparation for a new start in life at Canterbury—might seem to require a number in itself: this new prospect was doubtless the 'move'

Chapters xiii–xv: finished and proofs read by 22 August 1849

(Personal History and Experience of David Copperfield—N° V.)

chapter XIII.

The sequel of my resolution.

His journey
Goes to his aunts
Miss Betsey—"Janet! Donkies!"
Mr Dick

chapter XIV.

My Aunt makes up her mind about me.

Mr Dick again
Mr and Miss Murdstone come
conversation—ends with his Aunt adopting him.
Trotwood Copperfield

chapter XV.

I make another beginning

old House at Canterbury
Mr Wickfield
His one motive. Agnes Wickfield
Uriah Heep.

---

ready for September, as Forster had been told in June, just as David's experiences at the blacking factory were the 'move' prepared for August. But though the briefness of the memoranda might be thought to indicate that Dickens saw clearly every turn in the path before him, a phrase in a letter to Forster written on 10 August, when nearly half the number was done, shows that all was not straightforward: 'I have not worked quickly here yet', he wrote from the Isle of Wight; '. . . Divers cogitations have occupied my mind at intervals, respecting the dim design'.[1]

The nature of some of these cogitations is revealed in the memoranda. The query about Mr Dick's history seems to imply a doubt whether this was the right moment to relate it. He may well have been faced with the temptation to make a mystery of

1. *Letters*, II 167.

Mr Dick's past. This would have involved the provision of a group of subordinate characters related to Mr Dick and the cumbersome apparatus of a sub-plot. Dickens was never averse to such additional complication, but in his mature work a mystery was of interest only in so far as it clarified another purpose, as Lady Dedlock's mystery clarifies the inescapable responsibility of her social class for the condition of such a slum as Tom-all-alone's. The purpose of Mr Dick is to illustrate and commend such humane treatment of the partly imbecile as Betsey Trotwood administers. It was not beyond Dickens's powers to demonstrate this purpose by means of a mystery; but he may have reflected that it could be made equally clear without, and that by revealing Aunt Betsey's treatment of Mr Dick at this point he contributed effectively to the exposition of her character on which he was then engaged.

Forster was the first to mention that Mr Dick's topical[1] obsession with King Charles's head replaced the Bull in the China Shop at proof stage. But an even more significant alteration in proof has escaped notice. David's original vision of Mr Dick was of 'a florid, pleasant-looking gentleman, with a grey head, putting his tongue out against the glass, and carrying it across the pane and back again; who, when his eye caught mine, squinted at me in a most terrible manner, laughed, and went away'. The tongue is removed in proof, and the terrible squint is softened to an eye shut up 'in a grotesque manner'. If Dickens had not softened this description, he might well have been charged, as Coleridge charged Wordsworth in 'The Idiot Boy', with not taking sufficient care 'to preclude from the reader's fancy the disgusting images of *ordinary morbid idiocy*, which yet it was by no means his intention to represent'.[2]

Another point of interest in the memoranda is the note, 'Introduction of the real heroine'. It might be deduced from this note that Agnes Wickfield is to serve not merely as David's 'good angel', a rôle in which David commends her performance all too frequently, but that she is eventually to become his wife. A 'real' heroine also implies an illusory heroine, and though he may have been thinking of Em'ly in that part, it is more probable that he had already had Dora Spenlow in mind. If Agnes, then, as the real heroine, is destined to marry David eventually, Dora is also

1. 1849 was the bicentenary year of Charles I's execution.
2. *Biographia Literaria*, ed. J. Shawcross (Oxford, 1907), II 35.

destined to make way for her, assuming that she is indeed to marry David in the first place. Yet Forster records[1] that in the latter part of the story 'his principal hesitation occurred in connection with the child-wife Dora, who had become a great favourite as he went on', and this is confirmed by a letter of 7 May 1850, written during the course of Number XIV, 'Still undecided about Dora, but MUST decide to-day.' This hesitation may be explained as an attempt to avoid a harsh but necessary decision made at an earlier stage. But there is a truly Dickensian alternative. Had Dora been allowed to live, Agnes might have maintained her part as 'the real heroine' by educating Dora, by superintending the household, and by caring for the children, the very part which Georgina Hogarth—'my little housekeeper', as he calls her in a letter of 29 August 1850[2]—was playing in Dickens's own family. Such a development in this 'autobiographical' novel would have been embarrassingly close to life; but it would have had the advantage of saving Dora, and Dickens may well have reviewed this possibility before deciding upon her fate.

(*Continued overleaf.*)

1. Forster, VI vi. 2. *Letters*, II 229.

Number VI: October 1849

Dictionary

The good old Doctor & the young wife
Uriah Heep? qy Yes.
Mr Micawber? qy Yes. and Mrs
"Turn his attention to coals." The Medway Coal Trade

Mr Micawber's letter

The Progress from childhood to youth.

My aunt? qy No. only generally

Mr Dick? qy Yes. With the Dr.

Peggotty's half guinea to be repaid.

Mems for the Progress.
The cathedral

Miss Wilkins—No. Shepherd

Head boy.
Tail-coat
Loving a grown woman, much too old.

This number plan is appreciably more elaborate than the last, and shows that the story demanded more detailed planning at this stage. It is not difficult to see why this should have been. Two new themes are introduced—the themes of Dr and Mrs Strong's relations with Jack Maldon and of Uriah Heep's ambitions—whose connexion with David's story is of far-reaching complexity.

The Strong–Maldon theme engages his first attention. At first sight its relationship either to David's story or to the story of Steerforth and Em'ly may seem remote, but when in Number

Chapters xvi–xviii: finished about 20 September 1849

(Personal History and Experience of David Copperfield—N° VI.)

chapter XVI.
I am a new boy, in more senses than one.

Doctor Strong's
The Doctor and his young wife
Mr Jack Maldon Wife's mother. The old soldier
Mr Wickfield & Agnes.
Uriah Heep.
Mr Jack Maldon's going away. The cherry colored ribbon.
Close with her face.

chapter XVII.
Somebody turns up.

Mr Dick—The man who frightens my aunt.

Mr Dick & the Doctor walking up & down
Uriah Heep and his mother
Their lemon-squeezing process
Mr & Mrs Micawber. Mr Micawber makes Uriah's acquaintance.

chapter XVIII.
A Retrospect.

Two loves.
Miss Shepherd. In the responses—put her in
among the Royal family.
Fight with a butcher
Growing up—Agnes grows up.
In love with the eldest Miss Larkins
ring—Bear's grease—&c &c

XV Dickens explains what has been happening, it is clear that Annie Strong's experiences bear upon David's affection for Dora Spenlow. His eyes are opened by her words to see that he too has suffered from the 'mistaken impulse of an undisciplined heart'. There is little doubt that this was part of the original intention, although in Number VI the reader has not yet heard of Dora. The theme of The Undisciplined Heart had been touched long before Dora appears. David had told Em'ly in chapter iii that he 'adored her, and that unless she confessed she adored me I should be reduced to the necessity of killing myself with a sword'. His love for the eldest Miss Larkins was as extravagantly expressed:

> If the eldest Miss Larkins would drive a triumphal car down the High Street, and allow me to throw myself under the wheels as an offering to her beauty, I should be proud to be trampled under her horses' feet.[1]

Before Miss Larkins there had been Miss Shepherd, 'the one pervading theme and vision of my life'; and before Miss Shepherd, Agnes:

> I love little Em'ly, and I don't love Agnes—no, not at all in that way—but I feel that there are goodness, peace, and truth, wherever Agnes is.[2]

The distinction is already clear between the 'rock' on which his later love was founded and the mistaken impulses of his undisciplined heart.

Annie Strong's experiences serve to enforce this. She too had been deceived by childish love. When Dr Strong's proposal was made, she was as little able as David to recognize the future source of her happiness. ' "Mama," she said, crying,'—the report is Mrs Markleham's—' "I am extremely young . . . and I hardly know if I have a heart at all." ' But in this same chapter (chapter xvi), the very chapter in which David fails to recognize the substance of his love for Agnes, Annie Strong is brought by Jack Maldon's behaviour to recognize the difference between her old feelings for him and what she has since learned to feel for the Doctor. Jack Maldon's behaviour on leaving for India aroused that look of 'penitence, humiliation, shame, pride, love, and trustfulness' with which she regarded the Doctor, and which David was to remember 'a long time afterwards'. When at last he falls in love with Dora in Number IX, the reader feels no surprise because the quality had been foreseen and prepared for in Numbers I, V, and VI.

Did Dickens also foresee the use of Mr Dick to effect the reconciliation between Dr and Mrs Strong in Number XV? It is not impossible, since Dr Strong and Mr Dick are already placed in close association. The picture of these two men, each with his

1. This and other passages describing David's infatuation were removed from ch. xviii in proof when it was discovered that the 'over-matter' in No. VI extended to 96 lines of print.

2. Ch. xvi.

harmless obsession, walking together 'by the hour, on that side of the courtyard which was known among us as The Doctor's Walk', is a pleasing contribution to the pattern of the novel. It seems to suggest, as gently as possible, that the Doctor's notion of compiling a dictionary is as futile as Mr Dick's notion of writing a memorial, and as little likely to be completed. Dickens's purpose in creating Mr Dick should also be recalled. If he was aware of the best contemporary treatment of lunacy,[1] it seems not unlikely that he was already preparing to show Mr Dick engaged in the humane office of reconciling husband and wife.

Another strand in the pattern of the novel can be observed in the Strong episode and in other episodes of this number. In each of the prominent themes a shadow is cast upon a scene of domestic happiness: the Murdstones' shadow darkens the happiness of Blunderstone Rookery, and Steerforth is to darken the Peggottys' happiness. In the same way Jack Maldon casts his shadow over the Strongs, and Mr Dick reveals to David—at greater length before proofs showed the need for pruning—that an unknown man has been frightening Aunt Betsey. Uriah Heep's ambitions are announced lightly but surely, and they will cast their shadow over the happiness of Agnes and her father.

The memoranda disclose some uncertainty in the use of both Uriah and Mr Micawber at this stage, yet the pointedness of the coincidence by which Micawber discovers David at tea with the Heeps suggests that Dickens, in the moment of plotting Uriah's schemes, provides an instrument for unveiling them.

(*Continued overleaf.*)

1. A reviewer of *Maud* in *Fraser's Magazine*, Sept. 1855, remarks: 'The wonders which have been worked of late years, even in idiots and cretins, simply by drawing out their humanity, by interesting them and employing them, by giving them something to love, something to do, seem to open a boundless door of hope'.

Number VII: November 1849

Janet? qy?
Steerforth's mother? ⟨Yes⟩

Steerforth? Yes.

Little Em'ly? Yes.

The two partners? No
Mr Mell? No.

Lirrimer?
Littimer.

This brilliant and confident number shows Dickens in full sail with no apparent hesitation about the course before him. But the number plan reveals once more that he took his direction immediately before writing the number, and took it not without deliberation. A close examination of the number itself might have suggested as much, for complete as it is, it foreshadows doom.

David has now left school and is sent away for a change of scene to help in choosing a profession. Dickens must therefore take a last look at two Canterbury themes which he was not likely to resume in the near future. When David goes to take leave of Agnes, she mentions her anxiety about the 'gradual alteration in Papa' and Uriah's growing ascendency. Short as the episode is, it serves its purpose; but the passage had been longer before proofs showed the need for cuts, and two paragraphs describing a dinner

Chapters xix–xxi: finished about 18 October 1849

(Personal History and Experience of David Copperfield—N° VII.)

chapter XIX.

I look about me, and make a discovery.

Pave the way with Mr Wickfield
D° Agnes
D° Mrs Strong
Goes away to see Peggotty
First Fall in life Play.
Waiter Golden Cross Charing Cross
meets Steerforth

chapter XX.

Steerforth's Home.

Mrs Steerforth
Miss Dartle. "Threw a hammer at her?"
"Eh? But is it really though? I want to know

chapter XXI.

Little Em'ly.

The servant. Littimer.
Little Em'ly at Mr Omer's—Mr Omer "Two parties."
Peggotty
Mr Barkis a little nearer
Mr Peggotty's account of her being engaged to Ham.

at Mr Wickfield's had to go. These added some slight emphasis to the points made in David's conversation with Agnes. The other Canterbury theme concerns the Strongs and Jack Maldon, and after glancing at that, Dickens was ready to convey David to London for the principal subject of the number, his reunion with Steerforth.

The memoranda show Dickens in doubt whether to use Steerforth and his mother, Em'ly, Littimer, Mr Mell, and 'the two partners'. He decided against Mr Mell, who would presumably have served once more to illustrate Steerforth's churlishness, and who might have encouraged backward glances when so much lies ahead; and 'the two partners', Spenlow and Jorkins—though they had not yet received those names—were deferred until the following month. The remaining characters are employed and form the staple of chapters xx and xxi. Other characters enter, too. Em'ly's appearance involves the reappearance of the Peggotty, Barkis, and Omer households, who therefore did not require specific mention. But it is perhaps surprising that though Littimer is mentioned in the memoranda, Rosa Dartle is not. Littimer is to become an important agent:

> He was very often by [David observes, in a passage subsequently removed in proof] for his attention to Steerforth, at all times, was most remarkable. Without obtruding it, or watching him, he seemed to have the power of divining his wants, and supplying them at the very moment when it was agreeable to him that they should be supplied. He never showed the least sense of there being anything meritorious in this; neither did his master.

Miss Dartle, on the other hand, seems to have been regarded at this stage as a passive figure. She serves in this number as a chorus of sarcastic comment on Steerforth's brutalities. But her relative prominence in the summary, probably written after completing the number, suggests that she may have grown in importance while chapter xx was being written.

The future is foreshadowed in the Yarmouth gossip, retailed to David by the Omers, that Em'ly had not been keeping 'to her own station in life', that she 'wanted to be a lady . . . to do so and so for her uncle—don't you see?—and buy him such and such fine things'. It is foreshadowed even more ominously in Steerforth's remark that 'the sea roars as if it were hungry for us'.

Steerforth is delineated with great pains, and indeed with great success. The measure of his importance can be gauged by the number of mirror-characters who surround him to reflect facets of his personality—Mrs Steerforth, Rosa Dartle, Littimer, and, in the following number, Miss Mowcher. Even Mrs Gummidge is pressed into this service, for in a scene which, alas, was removed in proof[1] she succumbs to his undoubted charm and ceases to think of 'the old 'un'. But for all this superficial fascination, there is no difficulty in recognizing, thanks to a score of deft touches, that his feelings are false and his moral responses undependable. The most startling revelation is his reply to David's rhapsody as they leave the barge after interrupting the celebration of Ham's betrothal to Em'ly:

1. Reprinted by John Butt in 'David Copperfield: From Manuscript to Print', *Review of English Studies*, n.s. i (1950), 251.

'A most engaging little Beauty!' said Steerforth, taking my arm. 'Well! It's a quaint place, and they are quaint company, and it's quite a new sensation to mix with them.'

'How fortunate we are, too,' I returned, 'to have arrived to witness their happiness in that intended marriage! I never saw people so happy. How delightful to see it, and to be made the sharers in their honest joy, as we have been!'

'That's rather a chuckle-headed fellow for the girl; isn't he?' said Steerforth.

His final comment—'Daisy, I believe you are in earnest, and are good. I wish we all were!'—is scarcely needed to show what is brewing.

(*Continued overleaf.*)

Number VIII: December 1849

Aiguille and Tanguille Tranguille and Jorker	]	For the Proctors No. Spenlow & Jorkins
Miss Croodledey Miss Croodledy Miss Croodlejeux	|	No. Miss Mowcher.

His first time of getting tipsy.
Description of it exactly.

'A smashing number' was Dickens's comment to Forster on this instalment: 'His first dissipation I hope will be found worthy of attention, as a piece of grotesque truth.' That was written after completing the number on 20 November. Five days earlier he was still in chapter xxiii, turning over in his mind a suitable profession for David. 'I think it is necessary to decide against the special pleader', he wrote: '... I am not sure but that the banking house might do. I will consider it in a walk.' By 17 November he had rejected the banking house 'on account of the confinement: which would stop the story, I foresee. I have taken, for the present at all events, the proctor.'[1] None of this uncertainty is reflected in the summary, which was probably written, therefore, after completing the number. Yet the notes for chapter xxii at least are interesting since they show how consciously Dickens massed his

1. Forster, VI vi.

Chapters xxii–xxiv: completed 20 November 1849

(Personal History and Experience of David Copperfield—N° VIII.)

chapter XXII.

Some old scenes and some new faces.

Steerforth's misgivings] still tending onwards, Miss Mowcher
Em'ly's misgivings]

Ham Martha. The girl already lost.
Omer. haberdasher &c

chapter XXIII.

I corroborate M[r] Dick and choose a profession

Aunt Betsey—Afraid of fire
Proctor's —Doctors Commons
Chambers in Buckingham Street
M[rs] Crupp

Chapter XXIV.

My First Dissipation

Dinner Party
Guests
"A man" &c
Agnes at the Theatre
Amigoarawayso?

---

contrasts. The chapter which opens with Steerforth's misgivings closes with the misgivings of Em'ly as she sees herself mirrored in Martha Endell, 'the girl already lost'.

These two complementary scenes are divided by his most irresistibly and powerfully vulgar sketch, Miss Mowcher. She was undoubtedly to serve with Littimer as an agent of Steerforth's purpose; but before this could be brought about, Mrs Hill, a professional chiropodist and manicurist, recognized herself in this portrait, and instructed her solicitor to protest. Dickens promised that the character should be amended; but he pointed out, in a letter of 21 December,[1] that this could 'only be made in the natural progress and current of the story. Even if the next number were not already in the Press, it would be impossible to be made there, because the character is not introduced, and the course of

1. *Letters*, II 193.

the tale is not at all in that direction'. He kept his promise: the plan for Number X shows him attempting to make amends there —'qy Miss Mowcher? Impossible. Try next time'—and succeeding ('Miss Mowcher. Yes') in Number XI.

In so far as the summaries provided a record of contents of

Number IX: January 1850

No Steerforth this time. Keep him out.

Doctors Commons? Yes

Traddles? Yes

Dora Spenlow? Yes

Uriah Heep? Yes

The Micawbers? Yes

'No Steerforth this time. Keep him out.' With eleven numbers still ahead of him, Dickens presumably reflected that he must not bring the Steerforth–Em'ly theme to a too sudden issue, and also that the reader might well be kept in suspense. Instead of Steerforth, he reviews other possibilities, and accepts them all: old themes and old friends are to be kept in mind, and a new episode, foreseen at least as early as Number V, is now begun, David's subjection to the charms of Dora Spenlow.

For this episode Dickens was drawing once more upon per-

chapters, the detail in this number is surprisingly chosen. A guest at David's party, Markham, is recalled in his manner of speech ('"A man" &c'), as Rosa Dartle is recalled by a mannerism in the previous number plan; but the appearance of Betsey Trotwood's husband and his effect upon her are not recorded.

Chapters xxv–xxvii: completed before 21 December 1849

(Personal History and Experience of David Copperfield—N° IX.)

chapter XXV.
Good and bad Angels.

Start from last point, with Agnes—His good angel. Steerforth,
she tells him, his bad
at Papa's agent's—Mr Waterbrook.
Dinner—Aristocracy—Blood
Tommy Traddles.
Uriah Heep and Agnes—told to David at his chambers
sleeps there.

chapter XXVI.
I fall into captivity.

In love with Dora Spenlow
Miss Murdstone, her duenna
all his love
close with Mrs Crupp

chapter XXVII.
Tommy Traddles.

Traddles engaged
His furnishing
His story
M^r and Mrs Micawber.
all engaged to dine with David

---

sonal recollections. The evidence is contained in a letter written on 15 February 1855 to Mrs Winter, whose maiden name was Maria Beadnell:

> You may have seen in one of my books a faithful reflection of the passion I had for you . . . and may have seen in little bits of 'Dora' touches of your old self sometimes and a grace here and there that may be revived in your little girls, years hence, for the bewilderment of some other young lover—though he will never be as terribly in earnest as I and David Copperfield were. People used to say

to me how pretty all that was, and how fanciful it was, and how elevated it was above the little foolish loves of very young men and women. But they little thought what reason I had to know it was true and nothing more nor less.[1]

But though the account is true, it is not related uncritically, for it is witnessed by the affectionate yet steady eyes of an older observer. 'Some beautiful comic love' is a description of a later scene in the love-making.[2] It is beautiful; but it is also faintly absurd, and the presence of Mrs Crupp at the end of the chapter

Number X: February 1850

---

qy Em'ly to go? No. —Yes.

qy Aunt ruined?—Next time

qy Miss Mowcher? Impossible. Try next time

Littimer? Yes
Steerforth? Yes

First chapter funny

Then on to Em'ly.

Gauntlet to society
"Going out with the tide"

Divide last chapter in two

Mrs Gummidge

The number plan shows Dickens divided between the pursuit of two themes. Should he deal with Em'ly's elopement or with Aunt Betsey's ruin and its effect upon David's prospects? After

1. *Letters*, II 629. 2. Forster, VI vi.

ensures that the absurdity is recognized. '"It was but the gentleman which died here before yourself", said Mrs. Crupp, "that fell in love—with a barmaid—and had his waistcoats took in directly, though much swelled by drinking".' David protests, with justification; yet a reader might pause to reflect that love for 'the real heroine' would not be related in such a context. Agnes, moreover, had already been playing her part of 'the Good Angel' in the first chapter of this number, and was thus placed at the very beginning in some measure of competition with Dora.

Chapters xxviii–xxxi: begun 29 December 1849, proofs corrected before 23 January 1850

(Personal History and Experience of David Copperfield—N° X.)

chapter XXVIII.
Mr Micawber's Gauntlet

Mr & Mrs Micawber
& Traddles

Glimpse of Littimer
Mr Micawbers relieving himself by legal phraseology

Mrs Micawber's projects
Mr Micawber's letter.

Steerforth

chapter XXIX.
I visit Steerforth at his home, again.

Rosa Dartle.
"Never more to touch that passive hand"

chapter XXX.

A loss.

Omer and Joram—lead up.
Barkis is willin

chapter XXXI.

A greater loss.

The candle in the window
Ham comes alone & takes Davy outside
Her letter.

Close with Mrs Gummidge

some hesitation he decided that Em'ly should elope now, and that Aunt Betsey's ruin should be reconsidered next month. If Mrs Hill and her solicitor had not intervened, Miss Mowcher might have had a task to perform in assisting Em'ly's elopement;

but though there could be no place for a reformed Mowcher, there was obviously little hesitation about using both Littimer and Steerforth.

Before proceeding with Em'ly, the first chapter was to be 'funny'; and what more convenient than to take advantage of the opportunity provided in the last chapter of Number IX and stage a dinner, with Traddles and the Micawbers as guests, at which Mr Micawber should throw down his gauntlet to society. But the number is Em'ly's, and the comedy is interrupted by the Em'ly theme in the form of Littimer entering to inquire for his master. Before the chapter is over, Steerforth himself has arrived with the news that Barkis cannot last much longer, thus providing a motive for David to be in Yarmouth at the time of Em'ly's disappearance. Em'ly will disappear in the last chapter; thus room is left in the second to show Rosa Dartle's jealous love and, more important, to present once more the prophetic picture of Steerforth 'fast asleep; lying, easily, with his head upon his arm, as I had often seen him lie at school'.

When the last chapter came to be written, Dickens decided to divide it into two. A chapter must be given to Barkis, 'willin' ' to the end, but 'going out with the tide'; yet even here Em'ly is kept

Number XI: March 1850

M[r] Peggotty to begin his search. ✓
M[rs] Steerforth. qy Yes. And Rosa Dartle

Miss Mowcher. ✓ Yes
The Doctor and his wife. qy. No
Agnes? qy. Only an allusion
Aunt & M[r] Dick Yes
Is engaged to Dora. Yes (Miss Mills)
Tommy Traddles qy

What an idle time! What an unsubstantial, happy, foolish, time! of all the times of mine, that ⟨he⟩ Time has in his grip, there is none that in retrospection I can smile at half so much, and think of half so tenderly!

---

in view. She is seen through Mr Omer's eyes, as pretty as ever, working as well as 'any six', and clinging to her uncle 'tighter and tighter, and closer and closer, every day', but unsettled; and a later scene allows the reader to confirm Mr Omer's judgement from his own observation. This is the preparation for the final chapter in which Peggotty and her brother, Mrs Gummidge and David, are gathered together in the old barge waiting for Em'ly to come home with Ham. The talk turns upon Em'ly and shows Mr Peggotty's unchanged affection for her. The candle will always stand in the window to greet her return, burning as an emblem of unchanging love. Then Ham comes in alone, with a letter which explains what has happened. The light in the last moments of the scene is cast not upon what Em'ly has done, nor upon Steerforth's crime, nor even upon Ham, but upon Mr Peggotty, showing that Em'ly's elopement is to serve as a test of the heart's affections. Anger is expressed; but not shame: what Mr Peggotty is mainly impelled to do is 'to find my poor niece in her shame,'—the shame is hers, not his—'and bring her back'. The heart's affections stand up to the test; the emblematic candle will not cease to burn.

Chapters xxxii–xxxiv: completed 21 February 1850

(Personal History and Experience of David Copperfield—N° XI.)

chapter XXXII.

The beginning of a ⟨pilgrimage⟩ long journey.

chapter XXXIII.

Blissful.

The used-up young friend. Miss Mills—blighted affection. Sings about the echoes in the Caverns of Memory.

chapter XXXIV.

My Aunt astonishes me.

'Mr Peggotty to begin his search': that was the obvious opening for the number following upon Em'ly's loss. The second memorandum determines where the search shall begin, and the third finds the first favourable opportunity of making amends to Mrs Hill. These are the basic materials of the first chapter, but they do little to indicate what its tone and structure were to be. A letter written to Cerjat on 29 December 1849, and a passage in a letter to Miss Coutts written (4 February 1850) during the composition of this number, show the drift of Dickens's thought at this time: to Cerjat he wrote:

> I had previously observed much of what you say about the poor girls. In all you suggest with so much feeling about their return to virtue being cruelly cut off, I concur with a sore heart. I have been turning it over in my mind for some time, and hope, in the history of Little Em'ly (who *must* fall—there is no hope for her), to put it before the thoughts of people in a new and pathetic way, and perhaps to do some good.[1]

A full treatment of the moral and social problem of prostitution would have been beyond the scope of the novel, perhaps even beyond the scope of the novelist, though Dickens, as Miss Coutts's principal adviser on the home for fallen women at Shepherd's Bush, was in an exceptionally favourable position to study the problem. Besides, as he wrote to Miss Coutts,

> the sad subject . . . is difficult to approach, in pages that are intended for readers of all classes and all ages of life; but I have not the least misgiving about being able to bring people gently to its consideration. You will observe that I am endeavouring to turn their thoughts a little that way, in Copperfield.[2]

He was not interested in tracing, as George Eliot was to trace nine years later in *Adam Bede*, how one heedless act of vicious folly could bring disaster upon the community; but he could show how the community regarded the act. Em'ly had become an outcast. There was no question about that. But Dickens, with his mind on the girls of Miss Coutts's Home, was anxious to soften the Victorian reader's heart towards such an outcast. Mr Peggotty's heart had already withstood the test, and the reader is told once more that the emblematic candle 'must be stood in its old pane of glass, that if ever she should see it, it may seem to say "Come back, my child, come back!" ' But what of the other

1. *Letters*, II 194. 2. *Coutts Letters*, p. 165.

characters? Minnie Joram thought Em'ly 'a deceitful, bad-hearted girl. There was no good in her, ever!' Yet when David remonstrated, she 'tossed her head, endeavouring to be very stern and cross; but she could not command her softer self, and began to cry.' 'I was young, to be sure;' is David's comment, 'but I thought much the better of her for this sympathy, and fancied it became her, as a virtuous wife and mother, very well indeed.' As to Mr Omer, he 'had taken it so much to heart . . . that he had been very low and poorly all day, and had gone to bed without his pipe'. By contrast, Mrs Steerforth receives Mr Peggotty in a mood of stern selfishness and uncompromising condemnation. But Mr Peggotty is not downcast, and the words he is given show that Dickens shared that unusual power which Jeffrey had detected in Scott, namely, the power of displaying the noble qualities of humble characters.

Two passages foreshadow future scenes. When David asks Ham on what his thoughts are bent, he replies: 'On what's afore me, Mas'r Davy; and over yon.' 'On the life before you, do you mean?' David asks. 'He had pointed confusedly out to sea. "Ay, Mas'r Davy. I doen't rightly know how 'tis, but from over yon there seemed to me to come—the end of it like." ' Evidently the main incidents in the storm in chapter lv were already clear in Dickens's mind.

The second is a foreshadowing of the melodramatic scene in Number XVI (chapter l) where Rosa Dartle pours her reproaches upon Em'ly's head. The scene seems also to have been planned long in advance, for when Rosa and David part in chapter xxxii, Rosa declares that if ever she could reproach Em'ly with her infamous condition, she would go anywhere to do so.

Amongst the remaining memoranda it is noticeable that though the engagement to Dora is so enthusiastically chosen, Agnes is uppermost in Dickens's thoughts. 'The real heroine' cannot be overlooked, and the reader must keep her in mind, too, if only by 'an allusion'. The 'allusion' comes in the final chapter (which announces Betsey Trotwood's ruin), and is ambiguous. David had written to her announcing his engagement, and remembered

> that I sat resting my head upon my hand, when the letter was half done, cherishing a general fancy as if Agnes were one of the elements of my natural home. As if, in the retirement of the house made almost sacred to me by her presence, Dora and I must be

> happier than anywhere. As if, in love, joy, sorrow, hope, or disappointment; in all emotions; my heart turned naturally there, and found its refuge and best friend.

For what part was Agnes destined when those words were writ-

Number XII: April 1850

Agnes. ⟨Her ⟩ Yes
Dr & Mrs Strong? Yes
Jack Maldon? Yes.
Mr Micawber engaged by Uriah.

Progress of David to a working state, still tinged, romantically, by his youth and character, and overdone. No similar progress on the part of Dora. Poor little Dora, not bred for ⟨the world⟩ a working life
My aunt
⟨Miss Betsey⟩ "And not silly?"

Express that, very delicately

Carry the thread of Agnes through it all

After confirming the use of certain characters,[1] Dickens sets out the theme for the number in an unusually long memorandum. Aunt Betsey's ruin in the last chapter of Number XI pro-

1. The form of the memorandum relating to Jack Maldon seems to imply that the decision to bring him back from India was taken in the moment of planning. Compare the form of memorandum in No. XIV where he is not dissociated from the Strongs.

ten? They seem to look forward to David's later discovery that his love for Dora was the 'mistaken impulse of an undisciplined heart'; yet they are not incompatible with Agnes's rôle as the Georgina Hogarth of David's household.

Chapters xxxv–xxxvii

(Personal History and Experience of David Copperfield—N° XII.)

chapter XXXV.
Depression.

My Aunt.
"and not silly?
"Blind, Blind, Trot!"
Agnes
My Aunt's Property
Mr Wickfield and Uriah. Agnes—Blind, blind, blind

chapter XXXVI.
Enthusiasm.

David's New State. Forest of Difficulty
Glimpse of Rosa Dartle
Bring up Dr Strong and Annie, & Mr Jack Maldon. Mr Dick useful
Mr Micawber "a member of one of the learned professions
I.O.U. Foot on his native heath—Judge or Chancellor. Kettle Drums.
"Walks erect before his
fellow men"

chapter XXXVII
A little cold water.

< > Poor little Dora
"Oh Take me to Julia Mills and go away, please!"
Taking a Guitar case through the Forest of difficulty.
"I used to sit thinking of it of a night, sometimes,
until I felt quite grey

---

vides the motive for David to become self-supporting; but even though his resolve leads to little more than a part-time secretaryship to Dr Strong, what is tonic to David proves dispiriting to Dora, as the conclusion of the number amply shows. The contrast between the two heroines is completed by the part which Agnes is made to play. 'Carry the thread of Agnes through it all' is the direction; and accordingly it is Agnes who makes in the first chapter the only practical suggestion of the secretaryship, and who, in a general way, 'was like Hope embodied, to me':

> she filled my heart with such good resolutions, strengthened my weakness so, by her example, so directed . . . the wandering ardor and unsettled purpose within me, that all the little good I have done, and all the harm I have forborne, I solemnly believe I may refer to her.

The contrast between Agnes's practical support in the first chapter and Dora's impractical weakness in the last is strong enough. But Dickens was not content to leave it so. Agnes and Dora must be placed in even more marked apposition.

> 'Agnes!' I joyfully exclaimed. 'Oh, my dear Agnes, of all people in the world, what a pleasure to see you!'
>
> 'Is it, indeed?' she said, in her cordial voice.
>
> 'I want to talk to you so much!' said I. 'It's such a lightening of my heart, only to look at you! If I had had a conjuror's cap, there is no one I should have wished for but you!'
>
> 'What?' returned Agnes.
>
> 'Well! perhaps Dora, first,' I admitted, with a blush.
>
> 'Certainly, Dora first, I hope,' said Agnes, laughing.
>
> 'But you next!' said I.

The reader does not need exceptionally clear eyes to see that Agnes is 'the real heroine'. And Betsey Trotwood sees it too. She tenderly questions David about his love, makes him reflect whether Dora is not silly or light-headed; and when David protests that he could never love anyone else or cease to love her, Betsey Trotwood can only shake her head and smile gravely, murmuring, 'Ah, Trot! Blind, blind, blind!' At this point Dickens was forced to cut out in proof a sentence which glosses this remark:

> whether her tone of pity [he had written] was for me, or for herself, or for anybody else, I could not decide—did not ask myself, perhaps; but I know that it made me feel uneasy afterwards, and that it sounded in my fancy like a sorrowful strain of music I had sometimes heard at a distance, before that night.

Dickens relies heavily for his pointing upon these musical *motifs*. Betsey Trotwood's observation, which may be read as a comment both upon David's infatuation and upon his inability to recognize where his heart lay, is echoed at the end of the chapter in a passage describing Agnes sitting at the window and speaking to him of Dora:

> Oh, Agnes, sister of my boyhood, if I had known then, what I knew long afterwards!—
>
> There was a beggar in the street, when I went down; and as I turned my head towards the window, thinking of her calm, seraphic eyes, he made me start by muttering, as if he were an echo of the morning:
>
> 'Blind! Blind! Blind!'

This is the most prominent theme, and the minor detail stands in close relationship to it. If indeed Annie Strong represents one who has withstood the first mistaken impulses of an undisciplined heart, she is introduced here because her self-knowledge (supported by a visit to Agnes) contrasts with David's blindness.

The introduction of Uriah Heep and Mr Micawber is not inappropriate in a number dealing with Betsey Trotwood's ruin, even though no direct association is made. Uriah Heep is reported to be increasing his hold upon Mr Wickfield's affairs; and in preparation for Uriah's eventual exposure, Mr Micawber is shown on the eve of departure for Canterbury to take up his post as Uriah's confidential clerk.

(continued overleaf)

Number XIII: May 1850

The Doctor, Annie, and Mr Jack Maldon? No.

Agnes and her father? Yes

Mrs Heep? Yes. Touched

To carry on the thread of Uriah, carefully, and not obtrusively, also of David and Agnes

Mr Spenlow. Dead
Mr Peggotty's story of his search.
Miss Murdstone } qy Not yet
Mr Murdstone }

Traddles Next No

The two principal chapters, xxxviii and xxxix,[1] maintain the balance of Agnes and Dora established in Number XII. Ostensibly they deal with two partnerships, the dissolution of the firm of Spenlow and Jorkins by Mr Spenlow's death in chapter xxxviii, and the effectual subordination in chapter xxxix of Mr Wickfield to Uriah in the partnership of Wickfield and Heep. But the state of these partnerships is, in fact, used to show the

1. It was Dickens's frequent, but not invariable practice, to design his first two chapters of equal length and importance, leaving the final chapter as a short appendix to them. The following distribution of manuscript sheets between chapters may be noted: No. II, 13, 12, 5; IV, 13, 10, 6; V, 12, 10, 5; VI, 13, 10, 5; XI, 12, 11, 6; XII, 13, 10, 5; XIII, 10, 12, 5; XIV, 10, 12, 5; XVII, 12, 14, 4.

Chapters xxxviii–xl

(Personal History and Experience of David Copperfield—N° XIII.)

chapter XXXVIII.
A Dissolution of Partnership.

David found out
Mr Spenlow & Miss Murdstone
Will-making Two Maiden Aunts
Putney
Miss Mills's Journal. "Self and Young Gazelle. J.M."

chapter XXXIX.
Wickfield and Heep.

Touting in Doctors Commons.
Canterbury. Agnes.
Uriah and his mother. Why "Umble"
Mr Wickfield. Agnes.

chapter XL.
The Wanderer

Snowy night.
Martha.—a shadow of it.
Mr Peggotty.
His travels.
Letter from Little Em'ly. Close with him
going away again—through the snow—hushed.

---

effect upon Dora (and therefore upon David) of the dissolution of Spenlow and Jorkins, and the effect upon Agnes (and therefore upon David) of the subordination of Wickfield to Heep.

The memoranda indicate that this pattern, obvious as it now appears, did not immediately occur to Dickens as he set to work. His first impulse was to resume the Strong theme, but this he set aside. He then passed the Wickfields under review, and having accepted this theme for present treatment, he decided upon the nature of the episode and some of its threads. Mr Micawber was also to be used, but so far as planning was concerned, he could evidently be left to look after himself.

The longest and most detailed chapter is placed at the centre of the number. The memoranda for chapter xxxviii are even briefer, consisting of the single entry 'Mr. Spenlow. Dead'. The careful and ingenious balance of Dora and Agnes in these two chapters would therefore seem to have arisen after planning was complete. It was in the act of writing, evidently, that the detail of his diptych was determined: of Agnes, on one side, in whom David felt 'rest and peace', though he 'had perversely wandered

Number XIV: June 1850

David's Marriage to Dora

Back to the Strong incidents, and clear the way

M[r] Dick

Clear Julia Mills off

Bring Agnes and Dora together.

'Have begun *Copperfield* this morning', wrote Dickens on 7 May 1850; 'Still undecided about Dora, but MUST decide to-

away from the voice' of his own heart; of Dora, on the other, incapable of mastering her grief or of affording any support or encouragement.

The short concluding chapter gives an opportunity of keeping Mr Peggotty and Em'ly in mind. By introducing Martha Endell once more, Dickens was providing himself with the means of discovering Em'ly in a future number.

Chapters xli–xliii: begun 7 May 1850

(Personal History and Experience of David Copperfield—N° XIV.)

chapter XLI.
Dora's Aunts.

Traddles & David go to them
Their house at Putney
The old ladies like birds
arranged—Little Dora behind the door
"If I should like a nice Irish Stew for instance.

chapter XLII.
Mischief.

Uriah Heep, jealous of interlopers, works it out, about the Strongs
Old Doctor, generous & good. Agnes & Dora
Slap Uriah's face Dora—suppose—to David
Close chapter with M[rs] Micawber's letter describing change in Micawber

chapter XLIII.
Another Retrospect.

Let me stand aside, and see the phantoms of those
days go by me.
Licence—dressmaker—Agnes, Sophy, church
Peggotty in the gallery Dora Jip
House. Aunt don't live with them
"Are you happy now, you foolish boy?"

---

day.'[1] Neither the number begun nor the decision to be taken is

1. Forster, VI vi.

known for certainty; but unless he had got well ahead of the printer in previous months and had subsequently lost ground, the number must have been the XIVth; and the difficult decision is more likely to have been Dora's death than her marriage to David, which is announced with confidence in the memoranda, a confidence bred by the trend of the narrative in recent numbers. This is the most prominent incident of the number, and it necessarily finds its place in the final chapter. For there was much to be done before the ceremony. There were Dora's aunts to be reconciled to the match, and there was the contrast with Agnes to be maintained. The contrast is carried through by the decision to bring Agnes and Dora together. Not only is the reader intended to see Dora to her disadvantage, but Dora herself is made to recognize it, a recognition which prepares the way for her later recommendation of a second marriage.

Here perhaps is the first effect of the decision to get rid of Dora. But her fate affected not merely the fate of Agnes, but the future development of the novel. Dickens had contrived a number of entanglements: Em'ly has eloped with Steerforth, thus bringing sorrow to her family, and (since Steerforth's intentions are dishonourable) bringing shame and hardship to herself; Annie Strong is entangled in an old love affair, which the stupidity of her mother keeps alive, and which Uriah Heep reveals to Dr Strong in this number; Mr Wickfield and Agnes are entangled in Uriah's web; David is entangled in marriage with Dora, of whose incapacity he is becoming aware. The unravelling of one entanglement will affect the unravelling of the others. Em'ly could become another Martha Endell: Annie could break Dr Strong's heart: Uriah could marry Agnes: Dora could continue to live and make David more and more aware of his mistake. But if one of the solutions were rejected, all would be rejected, since the mood of the novel must be sustained: all shadows must be withdrawn from domestic happiness. Of these solutions one certainly and one probably must be rejected: Uriah, as much as Jonas Chuzzlewit or Carker, is a villain made for unmasking; and an ultimately happy future seems assured for Em'ly at a time when fallen women were being reclaimed at Shepherd's Bush by Miss Coutts or shipped off to a new life in Australia by Mrs Chisholm. If some such reflections as these occurred to Dickens, they would ease his decision to get rid of Dora and determine his interpretation of the story of Dr and Mrs Strong and Jack Maldon. A veil has been drawn in this number between husband and wife, which Mr Dick will remove; and thus the way is cleared for the interpretation, which can scarcely be deferred much longer than Number XV in the interest of David's recognition of his undisciplined heart.

Lastly, Mr Micawber's reserve, evident in Number XIII, has now become so pronounced as to make Mrs Micawber write to David about it. The exposure of Uriah seems imminent.

(*Continued overleaf.*)

Number XV: July 1850

M^r and Mrs Strong. To be adjusted—Mrs Markleham—Mr Jack Maldon

David's Married Life.

qy. M^r and Miss Murdstone? No. consider for next N^o

qy Little Em'ly? And through Martha??

qy My Aunt's persecutor? And any indication of Mr Micawber in communication with her?—No consider for next N^o

Mrs Steerforth and Miss Dartle. Carry Steerforth through by means of them.

The contents of this number were largely dictated by the contents of the last. The reader, impatient to learn something of David's married life with Dora, is provided with ample detail of their housekeeping. 'Carry through incapacity of Dora—but affectionate' is Dickens's direction; he does not add, 'Carry through the contrast with Agnes', though there it is, discreetly maintained:

> 'I wish,' resumed my wife, after a long silence, 'that I could have gone down into the country for a whole year, and lived with Agnes!'
>
> Her hands were clasped upon my shoulder, and her chin rested on them, and her blue eyes looked quietly into mine.

Chapters xliv–xlvi

(Personal History and Experience of David Copperfield. N° XV.)

chapter XLIV.
Our Housekeeping

< > Mary Anne—Paragon
Ordeal of Servants
First quarrel Carry through incapacity of Dora—but affectionate
Salmon. One pound six.

chapter XLV.
Mr Dick fulfils my aunt's prediction.

The Explanation brought round by Mr Dick
Shew the faults of mothers, and their consequences
"No disparity in marriage like unsuitability of mind and purpose"—"Saved from the first mistaken impulse of an undisciplined heart"—"My love was founded on a rock."
all brought to bear on David, and applied by him to himself
old unhappy feeling going
by, upon the wind

chapter XLVI.
Intelligence.

Miss Dartle—< > Garden seat—Prospect
respectable Mr Littimer, and his account of
Em'ly's having left Steerforth, and why
"Don't address yourself to me"—"Nor to me"—
"You have no mother? It is a pity she would have been proud of you
closing prospect, and mist like a rising sea. Next time seen, sea risen.—Then with Mr Peggotty following Martha

---

'Why so?' I asked.

'I think she might have improved me, and I think I might have learned from *her*,' said Dora.

But the memoranda show that Dickens's first consideration was to finish off the Strong sub-plot, which he had left so favourably placed in Number XIV. The entry 'Mr and Mrs Strong. To be adjusted—Mrs Markleham—Mr Jack Maldon' precedes 'David's Married Life', though it seemed proper to describe the housekeeping first. The scene is set in the following chapter for a passionate explanation by Annie Strong, not indeed so passionate as Edith Dombey's, though almost equally obscure. But the bearing of the scene upon the main plot is clear and is epitomized in the summary of chapter xlv, written in all probability after the chapter was completed.

The theme of the remaining chapter was determined after some deliberation. The number plan shows several topics being passed under review and deferred, until finally the Steerforth theme is chosen, the pursuit of Martha being picked up as a conclusion which will conveniently serve to open the next number. The summary may have been written after the chapter was com-

Number XVI: August 1850

Carry through, the unravelling of Uriah Heep. always by Mr Micawber.
Carry through, also, the married life ✓

Dora in declining health. First intimation? Yes.

Little Em'ly and Mr Peggotty. qy. To close the No with her discovery? Yes

qy Omer and Joram? No

qy. Mr and Miss Murdstone? From last Number
No.

qy. My Aunt's Persecutor? From last Number
Yes.

pleted, and one piece of external evidence seems to confirm this. No title had been found for chapter xlvi before the manuscript was sent to press, and the word 'Intelligence' is supplied in proof. But the title stands at the head of the summary in the number plan. If the summary, with the title, had been written before the chapter was composed, it seems unlikely that the title would have been omitted from the manuscript.

Chapters xlvii–l: written during July 1850

(Personal History and Experience of David Copperfield. Nº XVI.)

chapter XLVII.

Martha

Vauxhall Bridge
Oh the river oh the river!
Emily will be the means of her redemption.

My Aunt's husband
"This is my grumpy
frumpy, story Trot."

chapter XLVIII

Domestic.

Dora & David again—Page—transported page
Progress of his mind about his marriage—Tries to "form Dora's mind."
David's mind—old feeling—suppose not married—
Dora's illness begun—Jip growing old Carrying her upstairs

Little Blossom. O what a
fatal name it was, and
how the blossom withered
in its bloom!

chapter XLIX

Mysterious.

Mr Micawber's letter to David—fallen tower
Mrs Micawber's letter to Traddles. Oyster knife at the twins
Mr Micawber contemplating King's Bench
rascal-Heep—Gray's Elegy. Pastoral note.

chapter L.

Mr Peggotty's dream comes true.

Martha takes them to her
old street—about Golden Square
Scene between Emily and Rosa Dartle
"Uncle!"
covers her face with a handkerchief.

While at work on the number Dickens wrote to the Rev. James White (13 July 1850) '... I have carefully planned out the story, for some time past, to the end, and am making out my purposes with great care.'[1] It is difficult to accept the statement without qualification. He had indeed foreseen the implications of Dora's death and much of what is to occur at Yarmouth, but the number plans show that plenty of detail was left to be arranged from month to month. In Number XVI there is ample opportunity for such decisions. Two themes had been specifically deferred from the last number: one, 'Mr. and Miss Murdstone', is deferred yet again; but the other, 'My Aunt's Persecutor', is accepted and dealt with briefly at the end of the first chapter, whose main theme, the pursuit of Martha and through her of Em'ly, had already been determined by the manner in which Number XV was concluded. With this disposed of in the first chapter, the way is open for Em'ly's reappearance, and this also is decided in the memoranda, though without resolving how and where she is to be discovered. A hint had been offered in Number XI of a scene in which Rosa Dartle would load Em'ly with reproaches; yet the entry, 'qy Omer and Joram? No', following directly upon 'Little Em'ly and M[r] Peggotty', suggests that Dickens was contemplating her discovery in Yarmouth, or at least bringing her straight back from London; for it must be remembered that Mr Omer was physically incapable of leaving his shop. In the end he decided to stage the discovery in London and to leave the return to Yarmouth for a future number.

Yet though these points required consideration, the number plans indicate that his attention was primarily occupied with other matters. The 'unravelling of Uriah Heep' is to be 'carried through'—carried, in fact, to a point at which it can be completed in a later number; and in resuming 'the married life', a first intimation is to be given of Dora in declining health.

The unusually large number of corrections in the manuscript provides evidence of the trouble Dickens took in adjusting the melodramatic scene of Em'ly's discovery. Nor was he finally satisfied when he sent the manuscript to the printer, for he found several details to correct in proof. Besides some short additions to Rosa Dartle's part, he altered the timing of Mr Peggotty's arrival. In the manuscript Mr Peggotty arrives in time to hear the last of Rosa Dartle's tirade, and waits till it is over:

1. *Letters*, II 223.

Mr. Peggotty waited until she was gone, as if his duty were too sacred to be discharged in such a presence, and then passed into the room.

This was cancelled in proof and the following short paragraph substituted:

The foot upon the stairs came nearer—nearer—passed her as she went down—rushed into the room!

(*continued overleaf*)

Number XVII: September 1850

Dora to die in this N°? Yes. at the end. "I want to speak to Agnes." alone with her, before dying.

Smash Uriah Heep, by means of Mr Micawber.

Mr Micawber triumphant. restored to Mrs Micawber's arms.

Brought from last N°. Omer & Joram? Yes.

Mr and Miss Murdstone? Not yet.

The planning of this number cannot have caused much difficulty. Em'ly's discovery at the end of the last number demanded that the first chapter be reserved for her story, with a visit to Yarmouth to collect characters for the emigration[1] and to take leave

1. The contemporary reader was not likely to have been surprised by Aunt Betsey's proposal that Em'ly should go to Australia. The British Ladies' Female Emigration Society had held their first annual meeting in April 1850. 'It recognizes that a large emigration is going on', wrote a reporter in *Household Words*, 'and it seeks to provide an agency of moral improvement to the emigrants by establishing homes for the reception of female emigrants before they leave this country'. Under their auspices, as many as six parties of young women left Gravesend for Australia

Chapters li–liii: completed 22 or 23 August 1850

(Personal History and Experience of David Copperfield—N° XVII.)

chapter LI.

The beginning of a longer journey.

Mr Peggotty's narrative

Fever—forgot recently acquired language—"Fisherman's daughter "here's a shell!" / saved by Martha

David & Peggotty go down to Yarmouth

Clear the way for Emigration   Farewell of old boat

Mrs Gummidge

Chapter LII.

I assist at an Explosion.

Uriah Heep's office

Mr Micawber's letter—revelation—Traddles. my Aunt's property.

Mrs Heep "Be umble Ury, and tell all!

Emigration proposed by my Aunt

restoration of mutual confidence between M^r & Mrs Micawber.

Chapter LIII.   Australia.

Another Retrospect.

Three times—White line before each [?]

Speaks of herself as past.

Jip grown old. The chinese House before the fire. David looking at him

Present little Dora's death, through Jip's Death. David sees him lie down on the rug, and die—Agnes comes down—all over—

---

of Omer and Joram. The form of the first memorandum suggests

during the summer. It appears that many of them were redeemed prostitutes. One party, whose departure was reported in *Household Words* on 26 June, was described as consisting 'almost entirely of needlewomen, and most of them have been inmates of the "Home", and have received certificates of good conduct while domiciled there'. A 'Family Colonization Loan Society' was inaugurated during the summer by Mrs Caroline Chisholm for the purpose of lending money without interest to these emigrants, and it was in support of this Society that Dickens wrote an article, 'A Bundle of Emigrants' Letters' for the first number of *Household Words* (30 Mar. 1850): money is well spent, he declared, 'in sending a steady succession of people of all laborious classes . . . from the places where they are not wanted, and are miserable, to places where they are wanted, and can be happy and independent'.

a doubt whether Dora's death should be deferred, but the doubt must soon have been settled by the reflection that a decent interval must elapse between her death and David's marriage to Agnes in the last number. Her death determined, the most suitable position for it was the last chapter (liii), thus leaving the central chapter to be filled. But Dickens was already pledged by Mr Micawber's last letter in chapter xlix to unveil Uriah Heep at

Number XVIII: October 1850

To finish from last N°—Uriah
To bring up—M^r^ and Miss Murdstone? No. last No.
The Emigration N° = Mr Peggotty, Mrs Gummidge, Em'ly, Martha } Mr Micawber, Mrs Micawber, The children }

Agnes. Carry through.
Ham and Steerforth. Steerforth in a sinking ship in a great storm in Yarmouth Roads. Ham goes off in a life boat,—or with a rope round his waist?—through the surf. Both bodies washed ashore together? No.
a mighty wind.

To remember—the last parting—"he was lying easily with his head upon his arm".

Mrs Micawber—Her "family" and "never will desert Mr Micawber".

Close with David going on a tour abroad.

(Lapse between this N° and the next)

the earliest possible moment. The appointment for David to meet Mr Micawber was for 'this day week' and therefore could scarcely be deferred until Number XVIII. But there was no need to consider deferment, since the exposure of cunning by Micawber and Traddles, those two innocents in the ways of the world, makes a contrast of mood with the chapters before and after it such as Dickens loves to provide.

Chapters liv–lvii: finished between 17 and 22 September 1850

(Personal History and Experience of David Copperfield—N° XVIII.)

chapter LIV.
Mr Micawber's Transactions

Mr & Mrs Micawber
Her family.
Uriah Heep's business finished
Mr Micawber arrested—over and over again
My Aunt's money recovered. She composed.
Her husband. "He is gone, Trot. God forgive us all!

chapter LV.
Tempest.

David goes down to Yarmouth with letter from Emily to Ham
The storm
The wind—The spray—the coming to the sea
The town—Flying sand, seaweed—and flakes of foam seen in blotches.
Wreck. Bell at Broadstairs here, last night. Flying
Boat, blown down
I saw him lying with his head upon his arm, as I had often seen him lie at school.

chapter LVI.
Two chapters here. The New wound and the old

Home to Mrs Steerforth & Rosa Dartle.
"I loved him better than you ever did! I loved him better than you ever did!" Mother, a mere statue

chapter LVII.
The Emigrants.

The Micawbers. Preparation and Nauticality

arrested again
her family
Tween Decks
close with Emily & her uncle

Hungerford
Sunset

The number plan shows two small items to be disposed of before attention could be given to the principal episode, signalized by the entry 'The Emigration N°'. Finishing off Uriah, recovering Aunt Betsey's money, settling the Micawbers' affairs, and disposing of Aunt Betsey's husband provided enough business for a chapter, which as a chapter of mere business is suitably placed first. The emigration itself must conclude the number. Thus the central chapter is left for the disposal of Steerforth in the great storm for which preparations were made in the first number of all. But an additional chapter was then required, to provide for David's breaking the news to Mrs Steerforth and Rosa Dartle.

No scene in the book was given such careful preparation as the storm scene. The number plan shows the outline of events being sketched on the left-hand side, with a separate memorandum for the detail so frequently anticipated: 'To remember—the last parting—"he was lying easily with his head upon his arm".' Dickens then seems to have turned to the right-hand side to make a note of subordinate details, drawing for them upon a storm which conveniently rose 'at Broadstairs here, last night'.[1] The labour involved in writing this scene is conveyed in a letter to Forster of 15 September: 'I have been tremendously at work these two days', he writes; 'eight hours at a stretch yesterday, and six hours and a half to-day, with the Ham and Steerforth chapter, which has completely knocked me over'.[2] Two days later he told Wills that the 'most powerful effect in all the Story [is still] on the Anvil'.[3] Thus the writing of this chapter occupied at least four days.

Proofs showed that the number would end high on the thirty-second page. Honest dealing with the reader demanded that he should get full measure for his shilling, and the page must therefore be completed. Additions could be made most conveniently in the last chapter where they would cause least disturbance of type. Accordingly no more than one adjustment is made in the earlier chapters (the omission of a macabre detail at the end of the third paragraph of chapter lvi),[4] and the space is devoted to embellishing the last moments of the Micawbers.

1. *The Times* weather reports for 10–20 Sept. record no storms during this period.

2. Forster, VI vii. 3. *Letters*, II 234.

4. Steerforth's body has been covered with a flag—'While I tried to consider what it would be best to do, the wind plucked at the flag, as if it were eager to get underneath and see its work.'

The number ends, as is indicated in the summary, with a last sight of Em'ly and her uncle;

> surrounded by the rosy light, and standing high upon the deck, apart together, she clinging to him, and he holding her, they solemnly passed away. The night had fallen on the Kentish hills when we were rowed ashore—and fallen darkly upon me.

This marks an unusual change of intention, for the memorandum reads, 'Close with David going on a tour abroad'. But the calm, symbolic lights of the concluding picture could scarcely be improved, Em'ly suffused by the rosy expectations of a new life overseas, David returning to the darkness of his widowhood. Second thoughts were best.

(*Continued overleaf.*)

after Lapse—dreamily described—in Italy &c
David to come back from abroad
All his love for Agnes and all her love for him to be worked out

Traddles married, & living in chambers. Himself and his wife putting themselves to all kinds of inconvenience for her sisters

Uriah Heep "a Pet Prisoner"—continually singing hymns and exhorting everybody who visits him—regarded as a model Penitent—but quite true to himself & exactly the same infernal scoundrel as ever.

His Mother, ditto. Never were people so "umble".
No. Change that. Let him profess to be converting her.

Peggotty. Little Em'ly. The Micawbers

David and Agnes married.
Close with ⟨ ⟩ a Retrospect
What Dora said to Agnes, to come out at last.

Order
Absence
Return
Agnes
Interesting Penitents
Agnes
Visitor
Retrospect

To bring up.

Creakle, as a Middlesex Magistrate. remember his son
Mr Mell?
Mr and Miss Murdstone
Janet—Donkeys—Dr & Mrs Strong—Julia Mills

⟨order⟩

Transition state
return home? Murdstones? Agnes?
Agnes 1
Traddles and his wife
Interesting Penitents & Miss Mowcher?
Agnes 2. and marriage

Visitor?
Mrs Steerforth and Rosa?
Last Retrospect

Chapters lviii–lxiv: begun 22 September, completed 22 or 23 October

(Personal History and Experience of David Copperfield—N[os] XIX and XX.)

chapter LVIII.

Absence

His state of mind
Despondency changed by Agnes—Switzerland
Loves her and finds dreamily that he has long loved her.
Too late. For he made her his sister! Her, & her own noble heart

chapter LIX.

Return.

Gray's Inn Coffee House
unpromising appearance of England

Happiness of Traddles married. Hope for him, after all.

Mr Chillip

chapter LX.

Agnes.

Tells of the Murdstones.
Finishes them

My Aunt (1st time)
The old house
Looking out of a window how he had looked out as a boy
Brother and sister Agnes mother

chapter LXI.

I am shewn two interesting Penitents

Middlesex Magistrates Separate System
Uriah Heep & M[r] Littimer

The Beef & the Cocoa. "Hoping you and your families will amend & see your wickedness"!
"Everybody ought to come here"
Mowcher

chapter LXII.

A light shines on my way Agnes—

My Aunt (2nd time) David declares "I have loved you all my life"
"That only I should occupy this vacant place"

chapter LXIII.

A Visit

M[r] Peggotty. Tells of them all. "That's Em'ly"—M[rs] Gummidge
Port Middlebay newspaper. Micawber. D[r] Mell of Colonial Salem House

chapter LXIV.

A last Retrospect.

Wind up. Julia Mills &c.
Traddles a Judge
Close with Agnes.

Though the last number plan is densely covered with memoranda, it does not reveal all that had to be considered at the last stage. David, of course, was 'to come back from abroad' and 'All his love for Agnes and all her love for him' were still 'to be worked out'; the remaining characters, or the most important of them, were also to be paraded, as in the last scene of a pantomime, to make their final bow; but the stages of deliberation by which the final decisions were reached can only be inferred. The prominence given to Traddles in the memoranda is borne out by his prominence in the text; but though he seems at first to have been given the second chapter, at a subsequent stage (shown at the foot of the memoranda) he was evidently demoted to fourth place before being restored to his original position, where the description of his domestic happiness lends a more hopeful colour to David's prospects on his return.

It appears to have been only at the second stage of deliberation that more than one scene with Agnes was planned. The first stage seems to have envisaged a single episode, perhaps in the penultimate chapter, leading up to the marriage, followed by a final chapter of retrospect in which 'What Dora said to Agnes [was] to come out at last'. But if this inference is correct, the single episode was abandoned in favour of a more gradual process. Two visits to Agnes were then planned, and these two visits were to be separated by two other episodes. Perhaps it was felt that too much intervened between the visits, and in a revised order, enclosed within a box on the plan, this was remedied. It is the second of these visits which leads to the marriage and, eventually, to the revelation of Dora's last words.

Thus the memoranda appear to reveal three stages of deliberation, the essential difference between the second and third being a reduction in what intervenes between the two visits to Agnes and between the second visit and the last retrospect. But it was already decided at the second stage that these three main scenes should be interrupted by principal characters taking their final bow. Uriah Heep and his mother, Peggotty (but surely *Mr* Peggotty is intended), Em'ly, and the Micawbers stand out prominently in the number plan and are awarded two chapters; but several others are canvassed, and only the Dover donkeys fail to appear.

Uriah Heep owes his appearance in a Model Gaol to Dickens's

recollection of an article called 'Pet Prisoners',[1] which he had written for *Household Words*, 27 April 1850, censuring the system of separate confinement at Pentonville and the lavish feeding of the prisoners. The memoranda show that, by the time he had reached the second stage of deliberation, he had resolved to send Littimer there to join Uriah—after being captured by Miss Mowcher—and to put Mr Creakle in charge of them. This irrelevant excursus into sociology recalls an earlier manner, that of the disciple of Smollett.[2] But in spite of this, it affords a racy and economical disposal of four characters.

Although 'Visitor' is qualified with a query on its second entry in the memoranda, the form in which Mr Peggotty, Little Em'ly, and the Micawbers could be recalled admitted little scope for choice. A visit from so important a character as Mr Peggotty was more suitable than a letter, and by this stage he was committed to bearing news of Mr Micawber making good. However improbable this may seem, the tide of the novel was flowing too strongly in favour of retrieving past errors. The venial errors of David and Annie Strong can be retrieved in England; Australia is the place where more serious offenders and social misfits make good. Once the Micawbers are safe on the emigrant ship in Number XVIII, their fate is sealed.

There remain amongst the major characters Mrs Steerforth, Rosa, and the Murdstones. It appears that Mrs Steerforth and Rosa were at one time considered for a prominent position; but in the process of condensation which occurred after the second stage of deliberation, they were allotted a more modest place in the last retrospect. The Murdstones had been kept waiting in the wings since Number XIII, and even at the end their fate is to remain off stage. But just as Mr Creakle is economically recalled to present Uriah Heep and Littimer, so Mr Chillip, an even more remote acquaintance, is recalled to report that a second Mrs Murdstone is suffering like the first at the hands of her husband and his sister. The characters are thus presented at different distances in the final parade.

On 21 October 1850 Dickens reported to Forster that he was

1. Suggested, perhaps, by one of Carlyle's *Latter-Day Pamphlets*, 'Model Prisons', published in Mar. 1850.
2. See below, p. 178.

'within three pages of the shore'.[1] Two days later the novel was completed, and the last chapter, the preface, and a page of errata were sent off to Evans for printing.

1. Forster, VI vii.

CHAPTER VII

The Topicality of *Bleak House*

I

NONE of Dickens's novels is innocent of topical appeal. His naturally keen eyes were sharpened by a journalist's training to render his account of contemporary men and manners, and his sympathies were trained in the same school to detect social abuses. In the early novels he followed the practice of his master Smollett and kept shifting his scene to permit the light to play on a wide diversity of experiences. Thus in the first number of *Nicholas Nickleby* we are prepared, by meeting Squeers, for a visit to Dotheboys Hall; but we have already attended a public meeting held 'to take into consideration the propriety of petitioning Parliament in favour of the United Metropolitan Improved Hot Muffin and Crumpet Baking and Punctual Delivery Company'; and later in the novel we are to learn what life is like in a strolling players' troupe. There is no connexion between Squeers's slum and Crummles's more genial slum except that Nicholas Nickleby lives for a time in each—the Company Meeting he did not even attend—and there might have been even greater diversity of scene, if Dickens had acted upon an impulse, after a visit to Manchester, of striking a blow for the cotton-mill operatives.[1]

1. Dickens wrote to Edward Fitzgerald on 29 Dec. 1838: 'I went, some weeks ago, to Manchester, and saw the *worst* cotton mill. And then I saw the *best*. *Ex uno disce omnes*. . . So far as seeing goes, I have seen enough for my purpose, and what I have seen has disgusted and astonished me beyond all measure. I mean to strike the heaviest blow in my power for these unfortunate creatures, but whether I shall do so in the *Nickleby* or wait some other opportunity I have not yet determined' (E. Hodder, *Life and Work of the Seventh Earl of Shaftesbury*, ed. of 1888, p. 120). At the time of writing this letter, he had just completed No. X (chs. xxx–xxxiii), in which

This discursiveness of incident is gradually controlled in later novels, but it is not until the eighteen-fifties that a unifying principle can be detected in these heterogeneous topicalities. As late as *David Copperfield* such unrelated topics of contemporary discussion as model prisons, the redemption of prostitutes, and the treatment of lunatics, can be discovered cheek by jowl. But in the next novel, *Bleak House*, a great and largely successful effort was made to integrate the diversity of detail into a single view of society. The 'Condition-of-England question' was perfectly familiar. It was Carlyle who had raised it as long ago as 1839 in his *Chartism*, and he had recently presented another formulation of it in *Latter-Day Pamphlets*:

> The deranged condition of our affairs is a universal topic among men at present; and the heavy miseries pressing, in their rudest shape, on the great dumb inarticulate class, and from this, by a sure law, spreading upwards, in a less palpable but not less certain and perhaps still more fatal shape on all classes to the very highest, are admitted everywhere to be great, increasing and now almost unendurable.[1]

Carlyle goes on to define two attitudes currently adopted, one being to admit the miseries and pronounce them to be incurable except by Heaven, the other being to alleviate the evil by charities, 'to cure a world's woes by rose-water':

> A blind loquacious pruriency of indiscriminate Philanthropism substituting itself, with much self-laudation, for the silent divinely awful sense of Right and Wrong;—testifying too clearly that here is no longer a divine sense of Right and Wrong; that, in the smoke of this universal, and alas inevitable and indispensable revolutionary fire, and burning up of worn-out rags of which the world is full, our life-atmosphere has (for the time) become one vile London fog, and the eternal loadstars are gone out for us!

There is no need to ask whether Dickens recalled these particular passages. This in general terms was the diagnosis he accept-

---

Nicholas returns to London, after leaving Crummles's troupe of players, removes his sister from Mrs Wititterly's, and establishes her once more with his mother in Miss La Creevy's apartments. In the following number (chs. xxxiv–xxxvi) he begins life afresh as a clerk in the Cheeryble Brothers' counting-house. The originals of the two Cheerybles are well known to have been Daniel and William Grant of Ramsbottom and Manchester (F. G. Kitton, *Charles Dickens: His Life, Writings, and Personality*, 1902, p. 65). By placing the Cheerybles' business in Lancashire and sending Nicholas to work there, Dickens would have taken a satisfactory stance for striking his 'blow' in *Nickleby*.

1. 'Model Prisons', Mar. 1850.

ed of the troubles of mid-Victorian England; and in *Bleak House* he set himself to translate this diagnosis into the terms of his own art, choosing individual characters and groups of characters to represent 'the great dumb inarticulate class', those who regarded social iniquities as inevitable, and the rose-water philanthropists; finding symbols in the images of fog and fire; and representing by a plot the way the evil spreads upwards till it impinges 'on all classes to the very highest'.

'The great dumb inarticulate class' is represented by Jo the crossing-sweeper, and to a lesser extent by the brickmaker's family. These are the typical inhabitants of Tom-all-Alone's, a typical slum. They are the victims of our social iniquities, and in a different way they are victims of such ineffectual philanthropists as Mr Chadband and Mrs Pardiggle. The class who admit that the country is in a parlous state are represented by Sir Leicester Dedlock and those attending his house parties at Chesney Wold. These Regency survivals are content with their old-established ways—just as the lawyers are content with their antiquated routine—and are scornful of such men as Mr Rouncewell who tackle the problem by providing productive work. Fire will sweep away the confusion of the Law, as Spontaneous Combustion disposed of Lord Chancellor Krook; and Chesney Wold will slowly decay in the persistent rain. But before that happens, its secrets will have been found buried in Tom-all-Alone's, for that is where Lady Dedlock's lover lay and that is where she herself comes to die. Tom-all-Alone's must have its inescapable effect upon society; this is as unavoidable, in the present state of affairs, as the smallpox which Esther catches from Jo. It is not surprising to find that 'Tom-all-Alone's: The Ruined House' was the first title drafted for the novel in the manuscript.

The fable has indeed been frequently interpreted, but what has hitherto been overlooked is the topicality of Dickens's particularization. This was a fable for 1852, related to a large extent in terms of the events, the types, and the social groups which the previous year had thrown into prominence.

II

1851 was the year of the Great Exhibition in Hyde Park. It was also a time of public anxiety caused by the establishment of the Roman Catholic hierarchy in England during the previous twelve months. Dickens was aware of both. As to what Lord John Russell called 'papal aggression', he seems to have followed the Prime Minister's lead in blaming it upon the Puseyites: 'if the Universities', he wrote to Miss Coutts on 22 August 1851, 'had been forced to adjust themselves to the character of the times, we never should have had to bless Oxford for the intolerable enormity it has dug out of the mire'.[1]

The principal representative of the Puseyites in *Bleak House* is Mrs Pardiggle. Her allegiance is not asserted, but it is clearly enough implied, in the names she has given to her sons—Egbert, Oswald, Francis, Felix, and Alfred, the names of saints or heroes of the primitive Church—and in her custom of pressing her young family to attend Matins with her '(very prettily done), at half past six o'clock in the morning all the year round, including of course the depth of winter'. But she is not the only Puseyite in the novel. Other suspects are the ladies who pestered Mr Jarndyce for a subscription 'to establish in a picturesque building (engraving of proposed West Elevation attached) the Sisterhood of Mediæval Marys',[2] and the ladies and gentlemen of the newest fashion assembled at one of Sir Leicester Dedlock's country house parties. Theirs was a 'dandyism' in religion:

> in mere lackadaisical want of an emotion, [they] have agreed upon a little dandy talk about the Vulgar wanting faith in things in general; meaning, in the things that have been tried and found wanting, as though a low fellow should unaccountably lose faith in a bad shilling, after finding it out! Who would make the Vulgar very picturesque and faithful, by putting back the hands upon the Clock of Time, and cancelling a few hundred years of history.[3]

Bearing in mind the terms of his letter to Miss Coutts, we must attribute this attack upon the Oxford Movement in 1852 to Dickens's disgust at the establishment of the Roman Catholic hierarchy in England in 1850. The Puseyites were to blame for this 'intolerable enormity'.

No one in 1851 could escape being aware of the Great Exhibition, least of all the editor of a weekly journal. But readers of *Household Words* could not complain of being satiated with

1. *Coutts Letters*, p. 186.

2. *Bleak House*, ch. viii. The first Anglican Sisterhoods had been founded in the eighteen-forties. Miss Sellon's Sisterhood of Mercy at Devonport had been in the news in 1849 owing to an inquiry conducted by the Bishop of Exeter. See H. P. Liddon, *Life of Pusey*, III (1894), ch. viii.

3. *Bleak House*, ch. xii.

description and comment. The third in a series of articles by Charles Knight on 'Three May Days in London' was devoted to the Great Exhibition, and William Howitt was allowed to describe a 'pilgrimage' to Hyde Park; but when his wife offered an article on the May Festival at Starnberg, Dickens wrote impatiently to Wills (10 August 1851):

> In the May Festival of Miss [sic] Howitt (very good) for the Lord's love don't let us have any allusion to the Great Exhibition.[1]

This is what earlier letters might have led us to expect. He is 'used up' by the Exhibition, he tells Mrs Watson on 11 July:

> I don't say "there is nothing in it"—there's too much. I have only been twice; so many things bewildered me. I have a natural horror of sights, and the fusion of so many sights in one has not decreased it;[2]

and he left Miss Coutts to take the children. In fact, he had always had 'an instinctive feeling against the Exhibition', so Wills was told on 27 July, 'of a faint, inexplicable sort'.[3] Some explanation of this feeling, however, may be found in an article, which he wrote for *Household Words* (published 4 January 1851), entitled 'The Last Words of the Old Year'. The Old Year lies dying; on his death bed he surveys his life, and makes his bequests to his successor. It is a melancholy retrospect. '"I have been," said the good old gentleman, penitently, "a Year of Ruin".' Farmers have been blighted, and the land destroyed; many valuable and dear lives have been sacrificed, in steamboats, 'because of the want of commonest and easiest precautions for the prevention of those legal murders'; forty-five persons in every hundred are found to be incapable of reading or writing; starving children who stole a loaf out of a baker's shop have been sentenced to be whipped in the House of Correction. '"I have seen," he presently said:

> "a project carried into execution for a great assemblage of the peaceful glories of the world. I have seen a wonderful structure, reared in glass, by the energy and skill of a great natural genius, self-improved: worthy descendant of my Saxon ancestors: worthy type of ingenuity triumphant! Which of my children shall behold

1. *Letters*, II 336. To complete the tally, mention must be made of two articles by Henry Morley, one on the future of the Crystal Palace (19 July) and one on the Catalogue of the Exhibition (23 Aug.) which was reviewed by Dickens, and one by Horne contrasting the Great Exhibition with the Little (Chinese) Exhibition beside it.
2. Ibid., II 327. 3. Ibid., II 333.

the Princes, Prelates, Nobles, Merchants, of England, equally united, for another Exhibition—for a great display of England's sins and negligences, to be, by steady contemplation of all eyes, and steady union of all hearts and hands, set right?" '

The Great Exhibition, he seems to infer, may encourage, rather than temper, the mood of self-satisfaction, which the mechanical achievements of the age have aroused. In a novel where the life of England in 1851 is otherwise fully represented, the Great Exhibition is deliberately, even conspicuously, excluded.

III

At the end of his survey the Old Year makes some bequests. Not all of them are relevant to this discussion, but a note of prophecy may be easily detected in the following:

"I bequeath to my successor . . . a vast inheritance of degradation and neglect in England; and I charge him, if he be wise, to get speedily through it . . . I do give and bequeath to him, likewise, . . . the Court of Chancery. The less he leaves of it to his successor, the better for mankind."

The centre of *Bleak House* is the great chancery case of Jarndyce and Jarndyce. Dickens himself had suffered from chancery proceedings in 1844, when he had attempted to stop publication of a plagiarism of *A Christmas Carol*, and had ultimately dropped a chancery suit against the bankrupt pirates. More recently he had published two papers, entitled 'The Martyrs in Chancery', in *Household Words*.[1] Those papers show that he was aware of the injustices of chancery as early as 7 December 1850, when the first of them was published; but they do not foreshadow the treatment of chancery in *Bleak House*. There he complains of intolerable delays and legal obfuscation: the articles revert to a theme which he himself had already touched in *Pickwick Papers*, chapters xli and xliii, and deal with the cases of men who have languished in prison over long periods of years, because as executors they had failed to defend a suit in which another party was interested, or to hand over property of which they were never in possession. His theme in the *Pickwick* chapters, and his contributor's theme in the *Household Words* articles, is long-term imprison-

1. The *Household Words* contributors' book shows that the author, A. Cole, was assisted in the second article by Dickens's assistant editor, W. H. Wills.

ment.[1] It is possible to see how that might have turned his mind to the theme of *Little Dorrit* or of *A Tale of Two Cities*, but scarcely to the theme of *Bleak House*.

What had directed Dickens's attention to the Court of Chancery in 1851 was the interest which everyone was taking in chancery that year. The reader of *The Times* who opened his newspaper on 1 January would have noticed a leading article on the subject, in the course of which the writer remarked:

> We believe that the time is rapidly approaching when the public necessities and the public will must triumph over the *inertia* of an antiquated jurisprudence and the obstacles raised by personal or professional interest . . . the community suffers . . . from a confused mass of laws, from costly and dilatory procedure, and from an inadequate number of Judges . . . This opinion has now become so strong and universal in the country that active measures for the reform of the law . . . are becoming the test by which a large proportion of the Liberal party are disposed to try the sincerity and the capacity of their present leaders. We could crowd our columns day after day with the remonstrances which are addressed to ourselves, especially with reference to the present state of the Court of Chancery.

The words are not such as Dickens would have used, but the indictment is Dickens's indictment. The writer points, as Dickens was a few months later to point, to the inertia, the confusion, the costly and dilatory procedure, and (most significantly) to the vested interests impeding reform, 'the obstacles raised by personal or professional interest'.

In *The Times* of 24 December 1850, there had been an even stronger protest, and once again the complaint has a familiar ring:

> If a house be seen in a peculiarly dilapidated condition, the beholder at once exclaims, "Surely that property must be in Chancery;" and the exclamation very correctly expresses the popular

1. In Sept. 1852, Lord Denman, a former Lord Chief Justice, attacked Dickens in a series of articles in the *Standard*, which were reprinted as a pamphlet with the title, *Uncle Tom's Cabin, Bleak House, Slavery and Slave Trade* (1853). Commenting on it in a letter to Lord Denman's daughter, Mrs Cropper, 20 Dec. 1852, Dickens wrote: 'The pamphlet . . . objects that I come in at the Death of Chancery and might have attacked it before.—The most serious and pathetic point I tried with all indignation and intensity to make, *in my first book*, (Pickwick) was the slow torture and death of a Chancery prisoner. From that hour to this, if I have been set on anything, it has been on exhibiting the abuses of the Law.' For the reasons for Lord Denman's attack see *Letters*, II 445 and note.

> opinion as to the effect of legal proceedings generally upon all property which unluckily becomes the subject of litigation in any shape... Success and defeat are alike fatal to litigants.

and again, later in the same article,

> the lingering and expectant suitors waste their lives as well as their substance in vain hopes, and death robs them of their wished-for triumph, if ruin have not already rendered it impossible.

Richard Carstone, Miss Flite, and Gridley, as well as Tom-all-Alone's can there be seen casting their shadows before. Gridley's case is known to have been based upon an actual case in Staffordshire. Forster mentions that a certain Mr Challinor of Leek had sent Dickens a pamphlet setting out its details after the publication of the first monthly number of *Bleak House*, and that Dickens had embodied the facts in a later chapter.[1] Challinor had already drawn attention to the case at a meeting of the Chancery Reform Association on 30 January and *The Times* carried a long report of it the following day. At that meeting a barrister told an anecdote which might have appealed to Conversation Kenge:

> A man young in his profession . . . came to tell his father-in-law that he had at last succeeded in bringing a suit long in dependence to a termination. "You simpleton," said the grave senior; "it was by means of that Chancery suit that I accumulated the money by which I was able to give a portion to my daughter, your wife. If you had known which side your bread was buttered on, you might have made that lawsuit a patrimony for your children's children";

and another barrister reported that in a case where the parties desired to get out at any sacrifice, 20,000 sheets of brief paper would have to be looked over before the estate could be sold.

Thus in December and January alone the columns of *The Times* contain most of the charges in Dickens's indictment of chancery. There was more to come. A new session of Parliament was opened early in February, and in the course of the Queen's speech it was predicted that the administration of justice in the several departments of law and equity would 'doubtless receive serious attention'. The announcement was welcomed; but a week

1. Forster, VII i. The pamphlet was *The Court of Chancery; Its Inherent Defects as Exhibited in Its System of Written Proceedings* . . . By a Solicitor. London. Stevens and Norton, 26, Bell Yard. 1849. Dickens wrote to Challinor on 11 Mar. 1852 sending him a formal 'receipt of his pamphlet and obliging note'. In a letter to Wills of 7 Aug. 1853 Dickens asked for details of the Day case, which had been instituted in Chancery in 1834 and was still incomplete (*Letters*, II 481).

later *The Times* had already heard rumours that legislation might be delayed till the end of the session, although 'the state of the Court of Chancery is an evil . . . of extreme magnitude'. The rumour proved to be correct. Several weeks were consumed in the search for a Prime Minister who would form a government, and when at last Russell was persuaded to resume office he had first to complete the discussion of the Ecclesiastical Titles Bill which the establishment of the Roman Catholic hierarchy had prompted. It was not until the Act had been placed on the statutes at the end of March that Russell was able to propose a measure of chancery reform. At first *The Times* was inclined to welcome any bill which promised to improve existing conditions:

> To the common apprehension of Englishmen the Court of Chancery is a name of terror, a devouring gulf, a den whence no footsteps return. Ask why such a family was ruined, why the representatives of a wealthy man are wanderers over the face of the earth, why the butlers, and housekeepers, and gardeners of the kindest master in the world, in spite of ample legacies in his will, are rotting on parish pay, why the best house in the street is falling to decay, its windows all broken, and its very doors disappearing, why such a one drowned himself, and another is disgraced,—you are just as likely as not to hear that a Chancery suit is at the bottom of it. There is no word so terrible to an Englishman as this. An honest, industrious man . . . will turn pale and sick at heart at the bare mention of Chancery. A suit in that court is endless, bottomless, and insatiable. (28 March.)

But second thoughts were not so favourable. Russell's proposals were discovered to be quite insufficient, and less than a week after its first article *The Times* was remarking that the bill was nothing and would come to nothing. *The Times* was right again, for within a month of introducing his bill, Russell withdrew it in deference to legal criticism in the House of Lords.

A revised bill was not ready until the middle of June at almost the last possible moment before the end of the Parliamentary session. Though the bill was welcomed by Lord Brougham as 'a step—not a great or a long step, but still a step—in the right direction',[1] and though it passed all its readings before Parliament was prorogued in August, criticism was by no means silenced. *The Times*, which was describing the feeling of the public as 'one of angry and restless impatience',[2] permitted itself to adopt a

1. *The Times*, 15 July. 2. Ibid., 4 July.

more sardonic approach to the question. A clever young leader-writer, Robert Lowe,[1] later to become Chancellor of the Exchequer, discovered a chancery suit which had been introduced as long ago as 1815:

> Thirty-six years [he commented] are something in the life of a man, of a nation, of a dynasty, or even of a planet, but in the history of a Chancery suit they are a brief interval . . . a mere decent pause in the slow and stately march by which parties proceed to what, by a fine irony, we are in the habit of calling "equitable relief." When this old suit was new, the counsel who have succeeded to its management were probably babes in arms, and the judge before whom it is heard a truant schoolboy. Since the parties first applied to this dilatory tribunal for the determination of their rights three Monarchs have succeeded to the aged Prince in whose reign it was commenced. . . The occupant of every throne in Europe, and every prominent office in the English church and State, has been changed, but still the inexorable Chancery suit holds on its way, permanent in the midst of never-ending change, the only immutable thing in an era of restless transition. . .

And he continues, in words which bring Richard Carstone to mind:

> It is usual to speak of lawsuits as embittering the lives of those who embark in them; but such an expression does but little justice to the hereditary curse which a suit in equity on the present system hands down to the children who are to inherit it. We leave our suits to our children just as we bequeath to them too often our mental peculiarities and bodily infirmities. The little plaintiffs and defendants grow up for the benefit of Chancery; and she adopts them as naturally as they succeed to us. (14 June.)

Bleak House was not begun until the end of November, though Dickens's letters show that as early as 7 September his 'new book [was] waiting to be born'.[2] By that date, Russell's Chancery Reform Act was a month old; but the public was still critical. Throughout those weeks when the new story was 'whirling through' Dickens's mind,[3] *The Times* kept hammering at the inadequacies of legal education, and at the eminent members of the legal profession who were thwarting legal reform. The opening of

1. *The History of The Times 1841–1884* (London, 1939), II 130.
2. *Letters*, II 341. The first reference to the new novel is even earlier: on 17 Aug. he had written to Miss Coutts, 'I begin to be pondering afar off, a new book' (*Coutts Letters*, p. 184).
3. *Letters*, II 349.

the law courts on 3 November had provided one more occasion for insisting that 'not one whiff of wholesome fresh air has been let into the Court of Chancery and its purlieus'.

Thus Dickens's indictment of chancery was more than merely topical. It followed in almost every respect the charges already levelled in the columns of *The Times*. In both we read of houses in chancery and wards in chancery, of dilatory and costly procedure, of wasted lives, and of legal obstructionists. *The Times*, as befitted a national newspaper, was concerned to report the efforts made in Parliament to procure reform, even while it deplored the delays in Parliament itself. Dickens had no faith in the powers of Parliament to bring any good thing about. He makes no reference to Russell's bills. But the behaviour of Parliament during these months had not escaped him. Some of the most brilliant scenes in the novel display, with evident mockery of Disraeli's manner, a country house party of the governing classes at Chesney Wold. Like their fellow guests the Puseyites, these are Dandies too—'of another fashion, not so new, but very elegant, who have agreed to put a smooth glaze on the world, and to keep down all its realities'. Among them is my Lord Boodle, who 'really does not see to what the present age is tending', who finds that 'the House is not what the House used to be; even a Cabinet is not what it formerly was', and who 'perceives with astonishment, that supposing the present Government to be overthrown, the limited choice of the Crown, in the formation of a new Ministry, would lie between Lord Coodle and Sir Thomas Doodle—supposing it to be impossible for the Duke of Foodle to act with Goodle'.[1]

IV

Lord Boodle was not the only politician to be voicing his discontent with Parliament and Government in 1851. Scarcely had the session opened in February before Russell was defeated and the country was without a government for a fortnight, while first one statesman and then another tried to form an administration. And when a government was formed, it was clearly too weak to last. It is not surprising that Greville should record in his diary that 'there is no respect for, or confidence in, any public men or man' and that 'there is a lack of statesmen who have either

1. *Bleak House*, ch. xii.

capacity to deal with political exigencies, or who possess the confidence and regard of the country'.[1] Throughout this period *The Times* was unsparing in its attacks upon Parliament and Government alike for failing to perform their duties. One leading article in particular has a familiar ring. Lansdowne, Stanley, and Russell, however much they differed in policy, were all 'wonderfully agreed about the very small number of men at all fit, or likely, for power'. Lansdowne in particular 'is so honestly persuaded that orthodox statecraft is vested in a very small clique, that he is convinced it would be a national calamity to let in new hands. His is a wholesome jealousy and depreciation of outsiders. It is the old quarrel between 'the trade' and interlopers, between fully qualified artisans and independent workmen'.

The moral may be taken in the words of Dickens or in the words of *The Times*, for it amounts to the same thing.

> It is an insult [said *The Times*] to a free people and a constitutional State to allege that the faculty of government is confined among us just to a score or two hands. What becomes of all our numerous institutions for self-government . . . if, with all this apparatus of political training, the sacred gift of government, is after all, an heirloom in two or three families? (5 March.)

and Dickens:

> as to some minor topics, there are differences of opinion; but it is perfectly clear to the brilliant and distinguished circle, all round, that nobody is in question but Boodle and his retinue, and Buffy and *his* retinue. These are the great actors for whom the stage is reserved. A People there are, no doubt—a certain large number of supernumeraries, who are to be occasionally addressed, and relied upon for shouts and choruses, as on the theatrical stage; but Boodle and Buffy, their followers and families, their heirs, executors, administrators, and assigns, are the born first-actors, managers, and leaders, and no others can ever appear upon the scene for ever and ever.[2]

Contemporary readers could be trusted with so obvious a reference; and when they reached chapter xl, published in March 1853, where Sir Leicester and his circle comment on the election campaign then in progress, they would readily recall the general election of July 1852, of which Greville considered that the most

1. *Journal of the Reign of Queen Victoria from 1837 to 1852* (London, 1885), III 391, 406.
2. Ch. xii.

deplorable feature was 'the exclusion of so many able and respectable men'.[1]

V

Dickens's indictment of Boodle and Buffy is that they are content to fiddle while Rome is burning: and *The Times* would have agreed. On 5 March it declared that the most serious evil of the political *deadlock* was 'the indefinite postponement or defeat of various measures of great public utility, but yet unconnected with the passions, the prejudices, or the interest of political parties'. A modern reader, recalling the conditions in which the brickmaker and his family lived and the filth of Tom-all-Alone's, might ask whether there could have been any more important 'measure of great public utility' than a bill for cleansing the slums. Thinking people in 1851 were fully aware of these horrors. Dr Simon's report on the Sanitary Condition of the City, presented to the Commissioners of Sewers, was reviewed in *The Times* at great length on 31 December 1850, and 2 January 1851. In that review the reader would have learned

> that the main conditions which constitute the unhealthiness of towns are definite, palpable, removable evils; that dense overcrowding of a population; that intricate ramification of courts and alleys, excluding light and air; that defective drainage; that the products of organic decomposition; that contaminated water and a stinking atmosphere—are distinct causes of disease and death . . . that each is susceptible of abatement or removal, which will at once be followed by diminution of its alleged effects upon the health of the population.

Sanitary reform was not so actively canvassed in the columns of *The Times* as chancery reform; but no careful reader could have overlooked it. He would have been impressed by the resolution with which Lord Shaftesbury was campaigning for better housing conditions; he would have noticed Shaftesbury's description, in *The Times* of 9 April 1851, of the squalor in the cheap lodging houses of London, and very probably he would have approved of the Lodging Houses Bill sponsored on 8 July by Shaftesbury, who pointed out the consequences of overcrowding in the spread of disease and the undermining of morality. He would probably have approved of Shaftesbury's bill, for *The Times* on 6 August

1. Op. cit., III 459.

declared that on sanitary questions there is happily a general measure of agreement. Perhaps it was because of this general agreement that *The Times* was less active in pressing sanitary reform than in pressing chancery reform where there were vested interests to be overcome; but even so, there was no attempt to minimize the ghastly truth. In a leading article written on 4 September, when Dickens was meditating his new book, *The Times* reported as established fact that

> In English towns generally half the attainable period of life is lost to all who are born... This loss of life is in no degree attributable either to the situation, soil, or climate of a locality, or to the density of a population, or to the employments generally prevailing. . . The destroying agent is typhus fever, generated by localized filth and excessive moisture... Bad drainage and immoderate dampness,—that is to say, too little water where it is needed, and too much where it is out of place, are the generating elements.

In illustration of those generating elements of typhus, 'localized filth and excessive moisture', no more is needed than two details in the description of Tom-all-Alone's and the brickmaker's house and garden: 'the stagnant channel of mud which is the main street of Tom-all-Alone's'; and in the earlier chapter of Mrs Pardiggle's visit: 'miserable little gardens . . . growing nothing but stagnant pools. Here and there, an old tub was put to catch the droppings of rain-water from a roof, or they were banked up with mud into a little pond like a large dirt-pie'.

Dickens did not need *The Times* to draw his attention to sanitary reform. The author of *Oliver Twist* knew something of 'the foul and frowsy dens, where vice is closely packed and lacks the room to turn'. This was an old campaign of his to which he proudly alludes in the Preface to a new edition of *Martin Chuzzlewit* in November 1849: 'In all my writings, I hope I have taken every available opportunity of showing the want of sanitary improvements in the neglected dwellings of the poor'. The recognition of his claim may have led to his choice as speaker at the dinners of the Metropolitan Sanitary Association in February 1850 and again in May 1851. At the first of these dinners the Bishop of London, who presided, referred to plans for the clearance of Jacob's Island, the very slum described in *Oliver Twist*, and paid a tribute to Dickens who had first drawn attention to this scandal. But in spite of the general measure of agreement on sanitary matters discerned by *The Times*, it was not everyone who recognized the need. A few days later Alderman Sir Peter Laurie, the Mr Filer of *The Chimes*, told a vestry meeting of the parish of St Marylebone that Jacob's Island existed only in Dickens's imagination. The opportunity was too good to miss; and having occasion to reissue *Oliver Twist* in a cheap edition the following month, Dickens made a sarcastic retort:

> Remembering that when Fielding described Newgate, the prison immediately ceased to exist; that when Smollett took Roderick Random to Bath, that city instantly sank into the earth . . . I was inclined to make this preface the vehicle of my humble tribute of admiration to Sir Peter Laurie. But, I am restrained by a very painful consideration—by no less a consideration than the impossibility of *his* existence. For Sir Peter Laurie having been himself described in a book (as I understand he was, one Christmas time, for his conduct on the seat of Justice), it is but too clear that there CAN be no such man!

The same Preface also bears witness to Dickens's abiding concern for slum clearance:

> I have always been convinced that this Reform must precede all other Social Reforms; that it must prepare the way for Education, even for Religion; and that, without it, those classes of the people which increase the fastest, must become so desperate and be made so miserable, as to bear within themselves the certain seeds of ruin to the whole community.

This shows that his mind was already alive to the wider issues involved. In his speech at the second Metropolitan Sanitary Association dinner he explored the subject further, and in his remarks can be detected some of the interrelated themes of *Bleak House*. The smallpox infection which Charley and Esther catch from Jo is the novelist's way of expressing a truth already perceived by the orator:

> That no man can estimate the amount of mischief grown in dirt, —that no man can say the evil stops here or stops there, either in its moral or physical effects, or can deny that it begins in the cradle and is not at rest in the miserable grave, is as certain as it is that the air from Gin Lane will be carried by an easterly wind into Mayfair, or that the furious pestilence raging in St. Giles's no mortal list of lady patronesses can keep out of Almack's.[1]

1. *The Speeches of Charles Dickens*, ed. R. H. Shepherd (London, 1884), p. 127:

Mrs Pardiggle visiting the brickmaker and Allan Woodcourt succouring the dying Jo are foreshadowed in the following questions:

> Of what avail is it to send missionaries to the miserable man condemned to work in a foetid court, with every sense bestowed upon him for his health and happiness turned into a torment, with every month of his life adding to the heap of evils under which he is condemned to exist? What human sympathy within him is that instructor to address? what natural old chord within him is he to touch? Is it the remembrance of his children?—a memory of destitution, of sickness, of fever, and of scrofula? Is it his hopes, his latent hopes of immortality? He is so surrounded by and embedded in material filth, that his soul cannot rise to the contemplation of the great truths of religion. Or if the case is that of a miserable child bred and nurtured in some noisome, loathsome place, and tempted, in these better days, into the ragged school, what can a few hours' teaching effect against the ever-renewed lesson of a whole existence? But give them a glimpse of heaven through a little of its light and air; give them water; help them to be clean; lighten that heavy atmosphere in which their spirits flag and in which they become the callous things they are; take the body of the dead relative from the close room in which the living live with it, and where death, being familiar, loses its awe; and then they will be brought willingly to hear of Him whose thoughts were so much with the poor, and who had compassion for all human suffering.[1]

It is interesting to note that during the next two years, while *Bleak House* was in the course of publication, Dickens was himself engaged in the preliminaries of slum clearance by advising Miss Coutts on acquiring ground in a suitable locality for building blocks of flats.[2] On 7 January 1853, he paid a visit to Bermondsey to inspect a possible site adjoining Jacob's Island, and sent Miss Coutts a description.[3] It is not unlikely that this visit served to

---

the point had been forcibly made by Carlyle (*Past and Present*, 1843, III 2) when telling the story of a widow refused charity by the Charitable Establishments of Edinburgh:

> The forlorn Irish Widow applies to her fellow-creatures, as if saying, 'Behold I am sinking, bare of help: ye must help me! I am your sister, bone of your bone; one God made us: ye must help me!' They answer, 'No; impossible; thou art no sister of ours.' But she proves her sisterhood; her typhus-fever kills *them*: they actually were her brothers, though denying it! Had human creature ever to go lower for a proof?

1. Ibid., pp. 128–9.
2. Letters of 13 Jan., 16 Mar., 18 Apr. 1852; *Coutts Letters*, pp. 191–200.
3. Ibid., pp. 219–20.

supply his mind with some details in the description of Tom-all-Alone's in *Bleak House*, chapter xlvi, published in Number XIV the following April.

Even without any external evidence showing that Dickens habitually read *The Times*, the internal evidence would be strong enough. Of the five subjects to which *The Times* kept recurring during the months immediately preceding the inception of *Bleak House*, three take a prominent place in the novel, and one of the remaining two is memorably represented. What is of greater significance is that both the policy of the newspaper and its interpretation of facts are represented without much distortion in the novel. Dickens followed *The Times* in deploring the ineffectuality of Parliament, its incapacity for dealing with the important issues of the day; he shared *The Times*'s view that the unhealthiness of the towns was a removable evil, and an evil which must be removed unless the whole community was to suffer; and he agreed with *The Times* in thinking that chancery reform was a crying need, and was being obstructed by certain lawyers who profited from the existing system.

VI

The characters are no less of their time than the action which they support. Mention has already been made of Mrs Pardiggle, the representative of Puseyism. She and her fellow-worker, Mrs Jellyby, are not the only managing females in the novel. There were also Mr Jarndyce's numerous correspondents amongst 'the Women of England, the Daughters of Britain, the Sisters of all the Cardinal Virtues separately, the Females of America, the Ladies of a hundred denominations', all of them consumed with 'rapacious benevolence': 'excellent people, you know', confessed Mr Jarndyce, in a passage removed in proof from chapter viii,

> excellent people, you know, . . . Mrs. Pardiggle and all the rest of 'em. Excellent people! Do a deal of good, and mean to do a good deal more. But they want one pattern out of all varieties of Looms, they *must* be in extremes, they *will* knock in tin tacks with a sledge hammer, they make such a bustle and noise, and they are so confoundedly indefatigable!

One or two of these women make a more extended appearance at Caddy Jellyby's wedding in chapter xxx, notably Miss Wisk, whose mission 'was to show the world that woman's mission was man's mission; and that the only genuine mission, of both man and woman, was to be always moving declaratory resolutions about things in general at public meetings'.

In no other novel does Dickens make so much play with female emancipation and female management, and perhaps in no other novel could he have used these themes so satisfactorily. Every reader of *Bleak House* can see in what directions the energy of these women might more properly have been turned; but the contemporary reader would have recognized their living prototypes. A few might have seen in Mrs Jellyby a representation of Mrs Caroline Chisholm, whose Family Colonization Loan Society, established in May 1850, won Dickens's support, but whose housekeeping and dirty-faced children haunted his dreams;[1] but more readers would have recalled the failure of an expedition in 1841 to abolish the slave trade on the River Niger and to introduce there an improved system of agriculture. Dickens reviewed the published narrative of the expedition in the *Examiner* on 19 August 1848. The expedition appeared to him an exemplary instance of the type of misguided philanthropy associated at that time with Exeter Hall in the Strand:

> It might be laid down as a very good general rule of social and political guidance, that whatever Exeter Hall champions, is the thing by no means to be done. If it were harmless on a cursory view, if it even appeared to have some latent grain of common sense at the bottom of it—which is a very rare ingredient in any of the varieties of gruel that are made thick and slab by the weird old women who go about, and exceedingly roundabout, on the Exeter Hall platform—such advocacy might be held to be a final and fatal objection to it, and to any project capable of origination in the wisdom or folly of man.
>
> The African Expedition . . . is in no respect an exception to the rule. Exeter Hall was hot in its behalf, and it failed. Exeter Hall was hottest on its weakest and most hopeless objects, and in those it failed (of course) most signally.

The Niger expedition succumbed to fever, the few surviving colonists of the model farm were murdered by 'King Boy', and 'King Obi' returned to his profitable trade in slave selling: Borrioboola Gha failed 'in consequence of the King of Borrioboola

1. See 'A Bundle of Emigrants' Letters' in the first issue of *Household Words*, and a letter of 4 Mar. 1850 (*Coutts Letters*, p. 166). See above, p. 166 n.

wanting to sell everybody—who survived the climate—for Rum'. The connexion between the actual and the imagined episodes would have been clear enough, even if Hablôt Browne had not inserted on his cover-design the figure of a woman embracing two black children, and by her side a man who wears a foolscap and carries a sandwich board bearing the legend 'Exeter Hall'.

The moral, as Dickens expressed it in his review, was that 'the work at home must be completed thoroughly, or there is no hope abroad. To your tents, O Israel! but see they are your own tents! Set *them* in order; leave nothing to be done *there*; and outpost will convey your lesson on to outpost, until the naked armies of King Obi and King Boy are reached, and taught'.[1] But Mrs Jellyby did not see her disappointment in that light; we learn that 'she has taken up with the rights of women to sit in Parliament . . . a mission involving more correspondence than the old one'.

The only occasion for surprise is that Mrs Jellyby did not reject the petticoat in favour of the trousers. In the early summer of 1851 *Punch* received the intelligence that an American lady, 'a Mrs Bloomer', had adopted male attire: 'so far so good', was the comment; 'when does the lady begin to shave?' Whether Mrs Bloomer's initiative was followed to any great extent in England is uncertain; but interest was excited, and the pages of *Punch* in the late summer and autumn were stuffed with fantastic prophecy of the 'tremendous accession of physical energy to the ladies if they once get into trousers'. *Punch* foresaw the new garb

1. Lord Denman, in a pamphlet already quoted (p. 183 n.), fell foul of Mrs Jellyby, through whom 'the attempt at commerce and cultivation is to be ridiculed as a wilder absurdity than even the preaching of religion'. In defending himself Dickens restates his moral, but surprisingly and untenably claims that he was 'inventing' the notion of an African expedition: 'Mrs. Jellyby gives offence merely because the word "Africa", is unfortunately associated with her wild Hobby. No kind of reference to Slavery is made or intended, in that connexion. It must be obvious to anyone who reads about her. I have such strong reason to consider, as the best exercise of my faculties of observation can give me, that it is one of the main vices of this time to ride objects to Death through mud and mire, and to have a great deal of talking about them and *not* a great deal of doing—to neglect private duties associated with no particular excitement, for lifeless and soulless public hullabaloo with a great deal of excitement, and thus seriously to damage the objects taken up (often very good in themselves) and not least by associating them with Cant and Humbug in the minds of those reflecting people whose sympathies it is most essential to enlist, before any good thing can be advanced. I *know* this to be doing great harm. But, lest I should unintentionally damage any existing cause, I invent the cause of emigration to Africa. Which no one in reality is advocating. Which no one ever did, that ever I heard of. Which has as much to do, in any conceivable way, with the unhappy Negro Slave as with the Stars.' (Letter to Mrs Cropper, 20 Dec. 1852, in the Free Library, Philadelphia.)

becoming generally adopted; but in the van of the movement was the 'most superior and very strong-minded woman, settling into the forties, and owning to thirty-six . . . full of enthusiasm for "isms", and of scorn for conventionalities', the type of managing female who asserts her equality with the male.[1]

It was not long before Dickens offered his comments. In an article entitled 'Sucking Pigs', published in *Household Words* on 8 November 1851, he showed his strong distaste, not so much for the change of fashion, as for the state of mind implied in the change and for the proselytizing fervour accompanying it. Even if a woman

> chooses to become, of her own free will and liking, a Bloomer, that won't do. She must agitate, agitate. She must take to the little table and water-bottle. She must go in to be a public character. She must work away at a Mission. It is not enough to do right for right's sake. There can be no satisfaction . . . in satisfying her mind after due reflection that the thing she contemplates is right, and therefore ought to be done, and so in calmly and quietly doing it, conscious that therein she sets a righteous example which never can in the nature of things be lost and thrown away.

This article was published a few weeks before the first pages of *Bleak House* were written, and assuredly it expresses the mood in which Mrs Pardiggle, Mrs Jellyby, and their associates were conceived. They did not adopt the bloomer costume, but in all other respects they were enlisted under the banners of Bloomerism. When it came to defining the missions at which they should work, Puseyism lay ready to hand in the year of 'papal aggression' (as the pages of *Punch* bear witness), and though it was three years since he had touched upon the Niger expedition, 'the Nigger question', as Carlyle called it, was still a lively issue, and Exeter Hall with all it stood for was still a powerful force.

VII

Another dateable character is Inspector Bucket, whose identity was soon guessed. The detectives were a recently-formed[2] branch of the Metropolitan Police Force, and Dickens himself

1. *Punch*, XX 220, XXI 168, 192. Mrs Chisholm herself was described by Lord Shaftesbury as having attained 'the highest order of Bloomerism' in that she had 'the heart of a woman, and the understanding of a man.' (XXI 156.)

2. In 1842; see G. Dilnot, *The Story of Scotland Yard* (London, n.d.), p. 207.

had given them ample publicity in *Household Words*. An article of 13 July 1850, on 'The Modern Science of Thief-taking', explained the organization of the branch and described instances of the detective at work; his duty, it may be noted, was 'not only to counteract the machinations of every sort of rascal . . . but to clear up family mysteries, the investigation of which demands the utmost delicacy and tact'. A fortnight later (27 July), an article entitled 'A Detective Police Party' recounted an interview in Dickens's Wellington Street office with Inspectors Wield and Stalker, and was designed to convey 'some faint idea of the extraordinary dexterity, patience, and ingenuity, exercised by the Detective Police'.

Inspector 'Wield' was to become familiar to readers of *Household Words*. In Number 18 (27 July) he is described as 'a middle-aged man of portly presence, with a large, moist, knowing eye, a husky voice, and a habit of emphasizing his conversation by the aid of a corpulent forefinger, which is constantly in juxtaposition with his eyes or nose'. (Mr Bucket also was 'a stoutly-built, steady-looking, sharp-eyed man . . . of about the middle age';[1] and as to his forefinger, 'when Mr Bucket has a matter of this pressing interest under his consideration, the fat forefinger seems to rise to the dignity of a familiar demon. He puts it to his ears, and it whispers information; he puts it to his lips, and it enjoins him to secresy; he rubs it over his nose, and it sharpens his scent; he shakes it before a guilty man, and it charms him to destruction'.)[2] In Number 25 (14 September 1850) his experience was called upon to supply three 'detective' anecdotes, and in Numbers 63 and 64 (7 and 14 June 1851) he appears again, the last time under his proper name of Field, and shows his familiarity with the criminal underworld and his easy jocular intercourse with its inhabitants. It was therefore not an unwarrantable assumption that Bucket, so similar in build and manner and so well acquainted with the warrens of Tom-all-Alone's, was a representation of Field. But when *The Times* on 17 September 1853, reprinted an article from the *Bath Chronicle* ('A Detective in his Vocation'), which credited Dickens with making 'much use of Mr Field's experiences in Inspector Bucket, of the *Bleak House*', and with being 'engaged in writing his life', Dickens issued a denial (20 September): 'Allow me to assure you that, amid all the news in *The Times*, I found nothing more entirely and completely

1. Ch. xxii. 2. Ch. liii.

new to me than these two pieces of intelligence'. Had Pope written this letter, he might have boasted of having equivocated pretty genteelly. Dickens may have had no intention of writing Field's life, and may not have 'availed' himself of Field's 'experiences', even though they extended to clearing up 'family mysteries'; but it seems clear that he saw Bucket as Field, and endowed him with Field's peculiar yet limited sagacity, his energy, his good nature, his mannerisms, and above all with his intimate knowledge of the haunts of vice. Tom-all-Alone's, which Bucket knows so well, is a slum overripe for clearance. A similar association of mind led Dickens to think of Field when Miss Coutts was looking for an appropriate slum to clear; but just as Allan Woodcourt, a doctor, sees the human problem of Tom-all-Alone's more clearly than Bucket, so Southwood Smith's advice was considered more dependable than Field's:

> I am disposed to doubt the efficacy of [Field's] peculiar sort of knowledge and sagacity in this stage of the matter. A locality chosen, I have no doubt that, at a small expence, his assistance in the beginning would be of immense service; or, a locality suggested, that his observations upon it would also be very important—for, if there were a serious objection, he would be certain to know it. But the habits of his mind hardly lead him . . . to the present point before us.
>
> . . . Dr Southwood Smith is the man, of all others, to consult first. His fever-practice has made him, for many years, well acquainted with all the poor parts of London . . . and he knows what work there is in this or that place; and how the people live; and how their tenements are held; and all about them.[1]

VIII

At least two more characters, Mrs Bagnet and Mr Rouncewell, can be shown to have been in the public mind as well as in Dickens's mind in the early eighteen-fifties. A brief note in *Household Words* on 6 September 1851 had drawn attention to the difficult conditions in which soldiers' wives were living. Only five per cent of private soldiers could marry; and if they did, they received no more than 7s. 7d. a week with no married quarters, though a sergeant would be permitted to curtain off a narrow

1. *Coutts Letters*, pp. 191–2. Letter of 13 Jan. 1852, written during the composition of *Bleak House*, No. I.

space from the public dormitory for himself and his wife. The contributor of this note was herself the wife of an officer. In twenty years' experience of her husband's regiment, she could not single out three respectable women, for in such conditions only 'a will strong in virtue can set temptation at naught'. These then were the conditions in which Mrs Bagnet had learned to practise her virtues, conditions which had recently been brought to light in Dickens's own journal.

Mrs Rouncewell's eldest son was a manufacturer whose sturdy independence we are asked to admire. Some trade he needs must practise, but Dickens seems not to have chosen haphazardly in making him an ironmaster. It is possible that he had been reading *The Times* reports of the ironmasters' quarterly meetings at Dudley. Those were difficult days in the iron trade, for the demand for iron was much reduced; but the action of the ironmasters was exemplary, as *The Times* showed in its report on 29 March 1851:

> A reduction of make, or a reduction of wages, [was] suggested, but [either way] the work people must be the sufferers. The ironmasters of South Staffordshire are, and ever have been, particularly anxious not to curtail the employment or reduce the remuneration of their men; to such an extent has this considerate feeling been exhibited that many works have been carried on which, if profit only had entered into the masters' minds would have been closed, for the purpose of giving employment and support to the neighbouring population.

Whether or not this report had caught his eye, Dickens knew the ironmasters and respected them. Having occasion, a year later, to advise Miss Coutts where to send her 'suggestion-paper' on slum clearance and the principles of building a model community, he recommended the 'large ironmasters—of whom there are some notable cases—who have proceeded on the self-supporting principle, and have done wonders with their workpeople'.[1] It seems probable, therefore, that when Dickens was deciding what trade Mr Rouncewell should practise, he recollected the behaviour of a large group of manufacturers which he could wholeheartedly admire.

1. 18 Apr. 1852; *Coutts Letters*, p. 199.

IX

As in *Martin Chuzzlewit*, *Little Dorrit*, and other novels, so in *Bleak House* there are certain indications that Dickens intended to place the action at a greater distance in time. Thus it has been observed that for the details of chancery procedure he was drawing upon his memories of his career as a reporter in the Lord Chancellor's court in the late 'twenties, that the Spanish refugees who were neighbours of Harold Skimpole in Somers Town (chapter xliii) were known to be living there at much the same period;[1] and that Esther wrote the last section of her narrative 'full seven years' after the story was ended.[2] Contemporary readers who were well acquainted with chancery procedure might be trusted to note the discrepancies between chancery as it had been and chancery as it then was; but it is safe to say that the majority would fail to notice them and that Dickens himself can never have intended them to be used in evidence of the date of the action. He was content to draw upon his memory of chancery procedure without reflecting, or perhaps even caring, whether in every respect his knowledge was up to date. Nor are those 'full seven years' to be taken at their face value, for he is repeating once more the device, already used at the end of *Dombey and Son* and *David Copperfield*, of distancing the action of the story in time so as to emphasize the calm of mind which rewards the surviving actors.

More difficult to reconcile is the appearance of the Spanish refugees,[3] and the description (chapter lv) of preparations for the coming of the railways to Lincolnshire, where at the time of the action no railways evidently existed. But neither of these isolated references is enough to counteract the strong flavour of contemporaneity in the action and in the characters. *Bleak House* began as a tract for the times, and the more fully this is recognized, the more fully we shall appreciate the 'esemplastic power' which imposed upon a mass of seemingly heterogeneous material a significant and acceptable form.

1. The Dickens family also was living in Somers Town (No. 13 Johnson Street) from July 1824 till January 1829 (Kitton, op. cit., p. 19 n.)
2. The case is argued by Humphry House in *The Dickens World* (London, 1941), pp. 30–3.
3. Though Dickens could have recalled them from his boyhood recollections of that district of London, it seems possible that his memory was stimulated by reading Carlyle's *Life of Sterling* (1851), where they are described in Part I, ch. ix.

CHAPTER VIII

Hard Times: The Problems of a Weekly Serial

I

HOUSEHOLD WORDS had been running for some eighteen months when *Bleak House* was completed at the end of August 1853. While Dickens was engaged with his book he had no time to write anything for his magazine more substantial than articles; but once the book was out of the way, he could listen to the persuasions of Forster, Bradbury and Evans, and Wills. 'There is such a fixed idea on the part of my printers and copartners in *Household Words*, that a story of me, continued from week to week, would make some unheard of effect with it that I am going to write one'; so he told Miss Coutts on 23 January 1854.[1] The decision had been taken some time earlier, however. On 20 January he sent Forster a list of fourteen titles for 'the *Household Words* story', begging him to look at them 'between this and two o'clock or so, when I will call. It is my usual day, you observe, on which I have jotted them down—Friday! It seems to me that there are three very good ones among them. I should like to know whether you hit upon the same.'[2] Though he had not yet set himself to write, it would seem that he had already discussed the theme of the novel with Forster; for if he had not, he could scarcely have expected Forster to choose between titles for a single story so strictly committing as these: *According to Cocker, Prove it, Stubborn Things, Mr Gradgrind's Facts, The Grindstone, Hard Times, Two and Two are Four, Something Tangible, Our Hard-headed Friend, Rust and Dust, Simple Arithmetic, A Matter of Calculation, A Mere Question of Figures, The Gradgrind Philosophy.*

1. *Letters,* II 537. 2. Ibid.

These rejected titles and those in the manuscript—*Fact, Hard-headed Gradgrind, Hard Heads and Soft Hearts, Heads and Tales, Black and White*—remain of interest, since they seem to indicate the limits within which the book would move. The irony implicit in *Something Tangible, A Matter of Calculation*, and *A Mere Question of Figures* suggests that the novel will open up areas of experience beyond the reach of Mr Gradgrind's philosophy, and the importance of feelings, disregarded by the political economists, is represented in *Hard Heads and Soft Hearts*, while *Heads and Tales* seems to forecast the opposition of fact and fancy so prominent in the scenes at Sleary's Circus troupe. These titles show that the story would appropriately appear in the columns of *Household Words*, whose policy Dickens had defined in an initial address (30 March 1850):

> . . . No mere utilitarian spirit, no iron binding of the mind to grim realities, will give a harsh tone to our *Household Words*. In the bosoms of the young and old, of the well-to-do and of the poor, we would tenderly cherish that light of Fancy which is inherent in the human breast; which, according to its nurture, burns with an inspiring flame, or sinks into a sullen glare, but which (or woe betide that day!) can never be extinguished.

The same day on which he consulted Forster about the title, Dickens sat down to plan the book. On a sheet of paper preserved in the manuscript he wrote first the date and then a memorandum on quantity, which reads as follows:

> One sheet (16 pages of Bleak House) will make 10 pages and a quarter of Household Words. Fifteen pages of my writing, will make a sheet of Bleak House.
>
> A page and a half of my writing, will make a page of Household Words.
>
> The Quantity of the story to be published weekly, being about five pages of Household Words, will require about seven pages and a half of my writing.

and at the head of the first number plan he has, subsequently, written:

> Write and calculate the story in the old monthly N^os^.

These calculations conceal the real difficulty. They amount to saying that one monthly number is the equivalent of four weeklies; but they do not emphasize that the weekly number is now the unit, and that within its brief limits characters must be presented, background sketched, and atmosphere created. A monthly number of thirty-two pages had been a convenient unit for two or three episodes; one or two episodes had now to be related in the equivalent of eight pages. It is no wonder that Dickens found himself hampered. In February he wrote to Forster:

> The difficulty of the space is CRUSHING. Nobody can have an idea of it who has not had an experience of patient fiction-writing with some elbow-room always, and open places in perspective. In this form, with any kind of regard to the current number, there is absolutely no such thing.[1]

The sense of this restriction never left him: 'I am in a dreary state,' he told Wills on 18 April, 'planning and planning the story of *Hard Times* (out of materials for I don't know how long a story)'[2] and in the end he was forced to enlarge his weekly stints to ten pages of his manuscript.[3]

But though the difficulties of the weekly number exasperated him, and though there is reason to suppose that some material was forcibly excluded, there is no doubt that Dickens was able to adapt his manner to the new conditions, and it might be argued that the discipline was good for him. The necessary shortness of the chapters is matched by an economy in detail, noticeable throughout the novel and especially obvious if the opening chapters of *Hard Times* are compared with the opening chapters of *Bleak House*. It is appropriate, no doubt, that the symbolical fog of *Bleak House* should be more leisurely presented than the symbolical fact of *Hard Times*; but it is difficult to believe that in any monthly novel Dickens would have been content with those mere eight but sufficient words which set the scene, 'a plain, bare, monotonous vault of a schoolroom'. The initial description of Mr Gradgrind's square appearance is conveyed in a traditional manner, but it is considerably shorter than the initial descriptions of Sir Leicester Dedlock and Mr Tulkinghorn in *Bleak House*, chapter ii; and more remarkable still, both in economy and in power, is the symbolically contrasting appearance of Sissy Jupe and Bitzer as the sunlight plays upon them:

> whereas the girl was so dark-eyed and dark-haired, that she seemed to receive a deeper and more lustrous color from the sun, when it shone upon her, the boy was so light-eyed and light-haired that the

1. *Letters*, II 543. 2. Ibid., 551. 3. See below, p. 216, n. 2.

> self-same rays appeared to draw out of him what little color he ever possessed. His cold eyes would hardly have been eyes, but for the short ends of lashes which, by bringing them into immediate contrast with something paler than themselves, expressed their form. His short-cropped hair might have been a mere continuation of the sandy freckles on his forehead and face. His skin was so unwholesomely deficient in the natural tinge, that he looked as though, if he were cut, he would bleed white.

It is not merely that Bitzer's body has been deprived by Coketown smoke of the life-giving sun, or that his mind has been repressed by a lifeless education, but that he is emptier and shallower than Sissy; there is no depth to him. The monthly novels are not without comparable moments. The juxtaposition of Miss Flite and the young wards at the end of *Bleak House*, chapter iii, is equally well contrived, she suitably enough at the *bottom* of the steep, broad flight of stairs, they looking down upon her, and her words are equally powerful to suggest more than they say,

> 'Youth. And hope. And beauty. And Chancery. And Conversation Kenge! Ha! Pray accept my blessing!'

This, however, is only a small part of a much larger episode. It lacks the rounded completeness of the scene in *Hard Times*.

But though Dickens recognized how his manner required adapting to weekly presentation, he was also determined to 'write and calculate the story in the old monthly N^os^'. This is shown not only by the memorandum but by the whole appearance of the manuscript. In it the novel is divided into five monthly parts, each separately foliated as his custom was when writing a monthly serial, and each represented by a separate number plan. The first of these makes clear that after deciding what shall happen during the month he arranged this material in chapters before distributing the chapters into weekly issues. He evidently felt the need to see these chapters grouped into units larger than a weekly number, even though the monthly unit could not force itself upon the reader's attention and might not even be apparent to him. These larger monthly units would serve as stages by which to measure the progress made and the distance still to be covered. Thus the opening words of chapter viii, the last of the first monthly 'part'—'Let us strike the key-note again, before pursuing the tune'—seem to indicate that the exposition is completed; and the ending of the second 'part' with Louisa Gradgrind's marriage to Bounderby, the third with Stephen Blackpool leaving Coketown, and the fourth with the breakdown of Louisa's marriage, all mark important stages completed in the development of the story.

Though the reader may appreciate the completion of the stage without observing that a monthly 'part' is completed also, his attention is called to still larger movements in the story by the division of the novel into 'books'. The device had frequently been used since its adoption from the epic by Fielding in *Joseph Andrews*. But Dickens had not hitherto employed it.[1] Perhaps he had taken notice of Thackeray's refinement in *Esmond* (1852) of not merely numbering his books, as the custom was, but of naming them. The second number plan of *Hard Times* shows him considering this device ('republish in 3 books? / 1. Sowing / 2. Reaping / 3. Garnering'). By then it was perhaps too late to adopt it in serial publication: we do not know whether the first weekly issue, without an indication of book number, was already in print when the second monthly 'part' was under consideration. But the notion was kept in mind, and when the novel was reissued in volume form it was divided into books with the titles already determined, the divisions coinciding with what had been the end of the second and fourth monthly 'parts'.

Of earlier novels, only *Dombey and Son* lends itself to a similar division, with well-marked stages reached at the end of Number V (the death of Paul), Number X (Mr Dombey's second marriage), and Number XV (the flight of Florence). But from *Hard Times* onwards each novel, except for *Edwin Drood*, is divided into books even in the serial issues. This is further evidence of the attention which Dickens was now paying to construction. He was quite justified in telling Carlyle that *Hard Times* was 'constructed . . . patiently, with a view to its publication altogether in a compact cheap form'.[2]

II

Dickens's first purpose was to establish the dominion of Fact and of its high priest, Mr Gradgrind. The draft titles show that Mr Gradgrind was to be the representative of a theory. It is therefore appropriate that he should first appear in his own school

1. Except in the serial version of *Oliver Twist*, of which ch. xxii in Part XI is numbered the first of the Second Book. The book-division of this novel was abandoned in the first 'volume' edition. 2. *Letters*, II 567.

impressing his theories upon the rising generation, who will show the effect of his teaching as the story develops.

Although Dickens had settled upon the name, opinions, and perhaps the nature of his principal character before beginning to write, he was still undetermined about his supporters. Mr Gradgrind was to have two children—the first number plan specifies 'Louisa Gradgrind' and 'Young Thomas'—who would doubtless exist to disappoint him in different ways; but whether his wife was still alive was not yet decided. Dickens was evidently tempted to produce another repellent widower with a sister in attendance, as Miss Murdstone had attended upon Mr Murdstone, and Mrs Chick upon Mr Dombey. The number plan shows his purpose settling: 'Mrs. Gradgrind—or Miss? Wife or Sister? Wife.' Having fixed upon that, he turned to consider the remainder of the household: 'Any little Gradgrinds?

Say 3. Adam Smith
Malthus } no parts to play'
Jane

Jane Gradgrind is later to play a small, yet not unimportant, part; and Mrs Gradgrind is to become one more of Dickens's ineffectual mothers, closer in type to Mrs Matthew Pocket in the future than to Mrs Nickleby in the past. Her entry is carefully timed—postponed from chapter iii ('Mrs. Gradgrind—badly done transparency, with not enough light behind it. No not yet') to chapter iv ('Now, Mrs. Gradgrind'). No member of his household could have had less effect upon Mr Gradgrind or upon his children, and that was perhaps the reason that she displaced the sister in Dickens's choice: she serves to emphasize more powerfully than any sister that Mr Gradgrind alone influenced the course of his children's career.

Gradgrind is to be recognized not only in his house and family, but also by the company he keeps. He is seen in school with a representative of the Department of Practical Art, who in his determination to remove flowers from the design of carpets and foreign birds and butterflies from the design of crockery, is as anxious as Gradgrind to submit the imagination to the chains of fact and real circumstance. But the representative of the Department of Practical Art has served a limited purpose by the end of chapter ii, and no more is seen of him.[1]

1. See further K. J. Fielding, 'Charles Dickens and the Department of Practical Art', *Modern Language Review*, xlviii (1953), 270–7.

Much more prominent among Gradgrind's friends is Josiah Bounderby, for whose appearance the reader's expectations are raised at the end of the first weekly number (chapter iii). 'What would Mr. Bounderby say?' cried Mr Gradgrind on finding his elder children peeping through a hole in the circus tent. But Dickens himself had not pronounced the name with equal confidence when meditating his number: "What will Mr. Bound say?" is the version on the number plan (and in the manuscript of chapter iii), subsequently altered to 'Bounder' and finally to 'Bounderby'. Dickens may already have known his man; certainly the very next entry on the number plan shows that he knew what parts he was to play ('Mr. Bounderby, the Bully of humility. Dawn of Bounderby and Louisa'), and in their partnership Gradgrind supplies the ethos of heartless calculation in which Bounderby can oppress the Coketown operatives; but the momentary hesitation over his name shows that Bounderby was not so prominent in Dickens's scheme as Gradgrind.

A final entry on the first number plan points to Gradgrind's third associate: 'The man who, being utterly sensual and careless, comes to very much the same thing in the end as the Gradgrind school? Not yet.' This was James Harthouse, who is not introduced until the third month. He is a young man of good family who had found army and diplomatic life a bore, and had now been persuaded by an elder brother in Parliament to 'go in' for statistics, make a place for himself amongst the 'hard Fact fellows', and canvass one of the industrial seats. Finding Coketown as much of a bore as the army and the diplomatic service, he whiles away his time there by attempting to seduce Louisa Bounderby. If Dickens had already foreseen this rôle, it is surprising that he should have contemplated introducing Harthouse in the first month, since he could not perform his function in the plot until Bounderby and Louisa were married. A possible explanation is that Dickens, with his mind on the fable, needed Harthouse as a supporter to Gradgrind; but recognizing that Harthouse could best be employed as a seducer of Louisa, he permitted the requirements of the fable to give place temporarily to the requirements of the plot.

Bounderby also has his supporter. Just as Captain Cuttle is incomplete without Mrs MacStinger and Captain Bunsby, and Mr Toots without the Game Chicken, so Bounderby is incomplete without Mrs Sparsit. The distance he has reached from the humblest origins, born in a ditch and abandoned by his mother, is most readily measured by his now employing as a housekeeper this lady of seemingly the highest family connexions. But Mrs Sparsit's aristocratic connexions are of doubtful authenticity, and so are Bounderby's origins. The reader is left to guess this and merely to suspect that the eminently respectable countrywoman, Mrs Pegler, is betraying a suspiciously maternal interest in a most unlovable mill-owner. Dickens is already preparing the ground for the scene of Bounderby's exposure, or rather of his deflation, for at his first appearance he is seen to have

> a great puffed head and forehead, swelling veins in his temples, and such a strained skin to his face that it seemed to hold his eyes open, and lift his eyebrows up. A man with a pervading appearance on him of being inflated like a balloon, and ready to start.[1]

But though all but the most unsophisticated reader can see that a rich retribution is in store for Bounderby, this assumption of humility on his part and of gentility on Mrs Sparsit's serves a more immediate purpose. Here at the very centre of the dominion of Fact are people indulging in Fancy, a peculiarly repulsive Fancy maybe, but Fancy still. Here, in the punning of one of the rejected titles, is a man proud of his head but flourishing his tale. This apposition of Fact and Fancy is forcibly presented throughout the first three weekly parts. The young Gradgrinds have been brought up on Fact, but when we first meet them they are contriving to satisfy their starved Fancy by peeping through a hole in a circus tent. Coketown too is 'Fact, fact, fact, everywhere in the material aspect of the town; fact, fact, fact, everywhere in the immaterial'; but in an obscure corner of Coketown, Fancy is ensconced in the shape of a circus. The district is so obscure that Mr Gradgrind and Mr Bounderby, like two evil characters in *The Pilgrim's Progress*, do not know where to find it and are forced to enlist the help of the clown's daughter. The circus people are lodged at an inn named, in a suitable frolic of Fancy, the Pegasus's Arms, and are expert in all sorts of fanciful behaviour, in dancing upon rolling casks, standing upon bottles, catching knives and balls, twirling hand-basins, and dancing upon the slack wire and the tight-rope. But for all that they are the salt of the earth:

> there was a remarkable gentleness and childishness about these

1. Ch. iv.

> people, a special inaptitude for any kind of sharp practice, and an untiring readiness to help and pity one another, deserving often of as much respect, and always of as much generous construction, as the every-day virtues of any class of people in the world.

And their leader, Mr Sleary, has a philosophy adapted to the world of Fancy just as Mr Gradgrind's is adapted to the world of Fact:

> 'People must be amuthed, Thquire, thomehow,' continued Sleary, rendered more pursy than ever, by so much talking; 'they can't be alwayth a working, nor yet they can't be alwayth a learning. Make the betht of uth; not the wurtht. I've got my living out of the horthe-riding all my life, I know; but I conthider that I lay down the philothophy of the thubject when I thay to you, Thquire, make the betht of uth: not the wurtht!'[1]

This is the milieu from which Sissy comes to be an inmate of the Gradgrind household, there to be educated in Mr Gradgrind's system. It is some measure of the man's inherent goodness that he receives her as an inmate. He is redeemable, and the course of the novel shows that he will be redeemed by Sissy. He fails to educate her head, but she succeeds in educating his heart.

III

Within a week of setting to work, Dickens had paid a visit to Preston. The Lancashire towns had been suffering from a succession of strikes, and *The Times* had kept its readers fully informed about them by frequent reports, leading articles, and correspondence. The Preston strike, which had begun in the summer, had been especially stubborn. Forster relates that the choice of subject for *Hard Times* made Dickens anxious to observe it at first hand; but he was disappointed, and reported to Forster 'I am afraid I shall not be able to get much here'.[2] If his intention had ever been to introduce a strike into the novel, he changed his mind and recorded his resolution in a letter (21 April) to Mrs Gaskell, who was also at work on an industrial novel and interested in avoiding an overlap:

> I have no intention of striking. The monstrous claims at domination made by a certain class of manufacturers, and the extent to which

1. Ch. vi. 2. *Letters*, II 538.

> the way is made easy for working men to slide down into discontent under such hands, are within my scheme; but I am not going to strike.[1]

If a strike was ever entertained, the decision not to strike must have been taken early. The only position for a strike in the novel as we have it would have been in the second or the third month; a strike could have made no difference to the course of the plot or to the relations of the principal characters; but the number plans never canvass the possibility. They are not even concerned with industrial unrest. 'Mill Pictures' are indeed mentioned, and Bounderby's slander upon the operatives is rehearsed ('Turtle and Venison & a gold spoon. "That's what the Hands want Sir!" —'); but the subject of principal importance here is 'Law of Divorce' and the name of the sufferer, first 'John Prodge?' then in succession 'Stephen? George? old Stephen?' and eventually, the notion of martyrdom winning approval, 'Stephen Blackpool'. Another memorandum keeps Harthouse in mind but still defers his entry ('Man of N° 1?—Not yet'). These are the principal memoranda; the others remind him to 'carry on' Tom, Louisa, and Sissy, the last designated as 'Power of affection'.

The weekly numbers in the second month confirm this impression. Four of the eight chapters, ix, xiv, and the whole of the eighth weekly number, are devoted to the children: Sissy, a mere child in matters of political economy and statistics but uttering such wisdom as is given only to babes and sucklings, and ingratiating herself so effectively with the family that Mr Gradgrind, though disappointed in her development, freely admits that she is 'an affectionate, earnest, good young woman—and—and we must make that do'; Tom selfishly pressing Louisa upon Bounderby; Louisa coldly accepting Bounderby's proposal made through her father, and eliciting from Sissy a look of wonder, pity, sorrow, and doubt.

The remaining four chapters 'open the Law of Divorce', in the words of the number plan.[2] The Matrimonial Causes Act came

1. *Letters*, II 554.

2. The subject was topical. In 1853 a Royal Commission had reported on the Ecclesiastical Courts, one of whose functions was to try divorce petitions before their submission to Parliament, and had recommended transferring their functions to other bodies. A second reading was given in the House of Lords to a Divorce and Matrimonial Causes Bill on 13 June 1854, seven weeks after Dickens's fifth weekly number where the Law of Divorce was 'opened'. In the Debate the Lord Chancellor admitted that Divorce on other grounds than adultery had been suggested in

into force three years after the novel was written, and permitted a husband to obtain a decree in a divorce court on the ground of his wife's adultery. Hitherto a divorce could only be obtained by Act of Parliament, and was therefore so expensive as to lie beyond a poor man's reach: Bounderby in fact reckoned it to cost 'from a thousand to fifteen hundred pound. Perhaps twice the money'. The plight of the poor man is depicted in Stephen's interview with Bounderby and in the two subsequent chapters which illustrate Stephen's married life. It is a plea for greater latitude than the Act of 1857 was to permit. Stephen's wife may have been an adulteress, but more emphasis is laid upon her habitual drunkenness, a condition chosen perhaps because it permits a more harrowing scene of martyrdom to be displayed. As for Bounderby and Mrs Sparsit, they are not merely scandalized by Stephen's wish to be free to marry again, but they point out that the law cannot help such as Stephen is. There is one law for the rich and one for the poor. If Dickens had in mind at this stage to point the contrast between Stephen and Bounderby, he takes no pains to press it upon the reader. Bounderby is not yet married to Louisa, and the time is still far ahead—twenty chapters, in fact—when Bounderby, like Stephen, will feel that he 'mun be ridded o' her', and will take the law into his own hands by returning Louisa to her father. The ironic foreshadowing of an event is characteristic of Dickens's art at this period, but there is no premonition in chapter xi of the power which Bounderby will possess over his wife but which Stephen does not possess, and in chapter iii of Book 3 he offers no reminder of chapter xi of Book 1. A novelist so adept at linking his episodes is unlikely to have overlooked such a favourable opportunity of pointing at least one of the morals in his story. It is more probable that the crushing demands of the weekly serial compelled him to leave it out.

The Law of Divorce is 'opened' in Weekly Number VI (chapters xi and xii). It is not until Weekly Number XI that Dickens approaches the question of industrial unrest. In the first chapter of that number (Book 2, chapter iv) we find the 'hands' assembled to listen to the popular leader, Slackbridge. 'Stephen won't join', adds the number plan, 'and is sent to Coventry'. Here without

---

various quarters, but that he considered that the Bill should be confined to adultery. Lord Redesdale, opposing the Bill, allowed that a divorce could at present be obtained only by the rich, but denied that there was 'the least expression of a desire for a cheap tribunal for granting divorces'. See *Parliamentary Debates*, 3rd ser. cxxxiv (1854), coll. 1–20. The Bill never reached the House of Commons.

doubt Dickens was drawing upon his Preston experiences, for he had attended just such a meeting and had noted the attitude of the strikers as they listened to a delegate from another district. He was inevitably contributing to the knowledge of his south-country readers in describing the scene, and he was also exercising their sympathies for the Lancashire operatives both here and in other scenes where the Coketown landscape is described; but he made little attempt to discuss the problems of industrial unrest. In fact he scarcely went beyond the comments of *The Times* reporter who, in an article of 8 November 1853, found in the Preston operatives 'a certain rough vigour and independence of thought and feeling which one cannot help respecting', and blamed the masters 'for a generally stern and unbending demeanour towards their operatives, which freezes their sympathy, and lays the groundwork for constant suspicion and occasional violent ruptures, like the present'. These characteristics are exhibited in Book 2, chapter v, the second chapter of Weekly Number XI, where Stephen expounds 'the Slackbridge question' (in the words of the number plan) to an unsympathetic Bounderby, who proceeds to discharge him. Stephen's exposition is certainly rough, vigorous, and independent, but it contributes little to the problem and perhaps was not intended to contribute much. Why Stephen was sent to Coventry by his fellows we are not informed—perhaps there was insufficient space to offer a reason; it is enough that he suffers a further degree of martyrdom by first adopting an independent line and then defending it before Bounderby. That is the limited service of this theme; Coketown with its troubles is merely the purgatory in which individuals suffer. After a scene in which Tom Gradgrind projects his robbery of Bounderby's bank and arranges for suspicion to fall upon Stephen, Dickens provides (in the words of the number plan) a 'Morning picture of Stephen going away from Coketown out of the cruel ashes on to the country dust'. So ends the twelfth weekly and the third monthly number, and at that point Stephen and the industrial theme walk out of the novel until Weekly Number XIX.

IV

Meanwhile Dickens was occupied in developing that much-favoured theme, the education of the heart. At the beginning of the third month (Book 2, chapter i), Bounderby has set up house in the country[1] with Louisa, and the stage is set in the number plans for the destruction of this nominal marriage:

Mrs Sparsit's life at the Bank? Yes
Bitzer, Light Porter Yes
Tom's Progress Yes
Louisa's married life—Dawn of knowledge of her immaterial self—Too late Scarcely yet.
Man dropped in N° 1? Yes. Percy Harthouse
Jem
James

Here are the means by which Louisa will return to her father's home at the end of the fourth month (Book 2, chapter xii), and say to him

> 'I do not know that I am sorry, I do not know that I am ashamed, I do not know that I am degraded in my own esteem. All that I know is, your philosophy and your teaching will not save me. Now, father, you have brought me to this. Save me by some other means.'

The movement in the third month is somewhat slow. One weekly number and much of another had to be devoted to Stephen's isolation; but two entries on the number plan suggest some infirmity of purpose ('Lover for Sissy? No. Decide on no love at all / Sissy and Rachael to become acquainted? No.'), and the time to show the 'dawn of knowledge' of Louisa's 'immaterial self' was deemed to be not yet ripe. In the event Dickens did little more during this month than establish Harthouse in a convenient relationship with Tom Gradgrind, and place Mrs Sparsit and Bitzer in a strategic position to watch what is to come.

The stream of action moves rapidly once more in the fourth month and reaches the climax at the end of the sixteenth weekly number without apparent hesitation. We should have suspected

1. In moving Bounderby out into the country, Dickens was doubtless describing what many a millowner was doing at that time. Though he does not specifically condemn the action, it may be assumed that he would disapprove since it would tend to separate the master still farther from his men. But the move to the country is convenient in several other ways: the bank is more readily robbed; Harthouse and Louisa are more clearly isolated; and Tom, the betrayer of the sister who loved him, is more suitably shown (in 2, vii) biting and tearing rosebuds, the emblems of love.

none had it not been for the number plan. The first three entries for the fourth month are confirmatory:

> Tom to rob Bounderby? Yes
> Louisa to be acted on by Harthouse, through Tom? Yes
> Louisa's danger slowly drawn about her. Yes.

Since these plans had already been sketched in the previous month, the entries here can only mean that now was the time to put them into force. But the following entries betray some doubt where else the course of the story might stray during this important month:

> Sissy? No?
> Rachael?
> Bring her with Louisa again? No.
> Stephen?
> No

It is not surprising that Sissy, whose healing powers will prove so valuable, should be passed in review at this point, though reflection must soon have shown that her time was not yet;[1] and to consider at least a passing reference to a now distant Stephen is equally understandable. But that there should ever have been a question of bringing Rachael to Louisa in her distress seems to imply some doubt of the final issue of Louisa's actions which the firm control of the narrative denies. A visit from Rachael before Louisa's flight could only have been distracting, for it is essential that Tom and Harthouse alone have power to direct the course she takes. A visit to Rachael after the flight, or even a chance encounter, could only have delayed the inevitable return to Mr Gradgrind with its decisive effect upon his belief in his system. Though we cannot tell how long these entries were deliberated, their rejection would seem to have been inevitable, and the remaining entries return to the heart of the action:

1. She makes a brief appearance at the end of 2, ix, the scene of Mrs Gradgrind's death. But though we see little of her in that scene, we are made to feel her presence both in the difference which Louisa notices in her sister and in the thought with which the dying Mrs Gradgrind struggles, a thought more effectively presented in the number plan than in the text itself: ' "Mr. Gradgrind must have forgotten some ology. Can't have had them all taught".' Though nothing in Mrs Gradgrind's life became her like the leaving of it, we recognize that the scene really belongs to Sissy.

To shew Louisa, how alike in their creeds, her father and Harthouse are?—How the two heartless things come to the same in the end?

Yes, But almost imperceptibly.

Louisa

"You have brought me to this, father. Now, save me!"

Louisa is therefore to be denied such guidance as Sissy or as Rachael (another fount of affectionate guidance) might have offered in a matter where the heart must decide. Tom had been the subject of all the little tenderness of her life;[1] Harthouse had used Tom to gain her confidence and having gained it had shown that he recognized the emptiness of her marriage. Louisa is to be reduced by degrees to a situation in which she can bear her marriage no longer; she seeks refuge in flight, and returns a broken creature to her father's house. Weekly instalments were desperately short for representing these degrees; and to help us in recognizing them, Dickens offers his readers almost apologetically the image of Mrs Sparsit's staircase:

> Now, Mrs. Sparsit was not a poetical woman; but she took an idea in the nature of an allegorical fancy, into her head. Much watching of Louisa, and much consequent observation of her impenetrable demeanour, which keenly whetted and sharpened Mrs. Sparsit's edge, must have given her as it were a lift, in the way of inspiration. She erected in her mind a mighty Staircase, with a dark pit of shame and ruin at the bottom; and down those stairs, from day to day and hour to hour, she saw Louisa coming.
>
> It became the business of Mrs. Sparsit's life, to look up at her staircase, and to watch Louisa coming down. Sometimes slowly, sometimes quickly, sometimes several steps at one bout, sometimes stopping, never turning back. If she had once turned back, it might have been the death of Mrs. Sparsit in spleen and grief.[2]

Mrs Sparsit, so often likened to a bird of prey, is an appropriate observer of this gradual descent, and the arrangement by which the reader views the relationship of Louisa and Harthouse through her eyes is admirably managed, for while he relishes her misapprehension of it, he is prevented from regarding it as a romance.

Yet there is something ambiguous in the relationship. Louisa is attracted to Harthouse, and in her final confession to her father

1. The words are Louisa's (2, xii). 2. Book 2, ch. x.

she finds herself unable to say whether or not she loves him. Those 'almost imperceptible' steps by which Dickens hoped to show her recognition of the identity of Harthouse's and Gradgrind's creeds are difficult to discover. Were they too jettisoned because the difficulties of space were crushing? The equation of Harthouse with Gradgrind suggested in the number plan is neither clear nor satisfactory.[1] He is closer to Bounderby. Gradgrind is honestly persuaded of the truth of his system, and for him there is hope as the next monthly part will show; but Bounderby and Harthouse merely use the system for their own ends, and for them there is no hope.

V

The fifth month is co-extensive with the third and last book named 'Garnering'. Gradgrind, of whom little has been seen, except in the last chapter, during the two previous months, is now to return to the centre of the action. He was first observed at the beginning of the novel impressing the system upon the rising generation; it is time to see how the system has worked. The reader has been made fully aware of its failure both in Louisa and in Tom, and in that premonitory scene of Mrs Gradgrind's death he has received some hint of another force at work in Stone Lodge during Mr Gradgrind's absence; but it is only in the last chapter of the fourth month (Book 2, chapter xii), when he sees Louisa 'the pride of his heart and the triumph of his system, lying, an insensible heap, at his feet' that Gradgrind himself begins to recognize the failure and its cause. The requirements of the weekly serial[2] ensure that the recognition is both swift and clear. Grad-

1. The best that Dickens offers to convince his readers of the likeness of the two men is a passage at the beginning of the first chapter of this month (2, vii):

> The not being troubled with earnestness was a grand point in his favour, enabling him to take to the hard Fact fellows with as good a grace as if he had been born one of the tribe, and to throw all other tribes overboard, as conscious hypocrites.
>
> 'Whom none of us believe, my dear Mrs. Bounderby, and who do not believe themselves. The only difference between us and the professors of virtue or benevolence, or philanthropy—never mind the name—is, that we know it is all meaningless, and say so; while they know it equally and will never say so.'
>
> Why should she be shocked or warned by this reiteration? It was not so unlike her father's principles, and her early training, that it need startle her. Where was the great difference between the two schools, when each chained her down to material realities, and inspired her with no faith in anything else? What was there in her soul for James Harthouse to destroy, which Thomas Gradgrind had nurtured there in its state of innocence!

2. The demands of the story required additional space for this last monthly num-

grind meets his daughter the morning after her return, and confides to her:

> 'It would be hopeless for me, Louisa, to endeavour to tell you how overwhelmed I have been, and still am, by what broke upon me last night. The ground on which I stand has ceased to be solid under my feet. The only support on which I leaned, and the strength of which it seemed, and still does seem, impossible to question, has given way in an instant. I am stunned by these discoveries. I have no selfish meaning in what I say; but I find the shock of what broke upon me last night, to be very heavy indeed.'

and later in the same chapter:

> 'Louisa, I have a misgiving that some change may have been slowly working about me in this house, by mere love and gratitude: that what the Head has left undone and could not do, the Heart may have been doing silently...'

Of course it had. The reader, who has previously seen what 'the Heart' had done even for Mrs Gradgrind, has already noticed its effect upon Jane Gradgrind, or rather has seen its effect through Louisa's eyes:

> 'What a beaming face you have, Jane!' said Louisa, as her young sister—timidly still—bent down to kiss her.
>
> 'Have I? I am very glad you think so. I am sure it must be Sissy's doing.'

Of course it is; and before the chapter is over, Sissy, the representative of 'the Heart', has begun to exert her influence over Louisa too:

> 'Forgive me, pity me, help me! Have compassion on my great need, and let me lay this head of mine upon a loving heart!'
>
> 'O lay it here!' cried Sissy. 'Lay it here, my dear.'[1]

The remaining chapter of Weekly Number XVII (Book 3, chapter ii) completes the victory of Heart over Head, or at least is so intended. Sissy, like Jack the Giant-killer, goes resolutely forth to dispose of James Harthouse and succeeds in touching him 'in the cavity where his heart should have been'. Both Harthouse and the reader agree that it is 'very ridiculous' that a stroller's

---

ber. Dickens's note at the head of the number plan reads: 'Weekly N^os to be enlarged to 10 of my sides each—about', i.e., an extension of about two and a half sheets of manuscript for each weekly number.

1. Book 3, ch. i.

child should succeed in evicting a parliamentary candidate from his prospective constituency; but that is how things happen in fairy tales, and Dickens could never entirely resist the satisfaction of giving the victory over the forces of evil to the children of light. Another consideration might also have influenced him. If, as he supposed he had made clear, Gradgrind and Harthouse were alike in their creeds, it was appropriate that Sissy, who had penetrated Gradgrind's complacency, should succeed in wounding Harthouse also.

After the scene to which reference has already been made, where Bounderby repudiates his marriage with Louisa, the story returns to the robbery of the bank, and therefore to the suspected Stephen and his reappearance, and to Tom the real culprit.[1] The suspense—'Still no Stephen' is thrice repeated in the number plans—is admirably contrived.[2] It is not merely a question of what can have happened to Stephen. That is perplexing enough when the bills have been posted offering Twenty Pounds reward for the apprehension of a man whom the reader knows to be innocent, and of whose innocence many characters in the story are convinced. But his disappearance has also an important bearing upon Tom. The reader knows him to be guilty, Louisa and Sissy darkly suspect his guilt, but as yet their suspicions are not shared by Mr Gradgrind, who does not therefore recognize what further humiliations may be in store for him.

Stephen's discovery is presented in one of Dickens's most allegorically lurid scenes. His hat is found by Rachael and Sissy at the mouth of an abandoned mineshaft. The faith and hope of

1. The anxiety which Dickens experienced in the composition of these episodes is reflected in a letter to Forster of which, alas, Forster (VII i) transcribed only an extract:

> Tavistock House. Look at that! Boulogne, of course. Friday, 14th of July, 1854. I am three parts mad, and the fourth delirious, with perpetual rushing at *Hard Times*. I have done what I hope is a good thing with Stephen, taking his story as a whole; and hope to be over in town with the end of the book on Wednesday night. . . I have been looking forward through so many weeks and sides of paper to this Stephen business, that now—as usual—it being over, I feel as if nothing in the world, in the way of intense and violent rushing hither and thither, could quite restore my balance.

Weekly No. XIX, in which Stephen is at last found, is endorsed in the number plan 'The great effect'.

2. It may be remarked that the suspense is scarcely interrupted by the capital scene of Mr Bounderby's deflation, for when Mrs Sparsit brings Mrs Pegler into Bounderby's presence she supposes that she has captured a material witness to the robbery and to Stephen's disappearance.

Rachael are insufficient and she gives him up as lost, but Sissy's charity is equal to the situation; she controls Rachael, and fetches help. After several hours, Stephen is brought to the surface, still alive, and makes a dying statement before the large throng which has collected in the torchlight. It seems that he had set out immediately to vindicate his innocence, had taken the nearest cross-country route to Bounderby's villa, and had fallen down Old Hell Shaft, a mine whose foul air had formerly killed many who worked in it:

> 'When it were in work,' [Stephen comments,] 'it killed wi'out need; when 'tis let alone it kills wi'out need. See how we die an' no need, one way an' another—in a muddle—every day!'

He had begun his journey in anger with Louisa and Tom for plotting against him as he thought; but while in Hell a star shone down upon him ('I thowt it were the star as guided to our Saviour's home'), and by its light he saw more clearly and therefore more charitably, making it his dying prayer

> 'that aw th'world may on'y coom toogether more, an' get a better unnerstan'in o' one another, than when I were in 't my own weak seln;'

and commending Mr Gradgrind to clear his name—'Yor son will tell yo how', the martyr dies with the appropriate reflection (picked out in the number plan)

> 'in our judgments, like as in our doins, we mun bear and forbear'.

The utter failure of his system has its physical effect upon Mr Gradgrind, as a similar failure had had upon Mr Dombey: 'aged and bent he looked, and quite bowed down; and yet he looked a wiser man, and a better man, than in the days when in this life he wanted nothing but Facts' (Book 3, chapter vii). But the system does not invariably fail, and almost as appalling as its failure is its success. Tom is to be smuggled abroad through the agency of Sleary and his circus troupe, and all is going well with their plans when Bitzer appears and arrests the culprit. We have now come full circle. In the first weekly number, the reader had seen Bitzer a model pupil returning model answers to Mr Gradgrind's questions; now in the last number Bitzer is 'true to his bringing up', as the number plan remarks, and once more returns model answers to the questions put to him:

> 'Bitzer,' said Mr. Gradgrind, broken down, and miserably submissive to him, 'have you a heart?'
>
> 'The circulation, Sir,' returned Bitzer, smiling at the oddity of the question, 'couldn't be carried on without one. No man, Sir, acquainted with the facts established by Harvey relating to the circulation of the blood, can doubt that I have a heart.'
>
> 'Is it accessible,' cried Mr. Gradgrind, 'to any compassionate influence?'
>
> 'It is accessible to Reason, Sir,' returned the excellent young man. 'And to nothing else.'

In response to a final appeal to the sense of gratitude for schooling received, Bitzer dismisses this 'untenable position' with the comment that his schooling was paid for and the bargain ended when he left. Dickens's point is made; but he cannot leave a dying story like that, and he cannot consent to the further punishment of a reforming character. Besides, Gradgrind in his unreformed days had taken pity upon Sissy and now he is to garner the reward which, by her presence in his house, he had already begun to reap. 'The Thquire thtood by you, Thethilia,' says Sleary, 'and I'll thtand by the Thquire'; Sleary knows a trick worth two of Bitzer's, and Tom escapes.

It is the end, except for that dip into the characters' future with which Dickens always assuages the curiosity of his readers. But before the epilogue is reached, he gives the last word to Mr Sleary, who had had to apologize on a previous occasion for being 'too muth of a Cackler'. The payment which he accepts for services rendered is altogether appropriate. It was a fundamental principle of the Gradgrind philosophy that everything was to be paid for; and Mr Gradgrind pays. Five pounds, it is true, went to Mr Childers, who had assisted Tom's escape; but Childers was a family man, and the money 'mightn't be unactheptable'. Apart from that, the philosopher of Fact 'very willingly undertook' to stand a collar for the dog, 'a thet of bellth for the horthe', brandy and water for Mr Sleary, and 'a little thpread for the company'. After so willingly paying in kind, and agreeing, it would seem, to 'give a Hortheriding, a bethpeak' whenever he could, the exponent of calculable Fact has to listen to a tale about the instinct of the faithful dog Merrylegs, and we can readily accept his giving tacit assent to the moral which Mr Sleary sees in the depths of his brandy and water:

> 'one, that there ith a love in the world, not all Thelf-interetht after

all, but thomething very different; t'other, that it hath a way of ith own of calculating or not calculating, whith thomehow or another ith at leatht ath hard to give a name to, ath the wayth of the dogth ith!'

What remains for this brandy-sodden Fairy Queen to do but to pronounce a benediction and repeat the philosophy of fancy:

'People mutht be amuthed. They can't be alwayth a learning, nor yet they can't be alwayth a working, they an't made for it. You *mutht* have uth, Thquire. Do the withe thing and the kind thing too, and make the betht of uth; not the wurtht!'

CHAPTER IX

From 'Nobody's Fault' to *Little Dorrit*

I

DICKENS completed *Hard Times* in July 1854. By October the familiar symptoms of restlessness which presaged the beginning of a new book were appearing once more:

> visions of living for half a year or so, in all sorts of inaccessible places, and opening a new book therein. A floating idea of going up above the snow-line in Switzerland, and living in some astonishing convent, hovers about me.[1]

Early in February 1855 he was still 'in a dishevelled state of mind,' seeing 'motes of new books in the dirty air';[2] both public and personal life bore hardly upon him—this was the worst phase of the Crimean War, the beginning of his friend Layard's agitation for administrative reform, and also of the reappearance of his old love Maria Beadnell. To her he wrote on 3 April (partly perhaps in the wish to escape from his embarrassing disillusionment with his 'Flora') to say that he was 'going off, I don't know where or how far, to ponder about I don't know what'.[3] A month later, the 'wandering-unsettled-restless uncontrollable state of being about to begin a new book' still persisted; but in a few days his plans were taking shape—Folkestone for the autumn, Paris for the winter—and the form and date of the new book were fixed—'a new, long, twenty-number Green book (publication to

1. *Letters*, II 596. Dickens had visited the St Bernard in 1846 and recalled it when writing Bk 2, chs. i–ii of *Little Dorrit* ten years later (*Letters*, II 803, 828).
2. *Letters*, II 620; 'January' is the editor's conjecture, but comparison with letters of 9 Feb. makes the later date more probable.
3. *Letters*, II 650.

begin in November)'. Its 'first page' was before him, with 'all kinds of notes' and 'a capital name'.[1]

The 'capital name' stands at the head of the early number plans, as *Nobody's Fault*;[2] and this persisted in his mind through at least five months, throughout the writing of the first eleven chapters. He announced it to Mrs Watson on 16 September, but said it would not be made public until the end of October. On 13 October, however, it was advertised as *Little Dorrit.*[3] Why did Dickens choose *Nobody's Fault* as a title, why did he change it, and how is the original title related to the completed novel? Though this work has drawn much critical attention in recent years, no one since Forster has attempted to answer any of these questions.

Forster's explanation is simple, but unsatisfying:

> The book took its origin from the notion he had of a leading man for a story who should bring about all the mischief in it, lay it all on Providence, and say at every fresh calamity, "well, it's a mercy, however, nobody was to blame, you know!"

(a notion evidently related, though the connexion is not made by Forster, to the notebook entry:

> The people who lay all their sins negligences and ignorances, on Providence).[4]

This man, unnamed, makes two brief appearances in the number plans; first in Number II (chapters v–viii):

> The man who comfortably charges everything on Providence? Not yet

and then in Number IV (chapters xii–xiv):

> Charging everything on Providence? No

Even there, he hardly looks like a 'leading man', for by that time most of the main characters have appeared, and he cannot be identified with any of them. The trait might be compatible with

1. *Letters*, II 658–9, 660. The 'name' is referred to in a letter of 8 May, and the 'Green book' in a letter to Mrs Watson (*The Dickensian*, June 1942, p. 165) of 21 May; but 'a new tree with the old green leaves' had been mentioned in a letter of 5 Mar. (*Letters*, II 639).

2. Later deleted and *Little Dorrit* substituted.

3. A good deal earlier, therefore, than Forster's 'on the eve of publication' (VIII i) which was 30 Nov. Forster (followed by Johnson, II 846) is also wrong in supposing that four numbers were then written; the fourth number plan is headed simply *Little Dorrit*, and No. IV, though begun in Oct., was completed only on 31 Dec.

4. Forster, IX vii; for the notebook, see p. 29 n. above.

the passivity of Mr Dorrit, or the hypocrisy of Casby, or the nonchalance of Henry Gowan; but Mr Dorrit appears by name in the notes for Number II, and Casby in the notes for Number IV; and none of these fulfils the other function mentioned by Forster, of bringing about all the 'mischief' in the book.[1] Indeed, such personal responsibility for evil seems foreign to the whole book as we have it. In so far as any individual is responsible, rather than 'society', it is Mrs Clennam; but she is fully aware of what she has done and sure of her righteous motives. More probably the notion of this man was only accidentally the 'origin' of the book, and had he survived into the written story he would have been a mere exemplum of the wider theme of 'Nobody's Fault'; the title could hardly have persisted through the writing of so many chapters if it was to be fulfilled only by this vanished character.

The general notion of 'Nobody's Fault' may also have been connected with an abandoned suggestion for Number I: that of people meeting and parting as travellers do, 'and the future connexion between them in the story, not to be now shown to the reader';[2] 'being in the same place, ignorant of one another, as happens in life; and to connect them afterwards, and to make the waiting for that connection a part of the interest'[3]—meeting, that is, through Providence, not their own contrivance. But only a trace of this remains, in the juxtaposition in Marseilles of the two prisoners with the travellers; for although the Meagles family, Clennam, and Miss Wade, 'meet and part as travellers do', the connexion between them *is* already shown, at least as much as one normally expects in any introductory chapter.

But the early number plans and Forster's information are not our only evidence of Dickens's preliminary view of the dominant themes of the novel. Some weeks before publication began, the design for the cover must have been discussed with Browne, and prepared by him. Unfortunately no correspondence survives,[4] and we do not know whether the original design carried the old title. Certainly the words *Nobody's Fault* in the centre would emphasize the irony of the design. Its two sides seem to typify society in decay, and images of doom are combined with com-

1. The one possibility is another character who disappears early from the notes —Miss Wade's father, suggested for No. III (chs. ix–xi), with a 'Not yet', and again by implication in No. IV: 'Miss Wade. Her surroundings and antecedents? No'.

2. No. I, memoranda. 3. Forster, VIII i.

4. A letter of 19 Oct. complains of hearing nothing from Browne, 'although I have communicated at full explanatory length'. (*Letters*, II 698.)

No. IX. AUGUST. PRICE 1s.

LITTLE DORRIT

BY

CHARLES DICKENS.

WITH

ILLUSTRATIONS BY H. K. BROWNE.

LONDON. BRADBURY & EVANS, BOUVERIE STREET.

AGENTS: J. MENZIES, EDINBURGH; MURRAY AND SON, GLASGOW; J. M'GLASHAN. DUBLIN.

placence and self-absorption. On the left is part of a crumbling castle, on whose tottering top is seated a sleeping man in an arm-chair with a handkerchief over his eyes and a newspaper on his knee. Against the castle lies a falling tree; the 'supporters' of the coat of arms are rats. This is 'the world' in its material aspect. Opposite stands part of a church, crowned by a raven, while a child plays leap-frog among the graves, and in a wheel-chair sits the life-in-death figure of Mrs Clennam attended by Flintwinch. So much for 'religion'. Overlapping these two scenes, and extending across the bottom of the design, is a motley crowd of travellers, each clinging to his belongings, all moving different ways, colliding, harassed, unhappy. Across the top of the design is what is virtually a political cartoon. Two aged figures, crippled and half blind, lead the procession, followed by a line of dotards and a dandy; Britannia in a bath-chair, asleep, is propelled by a line of men in fools' caps, followed by a crowd of toadies, behind whom are women and children; all, save the last, are smiling inanely. The centre-piece is Little Dorrit herself, at the gate of the prison, in a shaft of sunlight.

Here then, strongly emphasized, are the political, social, and ethical themes of the novel; there is no narrative line, as in the *Dombey* cover, but the inner meaning of the story is clearly 'shadowed forth'. For our purpose, the most interesting feature is the prominence of the political idea; it is clear from the cover-design that chapter x, 'Containing the Whole Science of Government' was foreseen from the start, and that its satire was a fundamental part of Dickens's conception of the novel—more so, perhaps, than the working-out of the story suggests, since the Barnacles remain rather episodic in the plot. To the readers of Number I, the prominence of the political satire must have been baffling; there is nothing so far in Marseilles or London to suggest a political theme. But the month was December 1855; the state of things pictured at the top of the cover had become dismally familiar to every reader. Its promise was fulfilled for them two months later in the brilliant sketch of chapter x, 'How Not to Do It':

> Sometimes, angry spirits attacked the Circumlocution Office. Sometimes, parliamentary questions were asked about it, and even parliamentary motions made or threatened about it, by demagogues so low and ignorant as to hold that the real recipe of government was, How to do it. Then would the noble lord, or right honorable gentleman, in whose department it was to defend the Circum-

> locution Office, put an orange in his pocket, and make a regular field-day of the occasion. Then would he come down to that House with a slap upon the table, and meet the honorable gentleman foot to foot. Then would he be there to tell that honorable gentleman that the Circumlocution Office not only was blameless in this matter, but was commendable in this matter, was extollable to the skies in this matter.

The chapter is the second in Number III, which Dickens was writing in the latter half of September. He was evidently pleased with it. He writes to Collins on 30 September:

> I have relieved my indignant soul with a scarifier[1]

and to Macready a few days later:

> In No. 3 of my new book I have been blowing off a little of indignant steam which would otherwise blow me up, and with God's leave I shall walk in the same all the days of my life; but I have no present political faith or hope—not a grain.[2]

The context of this sentence makes his despair more specific:

> As to the suffrage, I have lost hope even in the ballot. We appear to me to have proved the failure of representative institutions without an educated and advanced people to support them. What with teaching people to "keep in their stations," what with bringing up the soul and body of the land to be a good child, or to go to the beer-shop, to go a-poaching and go to the devil; what with having no such thing as a middle class (for though we are perpetually bragging of it as our safety, it is nothing but a poor fringe on the mantle of the upper); what with flunkyism, toadyism, letting the most contemptible lords come in for all manner of places, reading The Court Circular for the New Testament, I do reluctantly believe that the English people are habitually consenting parties to the miserable imbecility into which we have fallen, *and never will help themselves out of it.* Who is to do it, if anybody is, God knows. But at present we are on the down-hill road to being conquered, and the people WILL be content to bear it, sing "Rule Britannia," and WILL NOT be saved.

The last sentence is strongly suggestive of the 'cartoon' on the cover.

Dickens had been led to this position by the events of the past twelve months. The Crimean War began in March 1854; in October, William Howard Russell's revelations of mismanagement and disaster were appearing in *The Times*; in January 1855

1. *Letters*, II 694. 2. *Letters*, II 695.

the Roebuck Committee was appointed, and Lord Aberdeen's government fell—to Dickens, and to many others, merely substituting Coodle for Doodle.

The general evidence of inefficiency and corruption, 'a confused heap of mismanagement, imbecility, and disorder, under which the nation's bravery lies crushed and withered'[1], gave Dickens the material he wanted for the Circumlocution Office, in which he also made use of the abuses exposed by the Northcote–Trevelyan report of 1853. As usual, the sharp truth is softened by his artist's delight in the creation of a satiric fantasy; there is more relish than indignation in his picture of the Barnacles. But the full animus of his attack is seen elsewhere, and in the very months in which the novel was first forming in his mind—seen in his letters, in *Household Words*, and in his speech for the Administrative Reform Association.

The first reflection of his political disgust is in the scheme, communicated to Forster in August 1854, of 'occasional papers in Household Words called the Member for Nowhere',[2] which would have shown his 'contempt for the House of Commons'; this was reluctantly given up in the following month. Dickens instead made an indirect attack. Seeing that 'the war will be made an administrative excuse for all sorts of shortcomings'[3] and that 'the old cannon-smoke and blood-mists obscure the wrongs and sufferings of the people at home',[4] he proceeded to ventilate these wrongs in an article 'To Working Men', published on 7 October and followed by a series, by himself and Henry Morley, on public health and sanitary reform.

A letter of February 1855 shows him moving nearer the Barnacle idea:

> I am hourly strengthened in my old belief that our political aristocracy and our tuft-hunting are the death of England.[5]

and the same letter mentions his 'bright idea' for a political skit on the *Arabian Nights*, 'The Thousand and One Humbugs'. This series appeared a few weeks later;[6] the undesirable characters bear such names as Scarlitapa, Jobbiana, and Palmerstoon, or Twirling Weathercock. The last of these sketches brings us to the

1. 'That Other Public', in *Household Words*, 3 Feb. 1855; Dickens reverted to the subject in a satirical fairy tale, 'Prince Bull', in the issue of 17 Feb., where the wicked fairy godmother is called 'Tape'.

2. *Letters*, II 584–5. 3. *Letters*, II 600. 4. *Letters*, II 603.

5. *Letters*, II 622. 6. 21, 28 Apr., 5 May.

month in which the actual writing of the novel began; and its relation to his political preoccupations is clear from a letter which was written some weeks earlier:

> You see what we have been doing to our valiant soldiers. You see what miserable humbugs we are. And because we have got involved in meshes of aristocratic red tape to our unspeakable confusion, loss, and sorrow, the gentlemen who have been so kind as to ruin us are going to give us a day of humiliation and fasting the day after to-morrow. I am sick and sour to think of such things at this age of the world. . . I am in the first stage of a new book, which consists in going round and round the idea, as you see a bird in his cage go about and about his sugar before he touches it.[1]

In May the Administrative Reform Association was formed; Dickens immediately became a member, and on 27 June made a speech at the meeting at Drury Lane Theatre.[2] The Prime Minister had taken advantage of an earlier meeting in the same place to jeer at the Association's 'private theatricals'; Dickens made a telling comparison with the 'public theatricals' of politics:

> so full of "walking gentlemen", the managers have such large families and are so bent upon putting those families into what is theatrically called "first business"—not because of their aptitude for it, but because they *are* their families. . . We have seen "The Comedy of Errors" played so dismally like a tragedy . . .

At the same time he disclaimed any intention of changing his sphere of action from literature to politics:

> By literature I have lived, and through literature I have been content to serve my country; and I am perfectly well aware that I cannot serve two masters. In my sphere of action I have tried to understand the heavier social grievances, and to put them right.[3]

His mind was turning back to his novel, *Nobody's Fault*; by September the failure of Layard's movement was clear, and Dickens

1. *Letters*, II 712; undated; the editor conjectures 'November', but the 'day of humiliation and fasting' was 21 Mar., which makes this one of the earliest references to the new book. Compare also the letters to Layard on 10 Apr. (I 651–2) and to Forster on 27 Apr. (I 655–6).

2. A reporter who was present recalled the speech as 'a masterpiece of raillery and rebuke to a "how-not-to-do-it" Government' (F. G. Kitton, *Charles Dickens by Pen and Pencil, Supplement*, 1890, p. 45).

3. *Speeches*, ed. R. H. Shepherd. Forster, who probably did not approve, makes only a passing reference to the Association, making Dickens's share in its work merely an instance of the 'unsettled discontent' of this summer (VII ii).

was 'blowing off . . . indignant steam' in his description of the Circumlocution Office.

Enough has been said to demonstrate his concern with the evils of 1854–5, and his intention of exposing them in his writings;[1] it is necessary only to add that in the ironic formula 'Nobody's Fault', he was catching up a current notion. Revelations of mismanagement of the war at once led to the attempt to pin down the responsibility; which failed, as usual, owing to the skill of officials and ministers in 'passing the buck'. 'Who's to Blame?' was the question everyone was asking (it was the title of an article in the *Catholic Standard* by Newman in January 1855); and the answer was 'Nobody'.[2] If the man who was to assert that nobody was to blame survives in the novel at all, he is surely a Barnacle.

When he was half-way through *Little Dorrit* (a few weeks after writing the chapter 'A Shoal of Barnacles') Dickens summed up the situation in *Household Words* in an article called 'Nobody, Somebody, and Everybody':[3]

> The power of Nobody is becoming so enormous in England, and he alone is responsible for so many proceedings, both in the way of commission and omission; he has so much to answer for, and is so constantly called to account; that a few remarks upon him may not be ill-timed.

1. Much more of course would need to be said in a full study of the topicality of the novel, which would involve a fuller treatment of the Civil Service report of 1853 and would have also to include the 'Sunday question' (the Hyde Park riots on Lord Robert Grosvenor's bill receive their comment in the picture of a London Sunday as it strikes the returned traveller in ch. iii, and this relevance was generally recognized) and the contemporary rage for speculation in England and France, including the suicide of John Sadleir in Feb. 1856, reflected in the history of Mr Merdle. Several reviews of the completed novel were on partly political lines; see especially 'The License of Modern Novelists' (*Edinburgh Review*, July 1857); *The Train*, Aug. 1857; and two articles in the *Saturday Review*, 3 Jan. and 4 July 1857. The writer of the last of these concluded with the hope that Dickens would not again offer his readers 'the cold cabbage of Crimean inquiries and Royal British Banks, Administrative Reformers, Tottenham Court Road accidents, Messrs. Redpath, Cameron, and John Sadleir'.

2. Compare the cartoon in *Punch* (Mar. 1855, xxxvii 85) 'Mr Bull wants to know "the Reason Why"' and the title of a pamphlet of the autumn of 1854, 'Whom Shall We Hang?' That it really was 'nobody's fault' but the fault of the whole structure of administration became steadily clearer with successive hearings before the Committee. Roebuck wrote 'I felt corruption round about me, but I could not lay my hand upon it' (Asa Briggs, *Victorian People*, 1954, p. 84). A typical contemporary comment is 'there has been any amount of short-comings and blunderings, causing . . . a fearful and needless quantity of misery . . . yet it seems quite hopeless to attempt to find out who is to blame' (*Illustrated London News*, 24 Mar. 1855).

3. 30 Aug. 1856.

The hand which this surprising person had in the late war is amazing to consider. It was he who left the tents behind, who left the baggage behind, who chose the worst possible ground for encampments, who provided no means of transport, who killed the horses, who paralysed the commissariat, who knew nothing of the business he professed to know and monopolised, who decimated the English army. It was Nobody who gave out the famous unroasted coffee, it was Nobody who made the hospitals more horrible than language can describe, it was Nobody who occasioned all the dire confusion of Balaklava harbor, it was even Nobody who ordered the fatal Balaklava cavalry charge. The non-relief of Kars was the work of Nobody, and Nobody has justly and severely suffered for that infamous transaction.

In civil matters we have Nobody equally active. When a civil office breaks down, the break-down is sure to be in Nobody's department. I entreat on my reader, dubious of this proposition, to wait until the next break-down (the reader is certain not to have to wait long), and to observe, whether or no, it is in Nobody's department. A dispatch of the greatest moment is sent to a minister abroad, at a most important crisis; Nobody reads it. British subjects are affronted in a foreign territory; Nobody interferes. Our own loyal fellow-subjects a few thousand miles away, want to exchange political, commercial, and domestic intelligence with us; Nobody stops the mail. The government, with all its mighty means and appliances, is invariably beaten and outstripped by private enterprise; which we all know to be Nobody's fault. Something will be the national death of us, some day; and who can doubt that Nobody will be brought in Guilty?

II

Meanwhile the novel had become *Little Dorrit*: a title which, Dickens said, 'has a pleasanter sound in my ears, and which is equally applicable to the same story'.[1] Its application is however very different. 'Nobody's Fault' represents the 'one idea and design' of social criticism of which 'Society, the Circumlocution office and Mr. Gowan' are 'three parts';[2] *Little Dorrit*, the optimism about humanity which sets the rest in perspective. In her Dickens repeats, more subtly, a leading idea of *Oliver Twist* and *The Old Curiosity Shop*: that of the strength and indestructibility of natural, innocent virtue. As with Oliver and Nell, her goodness,

1. To Mrs Watson, 10 Nov. 1855. (*The Dickensian*, June 1942, p. 166.) Mrs Watson was one of the few to whom he had confided the original title.

2. *Letters*, II 766.

with such an upbringing, may be thought implausible; but it must be seen as expressing what still survived of Dickens's own indestructible faith—expressing it almost allegorically, with the validity of fairy tale. It seems likely that Little Dorrit was not at first intended to be so important a character; indeed, in manuscript, proofs, and letters we can trace the way she grew in importance, and even see her acquiring her name.

She was introduced in the third chapter, merely as an unknown girl seen in Mrs Clennam's room and inquired about by Arthur Clennam. In the manuscript her name does not appear; Affery only says 'Oh! *She*'s nothing; she's a whim of hers.' Her name is added in proof as 'Dorrit', which is then altered in a different coloured ink to 'Little Dorrit'. This change must have been made a good deal later, for her name is 'Dorrit' whenever she appears, in manuscript and proof, right up to chapter xii, and even in the memoranda for Number IV (chapters xii–xiv); the first appearance of 'Little Dorrit' in the manuscript is an addition made on the back of a leaf in that chapter. The text of chapter xii is indecisive as evidence, since she does not appear, and is referred to naturally by Plornish as 'Miss Dorrit' and only by Clennam (in the later addition) as 'Little Dorrit'; but the decision as to the title must already have been taken when that chapter was written, for the heading of the number plan, which stands on the right-hand side, is plain from the start as *Little Dorrit*. The dawning of the change may go back to chapter ix, where Maggie calls her 'Little mother', and which ends with Clennam's farewell in the prison yard:

> Little as she had always looked, she looked less than ever when he saw her going into the Marshalsea lodge passage, the little mother attended by her big child.

And it is noticeable that in chapter xiv, where Arthur asks if he may call her by this name, Maggie corrects him to 'Little mother'. The emphasis also falls on the name at the close of chapter xiii, which ends with her softly opening the door; and this was prepared for in the summary in the number plans:

> Lead up, through the state of Arthur Clennam's mind to "Little Dorrit"

in contrast to the general note in the memoranda, 'How he stands towards Dorrit?'

Having made his decision, Dickens went back and changed the name in all previous chapters,[1] which by now were in proof; and also added the title,[2] and presumably drafted the advertisement for 13 October. (It would be tempting to take the earlier advertisement of 6 October, where the novel was simply 'New Work by Mr. Charles Dickens', as defining the date of the change within a week; but such a preliminary advertisement in general terms was not unusual.) No change in her description in the early chapters was necessary; she was already a 'diminutive figure' with 'all the manner and much of the appearance of a subdued child'. But it is conceivable that if Dickens had had time to rewrite, he would have led up more clearly to the first appearance of the name in chapter v.

'I can make Dorrit very strong in the story, I hope', he had written to Forster on 16 September (during the writing of Number III);[3] and from this expectation dates the growing concentration upon her. That number in fact shows the double emphasis very clearly; the 'Little Mother' chapter (ix) being juxtaposed to 'Containing the Whole Science of Government' (x), in which Arthur, actuated by his interest in the Marshalsea family, applies to the Circumlocution office; and the further tangling of the threads is foreshadowed by his meeting there with Mr Meagles, the father of Pet,[4] who is to be the first object of his affections. Arthur Clennam's misunderstanding of his own feelings towards Little Dorrit is the result of his thinking of her as a child; so the diminutive is an essential part of the plot. It is also picturesque and symbolical—the small frail figure who is nevertheless the fount of moral strength; the protectress, the neglected, loved by all and, until the end, understood by none.

Dickens's decision was surely a wise one. He was writing a novel of individuals, not preaching a sermon or making a political speech; the pathetic, human appeal was more appropriate than the didactic 'Nobody's Fault', which in any case was almost

1. But he did not catch all the instances, so that there is a whole patch of ch. ix where she is still called 'Dorrit', surviving into modern texts.

2. No title appears on the proofs of I–III.

3. *Letters*, II 689. Mr William Dorrit is never called simply 'Dorrit', so there is no doubt that Little Dorrit is meant here.

4. 'Pet' was called 'Baby' in No. I, and this was altered only in proof; this also was a late revision (she is still 'Baby' in the memoranda of No. III) and it is very likely that it was consequent upon the addition of 'Little' to 'Dorrit', for two child-women in one novel would be awkward.

too narrowly topical.[1] On the most practical level of attracting sales, the new title had the advantage of recalling the most popular of all his characters, Little Nell; and its oddity was useful in arousing curiosity.

> For, let us say at once, that "Little Dorrit" is not a broom, not a village, not a ship,—as has been variously surmised at various tea-tables,—where the book in the green cover is as eagerly expected as the news of the last battle,—but a live flesh and blood little girl.[2]

Yet 'Nobody's Fault' survives, and not only in the Barnacles. Its meanings are multiple. Beginning as irony, a comment on the tendency to shift responsibility, it becomes a gloomy truth pervading all parts of the novel, as a ground-tone of despair about society. As in *Bleak House*, the calamities of the novel spring not so much from a single evil will but from the corruption of the whole condition of things: Mr Merdle and Mrs Clennam are themselves victims. The Marshalsea is more than a prison; it is a microcosm of the world. Gaining wealth, Mr Dorrit escapes only from one prison into another: the prison of society—with Mr Merdle's butler and Mrs General as half-comic jailers. We are shown the prison of poverty in Bleeding Heart Yard, the prison of administration in the Circumlocution Office, the prison of heredity and temperament in Mrs Clennam and Miss Wade. We are all each other's prisoners; there is no way out, for it is 'nobody's fault'. Individual happiness is possible for few; for the selfless servant of the community, like Daniel Doyce; for the Plornishes, against all odds, in 'Happy Cottage'; and for Arthur and Little Dorrit, when the curse of prison, wealth, and heredity is lifted from them. The novel ends with their marriage at the Marshalsea gates; but the very last words are not of them. They are of the crowds in the streets, the prisoners of society:

> They went quietly down into the roaring streets, inseparable and blessed; and as they passed along in sunshine and in shade, the noisy and the eager, and the arrogant and the froward and the vain, fretted, and chafed, and made their usual uproar.

1. As a 'formula' it was much more appropriate to the period when the first numbers were being written than to the time of publication.

2. *Athenæum*, 1 Dec. 1855. Can this be echoed by the inimitable Flora in ch. xxiii? '. . . and of all the strangest names I ever heard the strangest, like a place down in the country with a turnpike, or a favourite pony or a puppy or a bird or something from a seed-shop to be put in a garden or a flower-pot and come up speckled.'

INDEX

For Product Safety Concerns and Information please contact our EU representative GPSR@taylorandfrancis.com
Taylor & Francis Verlag GmbH, Kaufingerstraße 24, 80331 München, Germany

www.ingramcontent.com/pod-product-compliance
Lightning Source LLC
Chambersburg PA
CBHW081356090726
47908CB00011B/2692

* 9 7 8 0 4 1 5 5 6 9 0 9 5 *